Dear Visitor,

Voices of McDonald Observatory

*For RoseMary Wype,
I hope you enjoy these
stories. Karen Winget*

Karen Stewart Winget

*Karen Winget
2004*

Round Rock
Caddem Publishers

Published in the United States of America
by
Caddem Publishers
Suite 100
1822 Red Rock Drive
Round Rock
Texas
78664

ISBN 0-9742535-0-2

Printed in the United States of America

Cover picture: Star trails, a 15-minute time exposure of the night sky
with the Harlan J. Smith 107-inch telescope on the left; photo by author.
All photographs reproduced with permission.

For c a d d e m

and

To Frank, who gave everything to all of us without holding anything back, who always listened to everything we had to say, who encouraged us in every way, helped us build our strengths, overcome our weaknesses and, most of all, who believed in us. To Susan, who gave so much to McDonald Observatory, and gave us more than our fair share of Frank.

Susan and Frank Bash.
Photo by Joel Barna.

Acknowledgements

Thank you Norma Catt, my beautiful mom. You spent untold hours helping me transcribe the 115-plus hours of oral histories; you did this without pay, of your own free will, and I would not have finished without you.

Thank you Chris Cotter, my merciful friend. You recognized a manuscript in need of an editor and compassionately took it on. You did this without pay, of your own free will, and made a difference in the quality of this book.

Thank you Frank Bash, my brave patron. You generously financed my needs during this project, but more important, you put the bit in my mouth and never touched the reins.

Thank you to the many people who supported me emotionally and physically during this project. Thank you Robert Petty, Patricia Stewart, Goldie Brown, Miguel Prado, Javier Cardona, and Emma Cantwell for giving me delicious meals and making sure I rested well during my stays at the Observatory. Thank you Rebecca Johnson, Frank Cianciolo, Mark Wetzel, and Angela Otoupal of the Visitors Center for answering questions and getting this book on the shelf. Thank you David Doss and David Reaves for quickly taking the pictures I needed. Thank you David Doss and Cecilia Davis for quickly answering my many questions during this project.

Thank you Margo Hamby, Delores Baldwin, Joel Barna, Sandi Preston, and Brad Armosky for answering my many questions and keeping Frank informed. Thank you Cindy Thompson and Tim Jones for help with photographs, new and archival. Thank you Ralph Elder for your kindness in helping me understand the Center for American History archives.

Thank you to my children and first daughter-in-law: Charles, Amanda and Dean for your enthusiasm and support; Davis for finding some of the errors; Eric for sharing your bedroom with our office; and Maegan for waiting for that puppy. Thank you Don, my publisher—who knew you could do that? Thank you Kris and Eryn for your last minute proofreading and several delicious meals. Thank you to my parents, Catts and Wingets, for fielding children on occasion.

Thank you each narrator for your fearless devotion to this project. Thank you to every person who said, "I am glad you are doing this project." Thank you for every smile. This is the nourishment I needed to keep going...

CONTENTS

Preface

I didn't really write this book past the section on W. J. McDonald. The true authors are the persons belonging to the oral histories recorded for this book and placement in the archives at the University of Texas. You will meet each one on the following pages. If you are looking for a documented history or astronomy textbook, this is not it. If you are willing to let this astronomical observatory come to life through the voices of its people, and enjoy some gentle astronomy and living Texas history—then this is your book.

The words in quotes in the chapter for William Johnson McDonald are his words as reported by his friends, acquaintances, and relatives; they are derived from the sources listed in the few footnotes necessary to convey this information to the reader. I wrote the rest of the section on Mr. McDonald in the form of narration to remain true to the style of the book; I do not imply that he spoke the narration. I did not write these words without first researching documents concerning W .J. McDonald[1] and spending many hours in the dome of the 82-inch telescope looking through his books, a very small portion of his personal library that included his plant dissecting kit. From these documents came my impressions of W. J. McDonald to create his narration. McDonald's vision established the character of the McDonald Observatory. The McDonald will was contested but his wishes were not denied; the McDonald Observatory became a reality.

In the remainder of the book, each section is written from the oral histories of the people of the Observatory. I conducted a planned oral history interview with each narrator, with the exceptions as noted in the text. Working from the transcriptions, I organized and edited their narrations to tell the following stories. When you read their voices, they are speaking directly to you. Remember as you read, the spoken word looks different on paper. The spoken word is endearing and a characteristic of being human. Each narrator was allowed to edit their

---

[1] *Big and Bright, A History of the McDonald Observatory*, by David S. Evans and J. Derral Mulholland, 1986; *Biography of William Johnson McDonald* by Mamie Birge Mayfield and Paul M. Batchelder; W.J. McDonald will; letters from relatives, friends, and acquaintances of McDonald regarding his passing; Mrs. Florence Rodgers et al., vs. Morris Flemming et al, Court of Appeals for the Sixth Supreme Judicial District of Texas, Brief and Argument for Appellees, 1927—this is a document from the McDonald will trial; The Paris News, Friday May 5, 1939, article by News Staff Writer, Maude Neville, Paris, Texas.

narration with strong encouragement to preserve their spoken word. Their original taped oral histories are deposited in the University of Texas Center for American History and are available for research. These brave narrators have provided a great service to oral history.

A few of the chapters contain moderate technical narration. Since the information is historically important for the astronomical community, I am compelled to include the information in the book. I suggest that when you come to a technical paragraph, you can read it or not, but please try the next paragraph—there may be a good story in it. I promise, if you skip the very technical portions of the book it will not affect your enjoyment.

This is not an official history. The views, advice and interpretations presented in this book are not necessarily the opinions of The University of Texas, the Astronomy Department, or McDonald Observatory. They belong to the narrators and myself. The errors are all mine.

The book in your hands now is the evidence of McDonald Observatory's human character. There are few material facts in this book. There are light years of human witness.

Karen Stewart Winget
Round Rock, Texas
July 2003

Chapter 1 The Observatory and Mount Locke

The McDonald Observatory

Dearest Visitor,

I know you have traveled a long way to visit. Thank you, your gracious company enriches my life. Today I saw your approaching vehicle as it leaned around my curvaceous mountainside. I heard you catch your breath as you first gazed up at me. I saw my reflection in your eyes. I feel your enthusiasm as you arrive at my feet. There are many things I wish to tell you, my dear visitor, and it is my hope that through my voices in this book I can embrace you so that you may touch the heart of your West Texas astronomical observatory.

May I tell you of my nature, my science, and my abilities? May I also tell you of my weaknesses and failures? I want you to know my essential character, the events that make me McDonald Observatory, and the things without which, I cannot be. I would like you to know my qualities, what makes me different from any other place you have ever visited. I want you to know the nature of my being and the nature of the land I have inherited that now outlines my figure. I hope your visit will include a brief travel through time in the lens of one of my long eyes. From there, you will see the wonders of the universe are the boundaries of my nature.

I want you to know the people of McDonald Observatory. They are people, like you, from all over the Earth who are with me every day working, playing, struggling, loving, living. It is through the nurture of these people that I have earned my character. They have lifetimes of endearing stories to share with you so when you leave here you can say, "Yes, I know McDonald Observatory. I have stood at its feet, been in its embrace, learned its attributes and history and then stood on its shoulders with my knowledge and looked at the universe, truly for the first time."

I hope you carry a portrait of your experience home in your heart and marvel at your knowledge every time you go outside at night and look up. Or every time you close your eyes and remember how you felt when you looked up from my feet at the darkest skies on this continent. Have you ever seen so many stars? Did you cry? Did you notice that on a moonless night your body cast a shadow on the ground not from moonlight, but from only starlight? Did you see the Andromeda Galaxy? Did you realize that the light falling into your eyes left the Andromeda Galaxy two million years ago?"

As you read these pages, please realize preserved here is the evidence of men and women, their deeds great and small. Over a century and a half ago, even before Texas was mended into the United States, a boy was born in Pin Hook, now Paris, Lamar County, Texas. His name was William J. McDonald. Eighty-one years later and after an interesting life, he died and left the bulk of his wealth to the University of Texas. After designated monies were given to relatives, his last petition was, "All the rest, residue and remainder of my estate, I give, devise and bequeath to the Regents of The University of Texas, in trust, to be used and devoted by said Regents for the purpose of aiding in erecting and equipping an Astronomical Observatory to be kept and used in connection with and as a part of the University for the study and promotion of the study of Astronomical Science."

Our McDonald died in 1926, at a time when astronomy was widely considered an eccentric pursuit. Had it not been for his vision, my existence would not be realized today. In 1939 my construction was complete and a "Dedication of the McDonald Observatory" was given. Homer P. Rainey, President-Elect of The University of Texas, said the following words about me:

"We are here to dedicate this observatory to the most ancient and purest of all the sciences. In doing so, may I express the hope that this observatory will stand as an enduring symbol of the insatiable desire of man to discover the secrets of the universe, and that it may also stand as a symbol of the freedom of man's mind to explore the boundless areas of truth without any restrictions whatsoever. To these ideals, I dedicate the McDonald Observatory in the name of The University of Texas, and I now declare it open to research."

The science achieved on this mountain has drawn the outline of McDonald Observatory; the unique messages from the men and women on the following pages have painted me with the colors of life.

These people know me intimately and have contributed to the structure of my life, and each other's lives. Please listen.

In highest regard of your company Dear Visitor, I am

Truly yours,

McDonald Observatory

Mount Locke

I currently stand 6,809 feet above sea level. **I am this country and I am a part of McDonald Observatory.** As your eyes search the expanse of my country, know that in the beginning I was an earthen cradle for the sea. I was soft and yielding for creatures of the saltwater. I remained this way for a time, graceful waves sweeping over me with ease and the peaceful unchanging quiet of day and night. A blanket of sea was everything I knew. Until without warning and with great effort and resignation, my mountains were heaved from the Earth's depths. My country screamed and tore. My contentment was shattered and replaced with heat and fear. There was violence and change. I would be different now and permanently severed from the sea.

Quickly, the stinging blanket of sea left me, and the drying earth redefined my shape. Slowly and deliberately, calm returned and an unfamiliar but gentle breeze touched my face and caressed my sides. I began to heal. I soon came to know a new blanket: a cover of grasses, trees, and fruits for the land animals and birds that now roamed my earthen boundaries and swam in the airs above me. I was good for these creatures and peace was abundant.

No longer sightless, deaf, and muted by the pulsing waves of the sea, I realize a sense of turning. Repeatedly I turn to face a great energy of white-hot waves that warm my sides and cause my fruited plain to grow. Then, over and over I am rested in darkness with a kinder, gentler, changing orb of light rising above me. The orb is accompanied by an infinite sparkle of familiar lights. Yet, in the darkness, these lights seem so far away that they cannot know I am here. Sometimes in the darkness between us, I can barely see my own soul. It seems I am alone, the only one. How can I know?

Time passed longer than I can remember until one day, I heard a whisper. A whisper of a new creature in the land, a marvelous and terrible creature that forever changes the character of my creation. A creature so different from the others that silence forever separates them. This creature has a voice understood only by its own kind, but somehow and sometimes in their eyes, I can see understanding and appreciation. With these creatures came a possibility of knowing—knowing if I turn here in solitude.

At first they were few, and most who came carefully left nothing behind. What my earth reveals of their existence blends so naturally in my country that their time here remains secret. Eventually, groups of these people came near and encountered each other. There were exchanges of voices. Sometimes they screamed in passion. More often they screamed in death. They came here in long snakes of wagons and horses and eventually they stayed, bustling like ants to make their own lifeless creations for living. They seemed soulless and without honor as they broke my trees, stole my fruit, and killed my animals. This was barely tolerable, but soon, I learned to marvel at their genius. They were not hurting each other any longer and I heard their voices as they looked up into the dark skies. They whispered the same question: I wonder what is out there, are we the only ones? How can we know?

Mt. Locke

Clouds echo oceans past, fill the valleys below Mt. Locke, and lap at the sides of Little Flat Top, Signal Peak, and Black Mountain. Photo from McDonald Observatory archives.

Chapter 2 McDonald the Man

William Johnson McDonald
Lawyer, banker, kind gentleman

I am William Johnson McDonald and I am a voice of McDonald Observatory. Dear Visitor, I am honored to address you. Knowing that you will come to this observatory to learn about the heavens justifies my life and belief in the best human qualities. During my life, I spent a lot of time watching how people live. I saw some just get dressed up to look like they were something when they really were just "jellybeans."[2] I have watched others struggle and work hard to make good of their life; these are the people who will change things and make them better.

My father was one of those who struggled. He was Dr. Henry Graham McDonald, a government physician to the Choctaw Indians when he marched with the Native American Indians from the southeastern states to a reservation here in this land. I believe it was called the Trail of Tears. Later, in 1844, I came screaming into this world just as the State of Texas was struggling for her place in a great union. She was scarred up a bit as usually happens when you work for something you believe is important and essential. "Christ came into the world as a carpenter and worked, and so conferred a supreme honor on labor. I think everybody ought to work, no matter what he has. You should live a clean, upright life, keep out of bad company, go to school, and let wild women and whisky alone. You'll notice if an old hen gets off her nest and gets to fooling around too much, the eggs won't hatch, so keep your mind on your business. In addition, don't always work for somebody else but get into business for yourself. The blacksmith who made a success of his business is just as much to be thought of as the man who made a million." And this is important too, "deal fair." Fair is not equal; fair is everyone gets what they need. Being a banker, I know that you shouldn't give too much or take too much. If you give too much, that person will find no value in it and proceed to be careless and lazy. On the other hand, don't take too much either. In collecting loans I was always "lenient as long as a man does his best."[3] "When the time comes in handling the notes due my estate, the Regents are requested to

---

[2] "jellybeans" This term is a quote from Delbert Payne, McDonald's last office assistant, taken from his testimony at the McDonald will trial from the document Court of Civil Appeals for the Sixth Supreme Judicial District of Texas.
[3] McDonald's friends and acquaintances published in The Paris News, Friday, May 5, 1939, article by News Staff Writer, Maude Neville, Paris, Texas.

use the utmost liberality and lenience in the matter of renewals and extensions consistent with safety."[4]

Dear Visitor, my idea for an astronomical observatory comes from my belief that we were born with a natural need to wonder—to experience the excitement of something surprising and unknown. In my time, I saw evidence of our need to wonder in the study of astronomy and the "great telescopes and observatories located in the colleges and universities up in the northern states. There was a lot of money up there and that's all astronomy really needed. Someday we may be able to see the gates of Heaven and then we will be able to see who was there. I believe astronomy will be the next great wonder and it just needs a little money."

My intention for an astronomical observatory fund was to make it possible for persons to raise their knowledge of astronomical science. I believe schooling is important, not just for personal enrichment or to enhance ones social character but you should mostly strive for knowledge to better your society and fellow human. The number of people is growing and you need to expand your knowledge in order to survive. So ponder, think, imagine, suppose. Don't let the boundary of your current knowledge make an end to your learning. I had to travel a long time and a long way to get to school. I had one of the first cars, and I even rode in it once, but vehicles were young then and full of untold trouble—it was just more sensible to take my horse and buggy to Massachusetts to attend astronomy classes at Harvard. A great fire destroyed most of Paris, Texas, and unfortunately, hundreds of my school and personal books were destroyed, including all of my personal belongings in my room. Some of my books, which reflect only a portion of my interests, survived, and I hope are available for others.

Folks appreciated much of my advice. But some scoffed and laughed at my ideas about the science of astronomy and its importance to being human. I worked hard and lived modestly, just as I preferred. I liked being close to nature because its origins and future have always been important to me. Still, some thought I was eccentric. In my will, I made bequests to some family members. I studied my estate and thought a good deal about how the major portion of it should go. And so I gave it for an "astronomical observatory because in my opinion, it would be lasting and beneficial."[5] Some believed that my sole interest in life was to pile up money and be stingy; only a few realized how deep my love

---

[4] This statement was taken from the William J. McDonald will.
[5] Statement taken from witness testimony of W.F. Moore, lawyer in defense of The University of Texas in the McDonald will trial. Rodgers et al, vs. Morris Flemming et al., document.

for science and learning really is. The terms of my will made this very clear and I am grateful for the people who defend my request. Again, Dear Visitor, I am so very satisfied and proud that you came here today.

John Dykema

I am John Dykema, grandnephew of William Johnson McDonald, Old Bill, and I am a voice of McDonald Observatory. My uncle, also named William J. McDonald, was your benefactor's nephew. I knew my uncle well and spent a lot of time with him. I remember the many stories he told me about William J. McDonald. One, in particular, was about his car, the first car in Paris, Texas. This is how he told me the story.

The first car

Old Bill, was a solitary, hardworking man who was enthusiastic about astronomy. He had many academic interests and enjoyed the idea of using technology to further astronomy; but otherwise, he had little use for modern technology. Old Bill was the first person in Paris, Texas, to buy a car. He must have been wealthy because everyone else always drove a horse and buggy. I took care of the details of my uncle's life and one day he called me and said, get the car and come over to "drive me to the office." No one in Paris, Texas, had ever driven a car before this day, but I was very wise for a fiftteen-year-old and very excited about driving a car—I had even seen some pictures of cars and read about them in magazines! But otherwise, I had no experience with them. Anyway, I drove him to the office all right and then the two of us just drove around for a while. After our outing, Old Bill instructed me to put the car back into the garage where it remained from then on. The car was never used again by William Johnson McDonald and not because our driving experience was particularly unpleasant, but a car in those days was of untold trouble and besides, Old Bill had other things to think about. It was his horse and buggy he drove all the way to Massachusetts to attend astronomy classes at Harvard, not the car."[6]

---

[6] This section is from a telephone conversation between Karen S. Winget and John Dykema, Mar 30, 2001.

Chapter 3 Early and Current Residents

Aparicia "Pat" Prado
Early, long-time, and current resident.
My name is Enedina Aparicia Estrada Talavera Prado and I am a voice of McDonald Observatory. Welcome to my home. Come, sit down; it is cool and comfortable in this house. And please call me Pat, it's so much easier for everybody, me included.

Early Texans
This house is on the main street going through Ft. Davis and we can hear the cars and trucks as they pass by. My husband, Ardy, and I live here now but this is really my grandmother's house. My father, Catarino Hernandez Talavera, and then my brother and I were born in this house, but it is still my grandmother's because it was her house first. Her name was Isidora Hernandez Talavera.

My grandfather, Alvino Talavera, came to Texas with his brother, Prescilliano, in 1871, to get away from Mexico and the situation the way it was there. That is when he says he came because I have a receipt where he signed for his citizenship of the United States in 1884 and he told them he was here since 1871.

Grandfather's brother, Prescilliano, stayed in Van Horn but Grandfather came on down to Ft. Davis because he had seen my grandmother at the Cibolo Ranch and he decided he was going to stay around. In June 1879 he and my grandmother got married. I never did get to know him; he died in 1929, before I was born. But I have gotten this information from my cousins that are older than I and are still alive. They are the ones that used to tell me Grandfather liked to play cards. This was when he was older and he couldn't work anymore, that's what he did, sit down and play cards with his buddies. But before that, he was a bricklayer and worked hard for his money because he had a bunch of kids and he had to support them.

St. Joseph's Catholic Church
Did you see St. Joseph's Catholic Church on your way through town? Grandfather helped build our Catholic Church. There was a church building there already but the Father, Father Brocaddus, decided that he wanted to build a bigger church. The Father had some money of his own and used it to start the funding. Of course, they had started from scratch, from the foundation, and my grandfather knew how to do that. So he and several other people worked in their spare time to get the

foundation down without charging the Father. That way, the Father had the money to provide the other things that he needed and they finished the church in 1899. My mother, her name was Merced Estrada, knew Father Brocaddus as a child. He married Mom and Dad in 1930; he baptized me in 1931 and then my brothers in 1933 and in 1935. Father Brocaddus made sure that my brother and I went to "la doctrina" three times a week.

Building the Fort

Then *my* parents, *my* mother's side, were here since 1850. The original one that came here in 1850 was her great-grandfather and when he came, he already had four kids of his own. His name was Eusevio Estrada. He had worked at the old Fort in around 1869 when they were hiring to build the buildings—the hospital and many other buildings. Many were hired to build it and when they finished, of course, they were let go.

Grandmother's house

My very first memory as a little girl was coming into this room I am sitting in now to spend some time with my grandmother because she lived with us all the time that she lived. This was her house to begin with. My dad got married but since my grandfather was dead, he took the responsibility of taking care of her. You did not put people in the nursing home back then.

I am in the living room now but it used to be her kitchen. This was two rooms and it was divided into the kitchen and that was the bedroom. She had a wood stove right here. She wouldn't cook on anything else and she didn't want gas in here. She didn't want electricity either. She didn't want anything that was new. When my daddy started putting the electricity in, it did *not* go in this room, this part of the house that was original. The only way I could get a Christmas tree for her and light it on her table was by having an extension and putting it on top of the table and letting her look at that. She wouldn't allow Daddy to put any of the necessities in here…well, to me electricity was a necessity.

By the light of Grandmother's lamp

And then her kitchen table was right here by this big window. That was her bed over there, and here she had a beautiful big dresser, heavy dresser, and she had a trunk on that corner. She still had her little lamp, which I have now. A little, beautiful, little lamp. It's small but gives a good light and we used to play cards on her kitchen table until late at nights for as far back as I remember. We would be playing and talking and listening to all her stories that she would tell me. It was nice. At the

9

time, to me, it was life. That's the way it was. I didn't know anything different.

Indian raids

Oh, she used to tell me a lot of stories about the Indians. I particularly remember the one when she was very young; it was twilight and she was going to go and get some water and bring it in. When she bent over to get the water out of the creek she heard a noise. It was an arrow that stuck on a tree, either right above her or on the side. It missed her only because she had bent down. She had told me these stories about how the Indians would attack this house. They would have to close this big window here with some panes, some wooden panes, so that the Indians couldn't get in. At first the Indians attacked often, but then later as they started moving them out, they just disappeared.

I started taking Texas history in the 7th or 8th grade and I read about the Indians in the schoolbooks. I thought, this is what my *grandmother* told me! So I started telling them, this *is* what my grandmother told me. This is *true* because my grandmother says it is.

A road up Mt. Locke and Observatory life in the 1930s

When I was little, too little for school, Daddy helped make the road better up to the Observatory. There used to be a highway; it was paved anyway, from Ft. Davis to the Observatory. But some of the route was real, real high, you know, because it had not been cut around or anything. They just had the easiest way up even if it was straight up. So they decided to make it different and that's when we lived where they have the visiting center now. This had to be like in 1936. I think it took about three years to make the road. We would drive up there on Sunday night and the next morning, Dad would go to work. We stayed there all week. While we were there, we were able to play outside with the deer. The little deer would come around and we could play with them. There were other kids there too. There were a lot of families that worked up there from every Sunday and then Friday night, come home.

The road didn't matter to me really, but my dad was very excited about it because he knew how to work on them and he enjoyed the work. He was always glad that he had helped to put it together. At one time he was the dynamite man. In order to cut those big mountains that you see on the side of the road, they had to start from the top and cut down so they could put in dynamite. They would dig in, drop the dynamite, and let it explode out. They cut the road down and around in the mountain and it really made a difference because you used to have to go almost straight up to get to the Observatory.

Living at the Observatory was very nice. I do remember one thing that made an impact on me one Friday night. When everything was done and we were ready to come back home in town, Mother had the car packed and everything ready to go. All we were waiting for was for Daddy to get there, wash off a little bit and then we could drive home. Well, that day he said "No, we are not going to wait for me to clean up, I'll do it at home." This was because it was fixing to snow and he wanted to come down the mountain before it started. But before we left it had already started so we hurried on down. When we came to halfway that is when it got bad because it had already snowed a lot. We didn't want to go back because grandma was here at home and we had to come to see after her, see about her. But, we made it home and Daddy was always saying, "Whew," because we had barely made it here just in time. That was one of the close shaves coming down.

School in Ft. Davis and class trips to the Observatory

When I was in school here in Ft. Davis, they were segregated. To me, it was normal because that's the way it had been done forever. We had what we called the Mexican School. Actually, we didn't have a name for it other than the Mexican School. At that time, we weren't Hispanics yet—we were Mexicans. Nothing but Mexicans allowed at the school, but all of our teachers were white. This was only through eighth grade, then everybody that graduated went to ninth grade in high school, and that is when we came together with the whites. In high school, we went up to the Observatory as a class and they showed us what to do and what to see. They didn't have star parties then but they let us go at night.

Generations link with McDonald Observatory

My husband, Ardy, and I lived in Austin, Texas, from 1966 until 1994. We had Ardy's Appliance Service on Oltorf. While we had lived in Austin for a while, we decided we needed to return to Ft. Davis to care for our parents. And anyway, we prefer Ft. Davis. It's home. Our son, Miguel, was born in Austin but now works in the Transient Quarters at the Observatory. He is cooking and taking care of the astronomers and seeing that they have a nice place to stay while they are working at the telescopes.[7]

---

[7] Oral History interview taken by Karen S Winget in the Pat and Ardy Prado home in Ft. Davis, Texas, on August 14, 2002. July 4th, 2000, Ft. Davis had a celebration to honor the descendants of people who came to the area over a hundred years ago and for the civilians who worked at Fort Davis. Pat received two certificates because both sides of her family, the Talavera and Estrada families, were honored.

Willa Battaile (Billie) Morelock Washington

Billie was an area resident in the 1930s and currently lives in Austin, Texas. Billie's husband is a descendant of President George Washington.

My name is Willa Battaile "Billie" Morelock Washington and I am a voice of McDonald Observatory. I was born in Canyon, Randall County, Texas, and my parents were Horace W. Morelock and Willa Battaile. I was born November the 27th, in 1916. I bet you are wondering why I am called Billie. Well, my brother did not like the fact that a lot of people took Willa and made Willie out of it. So he always called me his sister Billie and that is how he introduced me to people when I came to Austin, to the University.

Mt. Locke in a mid 1930s postcard. The postmark bleed-through encircles the future location of the 82-inch. McDonald Observatory archives.

Picnics, Packards, and jitneys at the top of Mt. Locke

My father, Horace W. Morelock, was president of Sul Ross University in Alpine, Texas, for twenty-two years in the thirties and forties. For many years before the McDonald Observatory was built, we had picnics up on the top of the mountain. You know, we *climbed mountains* like people *jog* these days. Herbert Kokernot, who was a wonderful friend of Sul Ross and a large landowner, had a Packard. He would put the women and children in the Packard and drive them up to the top. The men who would come, came up in what we called jitneys, which were little Ford motorcars. The road was so long to go up there, and so steep, that the water would boil out of the cars. They would have to stop half way up, let it cool off, then they put more water in and come jiggling up. I remember looking back there and thinking, why are they all sitting there with a bottle in their hand? What are they drinking? So I think maybe for them, being marooned on the road turned out to be more fun than anything.

First sight of the future site

Now as my memory serves me, the head of the Chamber of Commerce, and Dr. Elvey, a Chicago astronomer and member of the Observatory site team, made the ascension to the top of Locke Mountain to determine the possibility if it was a good site or not. This was the first place they looked. His findings were excellent and after three days study, he came to our home. I had never seen one before but they brought a telescope to our home—it being the highest point in the area outside the Davis Mountains. We were about forty miles away. We went outside and they said to me, "Come here, I want to show you something; look through there." And I looked through the eyepiece and he said, "Now, look as far as you can see" and then he said, "This is confidential, but I think we have found the place! We are going to recommend that the Observatory be there!" And that to me is something I will always remember—looking through there and being able to see all the way past Ft. Davis.

The Millers

Lillian "Bit" Miller, Keesey Miller and Lucy Miller, speaking to you from the Miller home on Cedar Street, Ft. Davis, Texas, in 1980 and Lillian Miller again in 2000.

I am Bit Miller and I am a voice of McDonald Observatory. Welcome to my home, Dear Visitor. I would like you to know that I came here long before the Observatory. I came out here when I was five years old; that was in nineteen and thirteen. I was born in Texas but we lived in Oklahoma for a couple of years. My given name is Lillian, but not many know that because I have been called "Bit" since a very early age; my little sister named me Bit because she could not say Lillian.

High and dry in Ft. Davis

My mother had complications from a burst appendix in Oklahoma. She got all right, but the doctor told my father to take her to a high, dry altitude climate. My aunt and uncle lived here in Ft. Davis because he had come up with tuberculosis and it was recommended that if you have tuberculosis, you should live in a dry climate. In those days, nearly everybody who lived out here came out here for that same reason. You can't find a higher or dryer climate anywhere around here.

Ft. Davis before the Observatory

When we came here in nineteen and thirteen, there were not very many jobs and there were very few houses up here in town; this house was here but it was not like this. So we rented a house on the Fort, the Fort Davis. We lived in number 11 of the officer's quarters. They were in very good condition at that time and everybody we knew lived there too. No, the soldiers had been gone for twenty-five years by the time we got here and the government didn't own the property; it belonged to a man from San Antonio. My father got a job building the hotel, Hotel Limpia, down here in town. He wasn't a carpenter, he was a tailor, but he had to do what he could find so he helped as a carpenter. I remember my little sister and I, she was three and I was five, we used to walk from our house at the Fort up here to the Limpia and bring his lunch to the hotel.

Picking out a Ft. Davis boy

While you are in Ft. Davis, when you are at the courthouse, if you look up the way toward the mountains, there is a church up there with a steeple and that was built in nineteen and four. The schoolhouse is right next door to it and that is where I started school. I finished there too; we only had ten grades so I had to go Sul Ross to get my certificate to teach. I was eighteen years old that day when I started Sul Ross. Keesey Miller had the garage, of course, and I guess it was two or three months before he asked me for a date. I married that Ft. Davis boy. We grew up together and I picked him out when I was nine years old. He didn't know it and I didn't either at that time. I do now.

I first taught school here in Ft. Davis at the Mexican School; we were segregated then. I also taught school in El Paso. Right after Keesey graduated from A & M, all in the world he wanted to do was work on cars, so he bought the Ft. Davis Auto Company and sold Ford cars. He was a mechanical engineer and he just loved it. Cars weren't so old in those days but you did have to fix them. And he could.

Singing in the choir at the Presbyterian Church

Later on, to find work, we went to Houston and then to Dallas. While we were in Dallas I got to attend the operas. I went to every one of them that I could. The first thing my father bought when we moved here in 1913 was a piano. I couldn't play it though, I had poor coordination, but I could sing and that is what I love to do. I sing now, here in the Presbyterian Church choir. You can come and hear us sing, please do!

Keesey had decided that Dallas was not for him so we came back to Ft. Davis and started the ranching business. We raised cattle meat for the people. We bought some cows and a few bulls and then raised the calves. We sold some of the calves and kept some for the next year. We also sold the cows that were too old because you have some more that you raised; that is just the way it goes and that is the meat business. At one point, the doctors were saying that meat isn't good for you, causes heart trouble and all that. Well, that hurt our ranching business some but it didn't kill us. What we learned to do was raise them without too much fat and to do that, you just have to feed them differently.

First hike up to the Observatory site by the cloth-tied path

I am not sure what I remember my first thoughts were about the Observatory because I just kind of grew up with it. My first *trip* up to the Observatory? Oh, I remember that real well. Two Yerkes Observatory astronomers, Dr. Christian T. Elvey and Dr. van Biesbroeck, came here to look for places to put an observatory. One of the reasons the Observatory would come here was there was so little light. We didn't have any streetlights. In fact, we just barely had electricity. They were looking for a place where the light wouldn't interfere with the observing.

Dr. Elvey and Dr. van Biesbroeck camped up on top of the mountain where the Observatory is now. Nothing was up there but their tent at that time. They invited my husband and me and my brother-in-law and his wife to come up there, to climb up that mountain some night and they would show us through the telescope what they had. There was no road up there, only a path and we had to climb by foot; there wasn't any other way. The two doctors tied white strings and cloth on the bushes to show us the path up there. It was a zigzagging path and it was *dark. Oh*, it was dark. We went up there and had a look through their telescope at some stars they were looking at. Dr. van Biesbroeck was serving me some hot chocolate. I was not too well acquainted with him at that time and I was so embarrassed because I turned my cup over on him. *Hot* cup of chocolate. Oh, my gosh, I was embarrassed. Well, anyway, that was quite an experience for us.

There was nothing up there in the beginning of course. Soon they had made a road up there all right but it was a wagon road, you might say, and it was bad. They had to build a better road and they tried to get water up on the hill, drill for water. There was none up there so they had to drill down below. And that's where Keesey helped out a lot, when they were drilling the well and building the road.

Surveying the Mt. Locke site. Taken about 1935. The tripod is over the exact center of the 82-inch dome. W. S. Miller is looking through the surveying instrument, Dr. van Biesbroeck is on the left. McDonald Observatory archival photo.

I am Keesey Miller, and I am a voice of McDonald Observatory. Now, before there was any road built and well drilled it is interesting to hear how the land was acquired in the first place.

Land from the hand of providence and a hand of poker

There was a trade out, land for land. It began with The Union Trading Company, of which my father, Walter S. Miller, was a mainstay. The land that the Observatory is now on and named Mt. Locke was owned by the Union Trading Company. The Union had acquired it from a rancher's debt at one time and they were going to make a park out of it. Well, the park board, the Texas State Park Board, didn't have any way to finance a park so the land just lay there unfenced within the ranches surrounding this territory. So they traded this land to the Lockes for similar acreage. The Lockes, of course, had some acreage there already. Dr. Locke won his original foothold of land up there at the U Up and U Down Ranch in a poker game. This wasn't an uncommon practice in that day and time. He was going from the east to the west on the train, got in a poker game and this fellow he won the little tract of land from said it had a lake on it and pine trees. Well, on his return trip he decided he'd get off and go see about the resort land that he'd won. And he found it; it was designated. It had a little dirt tank on it! That's all. That was the nucleus of his adding to the ranch. His granddaughter, Violet Locke McIvor, later held the land.

The first roads

I always said that Father spent $2000, wore out two automobiles, and untold time promoting both the location of the Observatory as well as the construction of the State Park Highway. He had more influence on that than any other one man in the community. He worked through Judge Love, who was a State Senator from the Dallas district. They didn't know how they were gonna get the road built but Judge Love was a pretty sharp politician and he introduced it into the legislature that they enact a law that the highway department build the State Park Scenic Highway. That is what he wanted and he didn't leave it that they had any options. He introduced it, it became law, and he saw to it that they built it. My father and the Senator, of course, wore out the first automobile transporting themselves and the Senator's cronies, cohorts and associates around the road before it was a road. He didn't have to make too many trips to where you'd need another car pretty bad.

Before the road was built though, there came two young people. A young man by the name of T.G. Mehlen, an Amherst astronomer I believe, and Christian T. Elvey, a Yerkes astronomer. They came down here together to pick out where the Observatory would go. Still, they looked like they were wet behind the ears, as far as astronomy is concerned. Elvey was a prince of a fellow. I don't know anybody that I became more closely attached to than I did with Elvey. They were pretty active with the Observatory and they were active in the community. At first they lived here in town and then they finally got a house and moved up on the hill.

I take credit for having located the Observatory—this is a side issue. The reason I take that credit is I operated a little shop down here back in those years, repairing automobiles. I was kind of a jack-of-all-trades. They came down here and told me what they wanted; they wanted two pointers so they could adjust them and set them on the piers to locate the true north and south. These were the alignments. So I made those pointers and fixed them so he could adjust them in pretty small increments so they could get pretty close. They used them on the piers and that's the reason I say, I located the Observatory—aligned with the north and south.

Early residence construction, with 82-inch dome in the background.
McDonald Observatory archives.

The first director, Otto Struve, and his wife, Mary

Another interesting sideline was the Struves, Dr. and Mary Struve. They came down next. He was the director for the Yerkes Observatory in Wisconsin, and at the same time was the first director of the McDonald Observatory. The Struves came down during the preliminary observations. They camped for two or three nights on top of Spring Mountain. I wasn't there but my father and Barry Scobee, he was a writer and eventually the Justice of the Peace here, went up to visit them one night. Mrs. Struve was going to serve them a meal up there and she put a can of pork-n-beans in the coals to warm them. She did not put a hole in the can and after the beans got so hot, the can exploded and threw beans all over the place. Mrs. Struve was quite a character. To be around her casually, there wasn't a humorous side that was visible, but after you got acquainted with her, why, she was pretty good, had a sense of humor and so forth.

Mrs. Struve did a wonderful thing for us. Before we bought this place, she was walking up the street during a snowstorm. This house was pretty well covered with snow and she took a picture of it. Like I said, we hadn't even bought the place then but after we bought it, why, she produced this picture, it is one of the furtherest back pictures of this house and she took it two or three years before we bought it. She remembered that well; that is just the personal side of Mrs. Struve. Dr.

Struve was pretty straight laced but he had a twinkle in his eye once in a while, too.

Another sideline and a little bit of the atmosphere that was around here at wartime was concerning Germans. I've always heard lots of rumors that got started along in those days and it's kind of interesting how some of the things cast reflections on the other. There was a big tall German boy by the name of Theodore Immega. He was an engineer and recent immigrant from Germany and was an assistant to astronomer Franklin E. Roach. He was Dutch from the ground up, kind of an odd character, too. He was, well, you couldn't quite put your finger on it…as far as his personality was concerned. Then there was Eppenauer, he was also German and had served as a chauffer to a general in his homeland in the World War I. When he came to the United States, he bought his ranchland in the Davis Mountains; he even supplied some materials for the Observatory. Unfortunately, he chose an Indian good luck symbol for his ranch brand, which resembled the swastika. Why, you put those things together and you can introduce anybody to the notion that would make them suspicious of what War activities might explode on an innocent observatory.

Yes, and there is more of a background than that. **I am Lucy Miller, and I am a voice of McDonald Observatory.** In World War I we were so close to the border of Mexico and there was a great fear then of the Germans invading the U.S., coming in out of Mexico. This carried into World War II times and anybody who had a German name was under suspicion. They even had to wear nametags for a while. Do you remember that, Keesey?

Yes, I remember. There was even talk between Elvey and Dr. Struve saying that the people who live around here are beginning to worry about the possibility of an invasion from Mexico and that they should get in touch with the Warner and Swasey people who installed the 82-inch mirror so that if they had to, they could pull the mirror out and bury it in the ground to keep it from being destroyed. The attack never came, of course, but those are the problems of rumors getting started. Lucy, did you want to tell our visitor something more about the early people at the Observatory?

Cossack Cavalry officer to first director
Yes, well, when the University of Chicago and The University of Texas made the contract to operate the Observatory for the first thirty years jointly, Otto Struve was the director, the first director. How he landed here is fascinating. Our Struve, his great-grandfather, his

grandfather, and an uncle, each won the Gold Medal from the Royal Astronomical Society.[8] His father had established a Russian observatory and was the director. When World War I broke out, young Struve became an officer in the Cossack Cavalry. He finally was able to leave the constant turmoil and wound up at Constantinople. He was just penniless, nothing to go on, nothing to live on, but fell into the hands of the Red Cross there. By many chances, his condition became known to the University of Chicago, which was looking for an astronomer to replace an astronomer who was going blind. They wired him money to come to America; he went to the University of Chicago and was immediately given the position. And that is just a little bit of the story of how he came to us.

The Hotel Limpia story

Now this is about the Limpia hotel...Espey and Keesey's parents ran it and all the traffic and personnel for the Observatory came and most of them stayed at the hotel. Their parents got acquainted with everybody. It had originally belonged to the Union Trading Company. The Union Trading Company was established by Mr. Clifford Keesey, who was a baker with the army. That was an enterprising man because he left the army and built this trading post. It was the bank, the post office and a general store where they sold everything. He became immensely wealthy. Espey told me that the original little adobe building was left there when they decided to enlarge it and they built the big building around it. He sold everything from coffins to groceries to whiskey. It was the saloon and it was the bank and just about everything else. Later on, because Mr. Keesey was old and had no children, he sold the store, which had been his alone, to a group of local merchants, ranch people.

Different people ran the hotel; it was such a thriving business in those days before the automobiles and roads had gotten good. It was largely people from Galveston and Houston who would come out here. They would send their families out here to get them out of the dangerous climate and sometimes they would come out on the railroad and stayed months there at the hotel in the summer—the wives and children would, and the husbands would come out in intervals to see them. The Limpia Hotel was the only boarding house and almost the only place to eat. There was a little cafe in the old building there. It was such a profitable thing that eventually they had to build what we call the annex down there. The current building is much larger than the original.

---

[8] Biographical Memoirs V.61 (1992), National Academy of Sciences, National Academy Press.

The Limpia was also the only place in the early days for the astronomers to stay at. All in all, we were very friendly with the astronomers in those days. Dr. Gerard Kuiper was one of the first Chicago astronomers and my husband's acquaintance with the Kuipers came from the day the 82-inch mirror was put in the Observatory. We knew it was coming, of course, and my husband went up there to see and watch it come in. He came home that night and told me that he had "been sitting on a log all day with a pretty girl in a red dress." That girl in the red dress was Sarah Kuiper, Dr. Gerard Kuiper's wife. Gerard was director of the Observatory after Dr. Struve. That was our first meeting of them and from that time on they became our close personal friends and we enjoyed that friendship for the thirty-five years. Now Bit, you can tell something more about our social life with the astronomers.

Astronomers absorbed into the Ft. Davis community

Oh, in those days we were real close to the astronomers, all of us were in Ft. Davis. There were not so many in those days, like there are now. We were all good friends. We got to know the astronomers and we knew everybody up there. We had a club. We didn't have the TV but we had what we called a "duck dinner;" it was from a cartoon of a duck dinner—you bring the ducks! So we had this duck dinner and everybody brought food. Then we played cards or whatever. The astronomers all belonged to the club with us. We expected them to be highfalutin and all that, but they were not that way. Not any of them.

In those days they came to church too; there were eight of them from up there in our choir and one of the astronomer's wives was our organist and choir director. We had a real good church attendance in those days, and members. And I didn't miss anything up there at the Observatory either; we were always invited. They were lovely folks. It's sad, but now they seem to have their own community up there and I don't see any of them anymore, except the ones that have been there a long time. There are so many of them now, too, I never meet any of them.

Dear Visitor, I would like you to see the Hobby-Eberly Telescope…well, I think you ought to see the first one first, and then go on up like I have. You know, I went up there first when it was just a tent and I spilled the hot chocolate on the doctor. That cloth-tied path up to the tent observatory started right there at that big curve, dead man's curve right at the bottom of the hill.[9]

---

[9] This chapter is a compilation of an interview of Keesey, Lillian, and Lucy (sister-in-law) Miller by John Derral Mulholland and Jerry Wiant, Dec. 27, 1980, and an interview

Camille Doss

Mountain observatory life

The voice you will hear tonight comes to you from the Camille and Dave Doss home in the Davis Mountains at the McDonald Observatory. From the Observatory road, walk down a wooded stone path to the chain link gate. Upon entering her living room, you are struck by the breathtaking view from three picture windows overlooking the valley below. Nature is up-close. Tonight, it is clouding up and there is a storm threatening.

I met him for the first time when I was eighteen. I was a student at Sul Ross and had come up to the Observatory with my family. I was standing outside of the 107-inch dome, looking down at House A because it was very picturesque. David came out of the dome side-door and frightened me. I turned around to look at him and he thought I said, "Hello." He came over and said, "Hi," and started talking to me. **I am Camille Doss and I am a voice of McDonald Observatory**. Shortly thereafter, we began dating and in 1973, we were married. We have lived here ever since. Our first year we lived in a trailer at the bottom of the mountain; in 1974 we moved to House E, and finally, in 1976, we moved into this house, House H. I was pregnant with our first child, Selena. Selena was the reason we put a fence around the yard and you have to come in a gate. You know, there were things about living on the side of a mountain that obviously are obstacles. We have a bi-level patio outside and I was always trying to put up barricades on the upper level so that when she played, she wouldn't step off accidentally. When she was three years old, she disappeared and I couldn't find her anywhere. She had toddled off to the 30-inch dome. That scared me; so shortly thereafter we put a fence up just to keep a boundary around the yard.

As the children grew up, we have three—Selena, Daniel and Tracy—they had the little three-wheel bikes and we would take walks around the mountain every evening. We've always had several cats and dogs, and whenever we would take a walk, the cats and dogs would follow us. Tourists would always be amused by our little entourage as we walked around the mountain, David and I walking, the three children peddling, the dogs panting, and the cats following and meowing. I think that is my fondest memory because it was so peaceful and carefree and everyone was happy. This was such a simple family time and is a lovely memory that I cherish.

---

with Lillian "Bit" Miller by Karen S. Winget, Sept. 24, 2000, with the exception of footnote 8.

It is remote here but I think David and I prefer it. I think the children liked it as well because we did a lot of things together. Danny was a Boy Scout, the girls were in Girl Scouts, and I was the leader. I gave my children a birthday party, all three of them, every year of their lives until they were ten years old. That meant I imported kids up here. I would drive to Ft. Davis, pick up the kids, and bring them to the house. We would have the party, then I would drive them home. It was a long day, but that was OK, because I wanted them to have a normal childhood and if it meant importing the kids' friends, I didn't mind doing that. I used to give Christmas parties up here for the Observatory children and we would have Santa come and bring gifts; it was fun.

We were also very involved in the First Presbyterian Church in Ft. Davis, the same one Bit Miller sings in. Have you seen it? It is right up against Sleeping Lion Mountain—very picturesque. David and I were married there and I became a member in 1984. Selena, Danny and Tracy became members in 1990. We participated in Vacation Bible School and Sunday School; the church has been a very integral part of our lives. Remote mountain living is not for everyone, not everyone would enjoy it perhaps, but I have come to cherish the way we live.

Dinner by moonlight with Harlan and Joan

Another of my favorite memories is of Harlan and Joan Smith; Harlan was the first Texas director of the Observatory. They invited us to dinner one night at their house, House A. Their dining room has large picture windows on two walls so there is a stunning view of the valley. There was a beautiful full Moon that night and Joan never turned on a light. She didn't need to; the moonlight was so bright. We sat there in the moonlight and ate our dinner and talked. We started talking about the Marfa Lights and told stories about ghost lights in the moonlight. It is such a wonderful memory of such a lovely time.

Harlan and Joan would come visit our house too. David kept beehives for many years and they came over because Harlan kept beehives in Austin and he wanted to see David's. So they came over and we talked about beehives and visited and they would always share their honey from Austin and we would share ours from Mt. Locke.

Keeping the mountain dark

Excuse me for a moment, I have to close the blinds, it is getting dark. You can't leave your blinds open because the lights in the house will interfere with the telescope viewing. Sometimes, when I go to visit friends, I get very antsy to close their blinds in the evening as well. Ever since my children were small, they have always wanted to have outdoor Christmas lights, but we were not allowed to at the Observatory. They would always ask for outside lights when they were small, but when they got older, they understood. When they moved to Alpine, their houses always looked like the Griswalds in the Chevy Chase movie because they could have as many Christmas lights as they wanted, so it's really rather funny to go by their houses and see them lit up.

David Doss

David, because of his job, has to get up in the night and assist the astronomers with equipment. This always amazed me about him. When the astronomers have a problem, they call David. If David couldn't talk them through the problem, then he would go up. He never lost his temper. He never griped about these calls. I know I would not have been as patient. He never got angry, he would just get up and take care of the problem. He loves his job. He knows this is his job, they need help, and they can't get their data if he doesn't get whatever they are working with fixed or running or at least try to. That's one thing that I have admired about David, his dedication. He is very dedicated to what he does and enjoys it, which is a plus for him. Not many people stay with a job for thirty years.

McDonald Observatory. Phtoto by Tim Jones, McDonald Observatory.

Fireworks and the 4th of July

Another David story, one of his favorite things, and we haven't been able to do it because of the drought, is the 4th of July fireworks display. David is a fireworks aficionado. We have a basement full of fireworks just waiting for a show. That was something he started and has loved to do but as I said, we haven't been able to do over the last few years because of the drought. We would go down to the old visitors center parking lot, and he would tell several people, "We are going to have a display and if you want to bring some stuff to shoot off, bring it over."

24

We would sit in our lawn chairs and watch David and friends put on a grand display of fireworks. It was spectacular and very enjoyable.

The view from Mt. Locke

If I am out walking, tourists ask me, "Do you ever get tired of this view?" I'd say, "No, I never do." I have had tourists tell me how lucky I am to live here and I'd say, "I know." When David retires, we have to leave our home and that is not a happy prospect. That's one of the bad things about living here, this house isn't ours and I know David and I will miss our home and our view. Like I said, there is nowhere else like this. I will miss the view; it is ever changing.

Sheri Eppenauer

I am Sheri Eppenauer and I am a voice of McDonald Observatory.

A caring community of friends

Our ranch, the Eppenauer Ranch, is a family trust. McDonald Observatory has been our neighbor and it is a caring community of friends. Whenever we needed help, from ousting a rattlesnake to putting out a fire, all we have to do is call, any time of the day or night, and someone will come to help. One year, this area suffered a fire that took two months to extinguish. The Observatory personnel, from the staff to the astronomers, worked day and night, side by side with the residents and finally put out the fire. They have the best fire people. Even though fires and the smoke are not good for observing at McDonald, fire is not the worst thing that can happen out here. Lightning starts the fires usually and the result is nature's way of replenishing the earth. Because of the location of the Observatory on the mountaintop, they can see a lightning strike, the resulting fire, and immediately call the landowner. Then they bring their equipment and help, which is all volunteer, and begin fire-fighting strategies.

One time our house burned to the ground. The people at the Observatory all came down and helped us clean it up. They are just all *good* people. If there were no Observatory, then we would have no neighbors, there would be no help, and it would be a void out here. The Observatory even purchased a school bus for the children. I am a schoolteacher and we have sent the children to the Observatory and the new Visitors Center. When they come back, they are full of new knowledge. We are truly intertwined with the Observatory.

We also help the Observatory out; it is a giving of both ways. If they needed something, like caliche, we would bring it to them. It also, at the same time, seems like another world. A world revolving around the white domes.   The life up there is very different.   In the evenings, they must blind all their windows with black shades. This is to not allow light to escape the house and destroy the astronomers' data.

We are also very proud and pleased that Mt. Fowlkes was named after our family, the E. H. Fowlkes family.   Edwin H. Fowlkes donated 200 acres of his Highland Springs Ranch, which included the point of highland then called Little Flat Top, to McDonald Observatory more than sixty years ago.   Little Flat Top was renamed Mt. Fowlkes in his honor and is where the Hobby-Eberly Telescope is located.

The essence of McDonald Observatory

McDonald Observatory is a quiet, scientific place that is not heard, but sees.   McDonald does its work without disturbing nature or the people.[10]

McDonald Observatory. The Hobby-Eberly Telescope is in the foreground and the Harlan J. Smith telescope (left) and the Otto Struve telescope (right) are visible on Mt. Locke. Photo by Martin Harris, McDonald Observatory.

---

[10] Telephone conversation between Sheri Eppenauer and Karen Stewart Winget, September 23, 2000.

Chapter 4 Early Scientists

Jesse Greenstein

Jesse Leonard Greenstein (1909-2002) pioneered several areas of astronomy in the 20th century. He played key roles in the discovery of interstellar magnetic fields and understanding the bizarre spectra of quasars as familiar lines with extreme redshifts. His expertise in theory and observations led to fundamental contributions to the understanding of stellar atmospheres through their spectra. He revolutionized the study of white dwarf stars.

My name is Jesse L. Greenstein and I am a voice of McDonald Observatory. Dear Visitor, I am speaking to you from Pasadena, California, in August 1980. At this moment in time, I am looking through some photographs and material of McDonald Observatory from the early years of the Observatory operation, being the 1930s and 1940s.

Pictures and people

Now, I know you cannot see these photographs, but let me just tell you a little bit about them. You might like to know about these people and the events—they have been very important in the astronomical world and I am sure you will recognize some of them as well as some of the instruments at the Observatory. The first photograph I come to is labeled, "Cleveland, Ohio, October 1937," and shows Sid McCauskey, myself, and Louis Green with Jason Nassau and Otto Struve seated in front. You have heard a bit about Struve before and I will tell you a little more about him in just a minute. This photograph was almost certainly taken in Nassau's house; the occasion was a visit by Struve to the Warner & Swasey Company to see how the 82-inch mirror testing was progressing. Warner & Swasey Company was the one hired to make the 82-inch mirror which was later named the Otto Struve Telescope. As things happen, the optician apparently misunderstood the nature of the patterns seen in the knife-edge testing of the mirror and each time an error was polished off the edge, it reappeared at the center. At the time I arrived, a good fraction of a year had been wasted in mis-correcting the mirror over and over. It is my memory that it was Gerard Kuiper who recognized the nature of the error, and after that point the mirror was rapidly processed.

The next pictures are of the winter of 1938 and early 1939 and reflect some of my visits to the Observatory before the 82-inch was completed. Otto Struve, Louis Henyey, and myself spent an evening in the library at Yerkes on a cloudy night and designed the nebula spectrograph, which was mounted on the 40-inch refractor first, and used by Henyey and myself for extensive investigations of reflection and emission nebulosities. We also obtained the spectra of a comet in the far UV. The optics were from the Cassegrain spectrograph of the unfinished 82-inch. Struve then planned the larger 150-foot nebula spectrograph using the same optics, which was built on the side of the McDonald Observatory on a slope which provided a proper angle to give it, effectively, a polar mounting. I went to use this on several occasions at McDonald.

Those few early years were of interest because with the nebula spectrograph, Struve really found the H II region, the glowing gas or interstellar medium, around hot young stars. This allows us to better understand the formation of stars. Bengt Strömgren, Denmark and Yerkes astronomer, later interpreted these so that the origin of the Strömgren spheres is in this somewhat makeshift instrument. The Rosette Nebula is an example of a Strömgren sphere.

Now I come to a somewhat "bloodthirsty" looking picture with a gun. The picture shows Arch and Ellie Garner, and I believe the gun is mine because I used to do target shooting. Garner was a very important figure in maintenance of the Observatory, the powerhouse, operation of the telescope when it eventually ran, and maintaining a generally high morale for visitors. He came, I believe, from northern Texas or Oklahoma, was part Indian in background and proud of it. He was unfortunately injured in a percussion cap explosion accident some years later and became, I believe, a schoolteacher. He was the absolute central figure in maintaining any kind of operations in those days. I remember a sticky relay, which required his climbing, in his pajamas, to the top of a ladder to poke it with a handle of a broom. He did everything.

The next picture is of the dedication of the Observatory in 1939. It is amateurish but is what I could get and shows many of the distinguished visitors. The group in front of the door starts with Henry Norris Russell, a Princeton astronomer, the next gentleman being, I think, the provost from the University of Texas, then Otto Struve, and Harlow Shapely of Harvard University. In another picture, standing on the catwalk of the Observatory, is Harlow Shapely. Another doorway picture shows Russell, J.S. Plaskett, Compton, Struve, and Shapely with an unknown in the back. My picture between the automobiles is Dean McLaughlin of the University of Michigan, Jan Oort from Holland, and Edwin Hubble.

We were, in fact, properly cognizant of the work of women astronomers in 1939, apparently, because in another photograph there is Cecelia Payne-Gaposchkin and Helen Sawyer Hogg.

Jesse Rudnick is on the picture with Karl Wurm and Albrect Unsöld. It should be remembered that the War, World War II, broke out a few months later. Unsöld was one of the first users of the coudé spectrograph; I was the observer for Struve and Unsöld and obtained many of the first high-resolution spectra taken with the one-half prism Littrow prism spectrograph, which gave roughly two Ångstroms per millimeter dispersion at H gamma. Unsöld and his students laid a classical work on Tau Scorpii which was done on plates taken in the first week or so of use of the coudé, with me and Struve, and, soon after the dedication.

Another group picture shows Albert Whitford, later director of the Lick Observatory, who had introduced photoelectric photometry and modernized by adding vacuum tube amplifiers. Karl Wurm is also shown with me in that picture.

The balance of these pictures are of a rodeo given by the local cowboys to celebrate the telescope's opening and especially to fascinate the European visitors.

The rodeo held for the occasion of the 1939 dedication, especially for the entertainment of the European guests. McDonald Observatory archives.

As I am looking at these pictures, of roughly forty-three years ago, some facts will be approximately right only. Let me attempt to give you a general impression of the state of Yerkes-McDonald before World War II began.

I came to Yerkes on my own funds as a National Research Fellow, a position I held for two years; I had met Otto Struve during a summer school at Harvard and found him very impressive. In those years he had invented the custom of bringing distinguished European astrophysicists to Yerkes and with the McDonald telescope approaching completion, also people with observing interests like Gerard Kuiper. I was half theorist, half observer myself.

Science, instruments, and firsts

Lacking the 82-inch telescope because it was not yet complete, I turned to collaboration with Louis Henyey, one the most brilliant Ph.D.'s from Yerkes. He was an outstanding theorist, had worked on theory of reflection nebulae, which was an interest that Struve and Elvey had had. Henyey and I made a good team in that I was more aggressive on obtaining observational data to illuminate some of these theoretical questions. It was Struve's wide curiosity that led to the construction of the nebula spectrograph on the 40-inch eventually at McDonald.

The ultraviolet quartz prisms and Schmidt cameras were available for the 82-inch Cassegrain spectrograph at that time, and we merely scavenged some lumber and designed and built the simplest possible light-efficient spectrograph. With it we obtained not only the spectra of reflection nebulae and of the Orion Nebula, which I studied in detail, but the first ultraviolet spectra of comets; the OH band at lambda 3060 Ångstroms was first seen with that instrument, and not very much more was done until space missions which showed Lyman alpha.

The great importance of the Strömgren spheres in the study of interstellar matter should not be forgotten; it essentially was the discovery that almost anywhere in the Milky Way one saw H alpha emission. With a McDonald nebula spectrograph, that made the idea of diffuse ultraviolet excitation and heating of the interstellar matter a generally acceptable one.

The first instrument available for the 82-inch was the Cassegrain spectrograph I mentioned, which was capable of giving ultraviolet and normal region spectra on film at reasonably good resolution, but also with a fast Schmidt camera, making it possible to reach faint stars.

The coudé spectrograph has long been replaced, but was initially a Littrow device with one-and-a-half glass prisms, therefore acting like a 3-prism spectrograph with a lens. The focal surface was highly curved and tilted and it was necessary to use film. This proved extremely difficult because unlike glass, film moves due to changes probably in humidity and possibly in temperature during exposure and there is almost no way of holding the film down. I experimented extensively for Struve at the very beginning of the use of the coudé. Some of the best spectra taken were with very heavy backing film of a type sometimes used in aerial photography, which as I remember, was nearly 3 millimeters.

With slow, high-contrast "process" Eastman emulsion, we obtained some beautiful spectra of bright stars, including Tau Scorpii, which Unsöld and successive generations of students analyzed and repeated in Germany using improved methods of radiation transfer and line-broadening theory.

Non-local thermal dynamic equilibrium problems were tackled by Swings from Belgium, who worked with Struve extensively, and with Karl Wurm who had to return to Germany with the outbreak of World War II. Struve's very international point of view resulted in having an outstanding group of senior European astrophysicists visiting on various occasions and for various lengths of time. Pol Swings was, in fact, caught in the United States by the German attack on Belgium and stayed through the War.

The first uses of McDonald that I remember are almost completely spectrographic; my attempts at photography at the prime focus failed because of a miserable support system and triangular images. I took some plates of the galactic center, however. Given the southern latitude, these plates should have been among the best ever taken, but the image quality was sadly deficient.

The observing scheduling for McDonald was almost always on a full-month basis, which was a fairly exhausting program. I remember once replacing Pol Swings, who, thin to begin with, had lost nearly 20 pounds in a month. We had problems with maintenance of the powerhouse through the entire night, since the workmen couldn't stay on duty, and eventually we had problems being our own night assistant after a certain number of hours.

The first few years were early for photoelectric astronomy, and most of the Yerkes interest was in astrophysics. Struve was interested in spectroscopic binaries and eclipsing systems, of course, the longer period contact systems with shells on which he worked so much with Swings. Much observing was done to cover these around their long cycles.

Insofar as I had any interest in spectroscopic astrophysics, it was more centered on the possibilities of obtaining stellar compositions. In this connection, I should say that the first suggestion that I work on a star of unusual composition was made by Otto Struve who told me that I should work on Upsilon Sagittarii. The system was then completely mysterious; Struve knew, I think from work at Mt. Wilson, that it showed little or no hydrogen. In 1940, I published my first paper on the composition of a star, and I believe it is also the first quantitative analysis of any star of peculiar composition made.

I also obtained a series of high-resolution spectra with the coudé of standard stars of various spectral types, together with some fainter objects with a longer camera on the Cassegrain spectrograph. The goal was to determine whether all stars had the same or different compositions, i.e., to apply the theory of ionization and excitation equilibrium with what little was then known about stellar atmospheres to the entire range of spectral types from B to G.

For me, much later, this resulted in my analysis of a metallic line star 14 Tau Ursa Majoris, and its comparison with stars of similar temperatures but of normal composition and differing luminosities. This series of papers in 1947 through 1948 was the invention of what I would call the Differential Curve of Growth method as a practical tool but it really started with my first observing sessions at McDonald in 1939 and 1940.

Otto Struve, first director

The dedication pictures show the wide and catholic interest that Struve had in astronomy. He invited the leading Europeans in several fields, the leading Americans and even brought some from Mt. Wilson, an observatory that had taken a negative or zero interest in Yerkes since Hale had left there many years earlier. I believe it would be a fair judgment to say that the work at Yerkes and McDonald in its first few years clearly established that team as far surpassing the Mt. Wilson Observatory, which had a larger and more experienced staff, but had no theoretical interest.

One could give Struve credit for two things. One, the invention of the combination of theoretical astrophysics and observations; and two, the importation of Europeans, if necessary, to do that; but also one must give him special credit for the incredible energy with which he carried on his own work as well as the administrative tasks that brought McDonald into operation. He did not have superb optical technicians or good optical advice. The only person with optical experience when I first arrived was Frank Ross, who had designed a type of lens used for astrographic purposes, and who was a practical lens designer. The new tendencies to the use of Schmidt optics was still untried, and in that area Mt. Wilson had leadership because of its superb optical technician, Don Hendrix, and, of course, the optical experts working on the 200-inch.

But for the period from 1935 to 1950, with a major interruption caused by the War, there is little doubt that the Yerkes-McDonald team was inventing modern astrophysics and observational astronomy.

One final curiosity comes back to me about my own work. I used the McDonald nebula spectrograph to obtain the energy distribution of M31, the Andromeda Nebula, into the ultraviolet, to predict the effect of red-shifting such an energy distribution into the normally-observed, blue-spectral region. In this I came into direct conflict with Edwin Hubble and Richard Tulman, who would use a far-too small so-called K correction to allow for the effect of the weakness of the ultraviolet continuum, as it was red-shifted. I had the courage to tell Edwin Hubble about my discovery, which was published and was correct; he was not amused.

The high dispersion spectrograph at McDonald was used by W.A. Hiltner, now at the University of Michigan, to prepare a photometric atlas of typical stellar spectra which was published. Struve and Swings continued observing with various dispersion spectrographs through World War II, although sometime in the early 1940s Swings went to Pasadena, where he became a member of an optical design group connected with a company doing work for the War.

George van Biesbroeck

van Biesbroeck was another important observer at McDonald; in addition to his visual measures of double stars, he took a series of plates centered on nearby, rapidly moving proper motion stars of low luminosity, to search for even fainter visual companions. This successful search published in the Astronomical Journal revealed some dozen of the faintest known stars; that is, the further extension of the late main sequence and of some white dwarfs. It is remarkable that double star observing continued much later at the Kitt Peak Observatory until we reached late eighties or early nineties.

War years

Struve continued observing steadily through World War II; I also did so, although I was unable to do any data analysis until about 1945. Kuiper also used the 82-inch, but left to do radar counter measures at Harvard. I believe the telescope was kept in steady use in spite of World War II.

Rationing and the lack of supplies made observing at McDonald during that period fairly hectic; a commissary with canned goods was maintained in the dome. On cloudy nights, the Texan night assistants would play and beat the astronomers steadily at pool, thereby winning the proper ration stamps to have midnight feasts of canned goods.

Some technical problems in telescope operation were encountered, and I do not know the subsequent history. The dome stoppage mechanism consisted of a heavy steel cable and a concrete block weight in a control room. In high winds, the dome drifted badly. There were some near accidents with the prime focus pulpits nearly hitting the telescope, since it had been designed with essentially no spare room. I believe there was no real shortage of fuel and the mountain kept in steady operation. Many good, younger astronomers used the 82-inch on a regular basis.

As I remember, Hiltner was also getting interested in photometry [measurement of light intensity over broad regions of the spectrum]. Hiltner might be a good informant about a slightly later period than the first few years, which I have emphasized.

Although I left Yerkes in June of 1948, I observed at McDonald as late as November 1947. My departure coincided with quite radical changes in the leadership at Yerkes; Struve had served long enough and wished to step down from several of his administrative responsibilities; in 1947 Henyey left; and I received offers from the Lick Observatory and the California Institute of Technology.

Yerkes, under Struve with the McDonald equipment, had been a magnificent adventure; for me the prospect of change was as much toward a new place and experience as away from Yerkes-McDonald. I never regretted the eleven years I spent in Williams Bay, Wisconsin, and commuting to Texas. It was a magnificent opportunity, and the McDonald Observatory was an enormously better location to do astronomy than I had known might exist.

I have a farewell gift from the Yerkes staff accompanied by the signatures of some fifty of my good friends there. It includes some of the finest observers, theorists, and friends that one could ask for.[11]

Paul D. Jose
McDonald Observatory resident astronomer in the 1940s.
I am Paul Jose and I am a voice of McDonald Observatory. Dear Visitor, welcome. I would like to be there in person to tell you about my years at McDonald but since that is not possible, I am recording this for you on July 24, 1978. I hope you enjoy my reminiscences. By the way, my last name rhymes with rose.

The 1939 dedication
I was trained as a professional astronomer and was living in Silver City, New Mexico, where I was teaching in a public school when I was invited to come over as a guest to Ft. Davis for the dedication of McDonald Observatory on May 5, 1939. The lectures took place in the dome of the 82-inch telescope and the speakers stood on top of the coudé room. The coudé room is located below and to the side of the great telescope and made a nice raised platform for speakers. We, the guests, sat on chairs on the observing floor and observing platforms. I remember I sat with Franklin Roach, the Observatory's first resident

---

[11] This oral history is not a face-to-face interview, but was dictated by Jesse Greenstein and collected by John Derral Mulholland in 1980. Dr. Greenstein passed away in late 2002.

astronomer. The only speaker whom I remember was Dr. J. S. Plaskett of the Dominion Astrophysical Observatory, and I remember he wore glasses with a black ribbon from them around his neck. He was discussing the figure of the 82-inch mirror and must have lost ninety-nine percent of the audience with his very technical discussion.

A photograph was taken of all the astronomers who were present and they were lined up outside across the front of the Observatory. There must have been twenty or thirty of us. I stood at the left end, next to Franklin Roach. I was not known to the person who identified the faces so was listed as a "newspaper man." During the dedication event, I stayed at the Limpia Hotel, which was operated at the time by Walter Miller, whose son you heard from earlier.

Job interviews

My next contact with the Observatory came as a different invitation, this time from Dr. Struve in the fall of 1945, asking me to come over from the Steward Observatory in Tucson, and interview for the position of resident astronomer for the McDonald Observatory. However, another astronomer, Arthur Adel, was selected and I understand that he, with his wife, reported for duty. Dr. Hiltner was observing at this time and the next morning after Adel's arrival, so the story goes, he awoke and told Dr. Hiltner that he was leaving. Hiltner thought Adel was just going downtown but it seems that Mrs. Adel refused to live in the isolation of McDonald and the couple immediately left the mountain, for good.

In the fall of 1946, I was again invited by Dr. Struve to come for an interview. I was now living back in Pennsylvania, teaching in the math department of my Alma Mater, Washington and Jefferson College. I came down during the Christmas holidays of 1946 and stayed on the mountain for several days to get more-or-less acquainted. Dr. Dershem, a retired physicist from the University of Chicago, was resident staff member in charge of the operation then. He was a good machinist and showed me much of the operation.

Russian astronomers and a Russian engineer

Just before my visit, a Russian engineer was at the Observatory and was making a detailed study of plans of the 82-inch telescope. The story is that he had come with a group of Russian astronomers to look over the telescope with the intent of having Warner & Swasey build a duplicate for Russia. When the group arrived at the railroad station in Marfa, the Russian astronomers got off the front of the car and the Russian engineer off the back. When they were all invited out to dinner in Marfa, the Russian engineer said that he had just eaten and would prefer not to join the group for dinner. Of course, he had not eaten, but being from the Socialist Republic of Russia, he was forbidden to sit with the more illustrious astronomers. When I arrived, the Russian astronomers had left but the engineer remained to study the plans of the telescope. He and I stayed in Cottage F. Between his Russian, my English, and with his Russian/English dictionary, we managed to make it possible to carry on *somewhat* of a conversation.

I recall that the engineer was in the dome with Dr. Struve one night while he was observing. They were carrying on a conversation in Russian and from the ground outside the dome, their voices sounded as if they were singing to each other. I understand that when the Russians approached Warner & Swasey about building a duplicate instrument, Warner & Swasey made the price so high that the offer to purchase was rejected. Warner & Swasey apparently didn't want to do business with Russia.

Early in 1947, Dr. Struve offered me the position of resident astronomer in charge of maintenance and I was scheduled to live in Cottage B. Before reporting to McDonald, I visited Warner & Swasey in Cleveland and discussed the construction and operation of the 82-inch. There were several engineers who worked on its design, and one of them commented that they build fine telescopes for the astronomers who don't take care of them after they are installed. Today, as you know, the 82-inch is still doing front-line science.

Night assistants

In these early days, there was no TQ [Transient Quarters] and it was a custom to have a night assistant whose family would operate a boarding house for the visiting astronomers. Charles Heyduck was the night assistant at the time and his mother ran the boarding house. They lived in Cottage D. Charles resigned sometime after I arrived and went to study at Sol Ross; Bill Bond followed him in September 1948 and his wife, Ruth, now ran the boarding house. Late on the night of April 17, 1950, Bill had an attack of appendicitis. I drove him to the Lockhart Clinic in Alpine around 2:00 a.m. and in due course of time, he was back to work. Bill resigned sometime in 1950 to go to the White Sands Missile Range.

The night assistant who followed Bill had stored all his furniture in a house near the well. I don't remember his name but I found and reported to him that his mattresses were full of bed bugs. He did not stay long.

Train travel and transformations

Travel in these days was mostly by train; it was necessary for someone from the Observatory to drive to Marfa or Pecos to meet incoming astronomers, and likewise, to take them back to the railroad. Pecos was by far the preferred meeting point since most of the visitors came from the east or north. On December 30, 1948, Helen and I went to Pecos to meet an astronomer from Poland. When she got off the train, she was dressed like a poor peasant and her luggage was accordingly not elaborate. She stayed in Cottage F, was so delighted with it, and commented that it was the nicest place she had ever lived in and wanted to know if she had it all to herself. The boarding house could not serve supper on one night during the week, so on occasion, we would invite the observers to have supper with us. This, I must say, provided some interesting experiences. One night, our astronomer from Poland arrived at our house in a very beautiful dress. I can't imagine how she had such a dress in the meager baggage she had with her. She was most interested in discussing politics since she was, at the time, in a free country where such discussions can be held.

I remember another occasion to drive to the train when we took a gentleman to Marfa. At the Marfa station we found a notice that the train would arrive *sometime today*. There had been a washout down towards Del Rio, but fortunately there was a chance to drive to Van Horn and get him to the Texas & Pacific train. We took a fast drive from Marfa to Van Horn and got to the station just minutes before the train departed. So much for chasing, I mean, meeting trains!

Electric power

Today there is dependable power at the Observatory, but in the early days electric power was DC. In the powerhouse there were two Kohler generators which burned butane and two other generators that burned diesel. The Kohler generators took care of all daytime operations, but the diesel carried the night load and required a babysitter all night long. There had been unsuccessful attempts through the Marfa office of the West Texas Utilities to get commercial power to the mountain. Thornton Page, a Yerkes astronomer, was on the mountain at a time when the commercial power was being discussed and it was decided the he and I should drive to Abilene to the main office of the West Texas Utility and join in the discussion. Page had a roadster, a red beard, and a red hat with a feather in it, so off we went to Abilene. At that time, he was a fast driver but years later he had a very serious car accident. From then on, he always advised people to drive slow, and with care.

Well, the mission to Abilene eventually bore results and the power line was constructed. I contacted the ranches along the route to participate in the cost of the power line; the Prude Ranch, the Merrill Ranch, the U Up and U Down, and the Eppenauer all participated which cut the cost to the Observatory, and the power line was energized on the 14th of September, 1948. The AC power certainly made life on the mountain easier and freed the babysitter for the old diesel.

Phone lines

The phone line was an item which required frequent and clever maintenance. Until the lines were strung up on poles, two hard-wire lines ran from the Observatory to town, across country in the shortest way possible. On occasion, the wires were twisted together by the wind or by horseback riders and it was necessary each time to go out and remedy the problem. At several points along the line, there was a fixture where one of the men could connect his portable phone and ring the Observatory until he had found between which two switches the trouble occurred. Then it was a case of walking the line to locate the trouble. One day we measured the resistance in the line between the Observatory and each of the switches, so if the lines were twisted it was possible to measure the resistance and get a good idea just where the trouble was. This worked...most of the time. A particular exception was a time when a hunter, who apparently was testing his rifle from the road along Limpia Creek, shot one of the wires in two. He could not *possibly* have seen the wire, it was just an accident, and I doubt it could ever happen again. I would like to have latched onto one of the old battery-operated, hand-crank phones that were on the mountain.

A V2 launch

I got a call one night from Clyde Tombaugh, who was working at the Flagstaff missile range. He asked me to watch for a V2 missile that was to be launched at 9:00 p.m. Mountain Standard Time on March 21, 1949. I looked forward to this and set up at an open window in the 82-inch dome to watch the northwest night sky. I waited and waited. Communications were not available to relay information on any delay in the firing and since nothing happened, after midnight I finally gave up and started down to Cottage C to turn in for the night. Just as I started down the walk from the dome, I saw a brilliant star rising in the northwest...I did get to see my first V2 launch from a distance of about 200 miles.

The Cook telescope

Dr. Kuiper had made arrangements to borrow the 10-inch Cook Telescope from the Cook Observatory in Philadelphia. This provided Tom Hartnett and I an adventure. In August of 1949, Tom and I had the old Ford one-and-a-half-ton truck fixed up and we took off for Philadelphia to load the telescope. When we arrived, we learned that we were not permitted to drive the truck across the beautiful Cook mansion lawn to load the telescope. So the telescope had to be dismantled and a moving firm came to carefully move each part across the lawn of the Cook mansion to our truck. This trip also gave Tom an opportunity to compare the Limpia Creek to the Platt River and see five-foot waves on Lake Erie, not to mention the general countryside compared to West Texas.

We returned to McDonald and after getting a road built across our West Texas lawn to the Cook telescope site, we constructed a rectangular metal building with a roll-back roof on the south side of the mountain. Although the building was square, we built a circular foundation for a possible future circular dome, which apparently was built later on the site.[12]

People

One of the reasons you picked up this book was to learn a bit about some of the people of the Observatory. The following are some of my reminisces about some of those folks. During the time I was at McDonald, there seemed to be constant reorganization of the administration; I guess because of the joint leadership of the University of Texas and the University of Chicago, Chicago supplying the astronomers and Texas supplying the money for operation until they could make their own astronomy department. When I arrived in July 1947, Dr. Struve mentioned that Dr. Kuiper would be the director and trusted that we could work together in harmony. Dr. Kuiper was director from July 1947 to July 1949. In 1949, a council was formed and composed of three members: Dr. Chandrasekhar as chairman; and Drs. Kuiper and Hiltner as the other two members. Dr. Chandra, whom I had never met, was always proper and cordial in the correspondence we had. This was about June 1950 and Dr. Struve resigned to go to the University of California at Berkley. I felt that he very reluctantly left the Yerkes/McDonald Observatories as he had a great attachment to the 82-inch telescope with which he had accomplished so much. Our contacts were always very cordial and I held him in high esteem.

---

[12] Communication from David Doss, Resident Engineer/Science Associate IV, on March 3, 2003: "As far as the Cook telescope, I have no idea where it is but its site is what we use to call the patrol camera [3-inch (0.08-meter) fisheye patrol camera, 1964] site. It is now the location of the Boston telescope. I had wondered why there was a circular pad under the rectangular building."

Dr. and Mrs. Struve were a very devoted couple. When Dr. Struve was measuring spectrograms, Mrs. Struve was very often by his side recording the measurements as he read off the micrometer readings. Dr. Struve kept a Chrysler two-door on the mountain. This car was the one which was way ahead of its day in its design—streamlined and a beautiful car to drive. Before Dr. Struve left for Berkley, he asked me to see about having the car engine rebuilt and the car body painted. This was done to his satisfaction. The Struves sold their furniture to some of the residents in Ft. Davis. We purchased their dining room table and chairs and we still use them constantly. The last day when Dr. Struve was loading his car to depart for Berkley, he had a sizeable piece of petrified wood, which he was placing in his car. But he decided that it was just too much weight to add to the already loaded car and the outcome was that I thanked him for it. I still have this piece and we have carted it around for several moves.

For several years, there were three families with children on the mountain, which created a school bus problem. My family lived in town during the school week, but there were the children of Mr. Crawford and Mr. Bond. Somehow they were taken to school each day, much of the time by Mrs. Crawford and then one of the men would at other times, take them down.

Thornton Page had married a woman who was a geologist. She took a great interest in the children and took them around the mountain, instructing them on the various rocks. Her instruction was so excellent that the Bond and Jose girls prepared boxes of rock specimens and sold them to the visitors during the summer and on weekends. Very enterprising.

One summer a gentleman and his son came down from La Mesa, Texas. The boy was interested in astronomy and his father wondered if there would be an opportunity for his son to spend a week or so at the Observatory and get a feel for the operation. I agreed that his son could come down during a time that I would be observing. So for a week, Martin Burkett and I spent the nights together observing. He cooked his own meals in the dome except for the few times we had him in for supper.

In February, 1949, Sir Spencer Jones, the astronomer royal, and Lady Jones were in for supper along with the Struves. The house at the Greenwich Observatory in which the Jones lived had been used by all the Astronomer Royals. Well, Lady Jones went into sort of a trance describing to us how the Ghost of Flamsteed, the first Astronomer Royal, would occasionally walk through their house at night. Fortunately, it did not seem that they brought the fellow with them to McDonald.

Now, let's come back to Kuiper. He was much interested in planetary work and built a planetary camera for the Cassegrain focus of the 82-inch. At the center of the plate, holding the camera, was a circular recess to hold a three-quarter-inch diameter lens to give enlargement to the progress. I suggested to Kuiper that he should have Joe Rodriguez make a retainer ring to hold the lens, in case because by accident, the plate and camera could accidentally be turned over when removing the camera from the telescope. He thought this would be unnecessary and I was much embarrassed to be the one to turn the camera over when taking it from the telescope. The lens fell out and became two pieces.

The roof at one of the houses near the well was to be painted and Kuiper wanted the color to be *just right*. So with a five-gallon can of red paint and a supply of pigments, he stirred in pigments, holding up the stirring stick until the color on the stick was *just right*. Well, the roof was duly painted and in a few days after drying, the Sun began to change the color to suit the Sun *just right*, not Kuiper.

In his planetary work, Dr. Kuiper made considerable use of the infrared spectrograph and the prime-focus camera. Bill Bond and I spent much time in getting spectra and direct photographs of Neptune and Uranus.

Tom Hartnett kept chickens and provided fresh eggs, especially to Kuiper. Tom was in need of a better chicken coup, so I purchased ten dollars worth of lumber so he could get the chicken coup in good condition. Kuiper reprimanded me *severely* for helping one of the Mexicans.

Dr. Hiltner was brilliant, but difficult. Since Kuiper grabbed off Cottage B as his domain, Hiltner grabbed off Cottage H and had considerable alterations and additions made. Then it was the usual battle of the budget and money was sometimes not available for equipment for maintenance. For example, there was no money to buy a set of small metric weights to use in changing the rate of the clock. Paper clips and brads became satisfactory for this...ho-hum.

Dr. van Biesbroeck was one of the favorites for the people on the mountain, especially the children. They loved him and he returned the love. He worked either at the prime focus for double-star photography or at the Cassegrain with the micrometer. At age sixty-eight and sixty-nine, he climbed around the bridge of the prime focus; this is tricky observing which often requires standing on the first rail of the bridge. He liked occasionally to come down to the house to photograph the Jose family.

Bengt Strömgren, from Denmark, and McDonald Observatory director for some years in the fifties, and his wife, are a very delightful couple: cordial, friendly, and very human. One day I had to drive to Marfa in the pickup truck, a beat-up job with a homemade plank bed and burlap sacks covering the springs on the seat. The Strömgrens went along for the ride and thoroughly enjoyed the trip, even sitting on the burlap-covered spring seats of the old pickup.

Dr. Pol Swings was a frequent visitor to the Observatory and we collaborated on several programs. I found him a very cordial person to work with. When Comet 1948L came around, I had started taking spectra of it, and when Swings arrived he encouraged me to continue observing the comet as long as possible until it would be lost in the twilight. There was one spectrogram of the comet which Dr. Struve became particularly excited about. He said it was the finest cometary spectra he had ever seen. In fact, he used it as an illustration in at least two of his books.

Dr. Otto Heckman, director of the Hamburg Observatory, visited the Observatory for several days to have a visit with Dr. Struve. He wanted to see Carlsbad Caverns, so I had the pleasure of taking him and spending the day with him. He was the type of person who expresses appreciation in a personal letter sent to us from Hamburg after his return.

Dr. von Weizsäcker, director of the Max Planck Institute, visited with Kuiper. It seems there was an effort to get him into the U.S. as a resident, but his record in Nazi Germany made it impossible to get him residency in this country.

There is a swimming pool and tennis court in the park at the bottom of the hill. Well, how they came to be is a good story. The water well for the observatory was pumped at infrequent intervals so that accumulation of rust had to be pumped out on the ground before clear water could be pumped up the hill to the storage tank by the 82-inch dome. One day some of the boys, Tommy Hartnett and Joe Rodriguez, suggested the possibility of building a storage tank near the well for this rusty water and suggested that I use the water for irrigating a garden. The tank was built and a garden space was laid out. Tom Hartnett and Bill Bond had the best garden; I had the worst. In a course of time, the water tank was converted to a swimming pool, and the garden to the tennis court. [13]

Well, now for the end of my story…One day around the middle of 1950, Dr. Kuiper and I were standing at the basement door at the west side of the powerhouse. The talks got a little rough; I lost my temper and let go with both barrels telling him what I thought of his self-centered attitude and the demands he made for his personal comfort ahead and

---

[13] Communication from David Doss, March 7, 2003. "There is a rock water tank near the current tennis court that was still being used as a swimming pool when I started to work here. It really shouldn't be considered a swimming pool since it's only about 8 feet across. The tank is about 100 yards from the old well site."

above the needs for the best maintenance possible for the equipment of the Observatory. This, of course, was the wrong thing to do.

The three and a fraction years I spent at the Observatory were busy years. I feel that much was accomplished and the conditions around the mountain were substantially improved. I enjoyed working with the telescope and making the acquaintance and friendship of many good men.

We kept our home in Ft. Davis which we had started shortly after coming to McDonald. Frequent trips back and forth and finally retiring in Ft. Davis have given me the opportunity to watch the Observatory grow beyond any expectations which I could have dreamed of in 1950.

Dr. Struve was a strong man and a joint operation between the University of Chicago and The University of Texas could have endured forever under him. However, my observation is that the University of Texas has created a fine staff and the future of the Observatory is assured.

Space pioneers von Braun and Strughold

Oh yes, before I go, I would just like to mention a couple of other fellows you should know have spent some time at your Observatory. On one of the public nights we held on the last Wednesday of the month, we had a group of four of the Germans who were stationed at Ft. Bliss for the rocket program. I forget the names of three of them but one was Dr. Werner von Braun. When his three companions addressed him, they all addressed him as professor. After we had closed the dome, von Braun and his three colleagues came down to the house and we talked until after two o'clock in the morning—a most interesting and inspiring conversation. During this conversation, von Braun was already thinking about a space satellite, a large rotating wheel in which habitation would be around the circumference where the artificial gravity would be approximately that at the surface of the Earth. My brother happened to be visiting with us at that time and he was tickled pink to sit in and ask questions. I sure wish I could remember the names of the other three men who were with him because I believe that our paths have since crossed, but never again did I have the opportunity to see von Braun.

Heinz Haber and Hubertus Strughold were working at the Brooks Aerospace Medical Center at San Antonio—I believe they were two of the Germans who came to this country after the War—they came over for a week or two to make use of the library at McDonald Observatory to get background material for their work on space medicine. Later on when I was working at Havan Air Force Base, I had the opportunity to run into Dr. Strughold. I don't recall of ever having seen Dr. Haber again.

Just a few more comments on operation and maintenance during my time. The metal cover on the inside of the 82-inch dome was held in place with stove bolts. These bolts gradually came loose and some were falling out. The best solution we could find were blind rivets compressed by a wrench. This was slow work. It was later discovered that many of the grease fittings on the rollers, which guided the windscreen cables, the cables for the elevator, and the rollers for the shutter, never had grease in them. So for some time, the men were "grease monkeys" climbing all around in the elevator and scaffolding which would reach to the top of the dome. On the ground outside the dome, there was a concrete walk and a walkway from the dome to the driveway. Considerable time has been spent laying the remainder of the sidewalks that are in existence today.

One day, the secretary, Dorothy Hinds, commented that more butane gas was being sold through the meters than we were purchasing. I suspected the altitude of the Observatory might be the problem because the meters were designed for sea-level operation. After corresponding with the meter manufacturer and a little figuring, we came up with a factor to correct for the altitude and hereafter, the cost to the users was reduced by about twenty-five percent. Several of the astronomers, when they learned of this, wanted a refund for past gas bills. These refunds were not given but from then on all gas usage was corrected for altitude.[14]

Al Hiltner

This is Al Hiltner and I am a voice of McDonald Observatory. Dear Visitor, greetings to you in Texas. Today is December 31, 1981, and I am recording this to you from Ann Arbor, Michigan. I shall make an attempt to recall a few points in regard to the living at McDonald Observatory in the early days of its operation. I was not there at the beginning of its operation; I came in about three years later. My first contact with McDonald Observatory was in October 1942. At that time I was to obtain spectrograms of the very brightest stars for a photometric atlas of stellar spectra. This photometric atlas had been planned between Dr. Otto Struve, R. Williams, and myself, and the reason it came about was that Williams and I had just completed the automatic spectrophotometer. This was a photometer that would give intensities directly from the photographic plate.

My family was with me and we had driven there via Colorado, which was a pleasant trip of course. We finally arrived there in October

---

[14] Reminisces of McDonald Observatory in the 1940s recorded by resident astronomer Paul D. Jose, received by John Derral Mulholland in 1978.

for a two-weeks run with the telescope. It was during the bright of the Moon, of course, and we had as it turned out, two weeks of really beautifully clear weather. I can only say I worked like a fool because of the long nights and then everyday I had to expose quite a number of comparison, or calibration, spectra.

Dr. Elvey was in residence at the time and just getting ready to go off to War research. Dr. van Biesbroeck was there too and one of the very delightful things I recall from this first encounter with...first visit to McDonald Observatory, was the pleasure of hiking with Dr. van Biesbroeck. In hiking the mountains we visited what was then known, I hope maybe it is still known, as Dr. van Biesbroeck's knoll. It is to the south and I believe he must have taken everyone there, and of course, that is the reason for its name.

The War years

During the War years, Struve was very strongly of opinion that astronomical research should go on and not be one of the fatalities of the War. So some of us tried to do both astronomical research as well as war research in optics at Yerkes Observatory. This was headed primarily by Henyey and Greenstein. Today, observing runs are rarely over ten days, but at that time we were assigned one month of observing at a time. After the one month of night...after night...after night...of observing, one could hardly look at the telescope.

The travel to McDonald from Yerkes during the War, and for a period thereafter, was really rather strenuous. In fact, it would take three days and two nights on the train to get there. And now, I guess, if we cannot get to our observing station on an overnight flight, we think it is much too far away. We can be in Chicago in the morning and if one really pressed it, one could be observing that evening.

Probably the most difficult time for the operation of the Observatory was during the War years. During this time, Dr. Dersham, from the University of Chicago, kept the Observatory together by the proverbial bailing wire.

I remember once that the synchronous motor for tracking the 82-inch telescope became inoperable for some reason or another and it got extremely hot. We decided before we really ruin it completely, we should discontinue its use and ship it back to the factory for repair. In the meantime, we switched to DC motor and ran it off batteries. And it's rather remarkable how well it worked, especially for spectroscopy, and the DC motor held its speed with a precision that one could even do photometry.

The lonely life at the Observatory

The operation at McDonald during the…particularly during the War years, was done with very few people. Today as you visit you will see many, many people. Also, there are many telescopes and a bustling Visitors Center. You have to remember that in the early days there was just the one telescope, the 82-inch. A night assistant worked just five nights and when his eight hours was up at three or four o'clock in the morning, he quit. Then the astronomer was alone for the remaining part of these five nights plus the other two nights of the week, which usually came on the weekend when everyone else had left the mountain. On more than one occasion, I found myself the lone occupant of the mountain and often wondered what in the world would happen if there was an accident. I doubt if we would permit such an operation to go on at this day and age, but these were during the War years and one took such risks, and right in stride of course.

One of the things that we were very short of during the War were observers. And particularly observers that would both observe and reduce their data. I recall one time Struve invited Sergei Gaposchkin to observe. The first night was total confusion because Struve was a day late and I had to leave early the next morning so as to meet Struve at his train that was pulling into Pecos early in the morning. So no astronomer was with Gaposchkin during the night—except that I tried to get him started and then I left him to do my packing—I had been there observing for a month. The night assistant was there, of course, but he was very limited in both knowledge of astronomy and the telescope. The night assistant was used primarily for guiding the instrument on long exposures with the spectrograph. That is, the astronomer was completely in charge of the operation. I recall that after going to bed, somewhere between 2:00 and 3:00 a.m., knowing that I could only get a few hours' sleep before the morning departure, the telephone rang. And, there was Sergei with this question, "Does the finder [scope] always invert the image?" I thought, what was he thinking, *always* as opposed to just *sometimes*? Well, you can imagine how much was accomplished that night. Fortunately, Struve arrived in time to help the following night and I think they went on and got some really very nice observations of some peculiar binary stars…binary stars that are now being investigated with new ideas with regard to the flow of material about these peculiar objects. I often wonder what Struve would think if he could come back now and look at the enormous amount of development that has gone on in his chosen field.

We often had to prepare our own meals while observing and Dorothy Hinds, the secretary on the mountain, would plan picnics and occasionally invite people over to her house for Mexican food. This was always a high point in any week, of course, or any observing period for me, to be invited to her house for a wonderful Mexican food meal that she made. And in fact, even today here in Ann Arbor we prepare food of the type Dorothy taught us to prepare while we were at McDonald Observatory. I sometimes say that 801 Bercher, that's our home address, is the best Mexican restaurant in Ann Arbor!

We would also take rides with Dorothy, north toward Kent, to watch for deer. The deer population was pretty heavy at that time and we would see well in excess of a hundred deer. There was no hunting on the grounds, of course, and to the best of my knowledge, the only hunter—at least the only hunter I ever saw on the grounds who shot a deer—was the local sheriff of Jeff Davis County. His excuse was that he had shot it off the reservation but the deer had run over onto our property. Well, the shot deer made it nearly to the center of the property, if that were the case.

Some astronomers from Yerkes considered living at McDonald after World War II, but it was never successful for one reason or another. No one stayed there much, I think, in excess of six months. I know Kuiper was there and I was there for a while, and I recall Kuiper lasted for about six months and I think the longest that I made it was something like three months before the scientific isolation, or maybe the isolation of the mountain itself, got to me.

I seem to recall only a few highlights after World War II. One was an observing run with the 82-inch, just when I was learning some photometry. It was so early in the photometry game that I still had a Galvanometer attached to the output of the 1P21 RCA phototube. It must have been about 1946 because a Russian astronomer spent a number of nights with me and he taught me a lot about photometry. He was so impressed with the 1P21 that I made arrangements so that he could get one and return it to Russia with him.

Another thing I recall, and these are all rather personal I am sorry to say, and that is the first pulse-counting photometer to be used at McDonald Observatory was a six-channel one for observing UBV colors and which we could observe both the star and the sky simultaneously. In other words, we had two apertures and the radiation from each aperture passed through a dichroic [color separation] filter in order to split the beams into the appropriate UBV colors. This system was one of the early pulse-counting photometers used in astronomy. The only other one I knew of at the time was used at Palomar, developed by Bill Bond. This particular set-up was used for measuring M13 and it was during a time when there was some controversy with regard to the main sequence and so there was joint effort between Sandage, Bill Bond, Harold Johnson, and myself. So I was working at McDonald and then later on I went to

Palomar, which I shall comment on. The limiting magnitude of the system when using it on M13, if there is such a limiting magnitude, if limiting magnitude can be defined, was around 22. I suppose I could put it more precisely by saying that the faintest star we observed was magnitude 22, although the information available was very small. [Magnitude is a measure of the amount of light coming from an object, the larger the number the fainter the object.] I later used the single channel on the 200-inch at Palomar, and my general impression was that the six-color instrument on the 82-inch easily out performed the single channel on the 200-inch.

When we originally installed the pulse counter, we had trouble with interference from relays used in guiding the telescope. Every push of a button would put in a few hundred counts, which confused the data greatly. In order to avoid this, what I did was to install some chokes and capacitors in the relay circuits and this quenched the DC arcs so that the telescope became very, very quiet as far as putting any undesired pulse counts into the instrument. The person in charge of the telescope was so impressed with what I had done with quenching the DC arcs that he raised a question about the bridge relays. There had been a long period of trouble, in fact, maybe fifteen years of trouble, with bridge relays freezing and so the bridge would continue to go up or go down as the case may be and he wondered whether or not something could be designed and installed in these relays so that they would not freeze. Well, I suggested a solution and the ground crew wound the chokes on sticks and placed them near the cabinets with the relays. I'll never forget their telling me of their experience when they first pressed the button. They had not tied the coils down and when the button was pressed to move the platform or the bridge either up or down, these unsecured chokes unwound like rattlesnakes. We soon solved that problem and so this removed fifteen years of frozen relays.

And, may I take this time to wish you all a very prosperous 1982; sufficiently prosperous that that 300-inch telescope will be forthcoming...Good luck.[15]

---

[15] Astronomer W.A. Hiltner on his experiences at McDonald Observatory in the 1940s. Cassette tape received by John Derral Mulholland, recorded by Hiltner, in Ann Arbor, Michigan, on Dec. 31, 1981.

Chapter 5 Early and Current Staff and Physical Plant

Cecilia Davis

My name is Cecilia Davis and I am a voice of McDonald Observatory speaking to you in the 82-inch dome building library; my office is in this building. I was born in Silver City, New Mexico, and we moved to Big Bend in around 1959. The first time I came to the Observatory was before I moved here. I was married then and my husband went to work for the Eppenauers as a ranch hand—a cowboy, and he wanted me to come up and see where he worked and see the area. I just thought it was beautiful up here. It was a beautiful spot and the scenery was gorgeous. My father and son, Cecil, had already moved to Ft. Davis because Cecil needed high school, so I applied for the physical plant secretary at McDonald Observatory. George Grubb hired me in January 1979. Astronomy didn't mean a whole lot to me because I had never really gotten into it. Then to apply for a job up here…that was really different. I did purchasing and receiving for the whole Observatory. We purchased anything the Observatory needed. Things I had never heard of in my whole life: like worms—I didn't know what a worm gear was. But, it was really interesting.

Fritz Kahl and I were talking about the mail the other night. They flew planes in; well, they had a plane that flew back and forth from Austin to Marfa, shuttling the astronomers and that was the way our mail went back and forth. We sent the mail out in these little bags to UT and they sent mail back to us whenever they had somebody coming out—two, three, four times a week. Then somebody went down to Marfa and picked up the astronomer and the mail, or we left a car down there, whichever seemed the most appropriate at the time.

At that time our offices were in House C, which was great, I had a fireplace and everything. Curt Laughlin was superintendent at the time and his secretary was Wana D. Box. She left two years after I came and Curt asked me if I would fill in until they could hire somebody and I said, "OK, until you can hire somebody." I am still here you know, I am the replacement. I went from secretary to senior secretary, then administrative assistant and now I am senior administrative associate. So back then I was running back and forth between House C and here, the 82-inch dome where Curt had his office. In fact I walked; it's up hill but it was good exercise and I'd run back and forth two or three times a day. Curt would call and need something so I'd come up here and help him, then I'd go back down and help George, then I'd come back up here.

One day they decided they needed the housing again where my office was and I said, "I am not moving out of here." George says, "Well, we can leave you sitting on the floor..." I ended up in an office in the dome and I think the worst I have ever felt was having to move out of House C.

Fire!

I live in Ft. Davis now, they said these houses were for people on 24-hour call and I said, "That's fine, I don't want to be on 24-hour call." I try to live a normal life after I leave here but sometimes I come back up at night. I am the dispatcher for the Observatory, but I don't allow radios in my house. I have been up here at night when there was a serious fire and they needed a dispatcher. Once in a while the firefighters are in a point where one truck can hear another truck, but they can't hear each other for some reason so I will just relay for them. Now they have a much better system. The Ft. Davis Fire Department can usually do the relaying or Marfa can relay so they have a better fire department.

Most of the fires are lightning strikes. Nearly every fire has been caused by lightning. Once in a while it is a careless camper, but I can think of only one of those and they had it put out in just a very short time. We've really had some serious lightning fires after I came up here. We nearly lost three men because they got trapped, but we managed. A helicopter flying over guided them out. He couldn't lift them out because of the winds that are caused by fires so they had to talk them out. Of course, I helped talk them out. That's probably the worst one I ever had. The men were surrounded and I guess when you feel surrounded like that you really can't see much of anything, but the helicopter could. I don't know how I'd react if I were them but it was pretty bad for me because, you know, you're sitting up here, you are blind—you can't actually see them, all you can do is keep talking to them and try to keep their spirits up. I started dispatching in the day but when the fires kept going, I'd stay up here because you just don't feel good about going off and leaving these guys.

The fire was not real close so we still had observers. The Observatory still worked, but it sure is dark when you've got the lights out like that for observing.

It didn't take long to talk the men out, couple of hours at the most. Part of the time I was relaying the information from the helicopter to the men. Part of the time they could talk to them direct and then, they'd lose contact again. One nice thing about being up this high, you can usually relay to areas that somebody else can't reach. Then other times, there are a lot of dead spots in these mountains.

Running the Observatory and helping the vampires

My position here at the mountain is quite unique compared to the observers' because I am here during the day. What goes on during the day is a lot different than what goes on at night. We call the astronomers vampires. We are the day people and they are the vampires. I'm sorry, that's not nice, is it. We feel like we keep the Observatory running. We know it is paperwork but it has to be done. Over the years it's really changed. I threatened them if they ever brought a computer in my office, I'd throw it out. And now, I can't live without it.

There is a Santa suit hanging in the closet here. Every year for Christmas we find some volunteer, an employee, to play Santa and we invite their children up. It's really up to each parent if they want their child to have a gift. They bring the gifts up to me and I stick them in the safe until it's time for Santa and our party, then Santa gives out gifts. We've got the suit, the beard, and the whole thing in the safe. It's probably the only dust-free area around here.

There are places and things you don't want to remember in life, but as a whole, I wouldn't change anything here…not a minute. I don't understand people that work in places they don't like. I don't know how they do that. Every job I have ever had I have loved every minute. And I have been here longer than I have been any place.

"…Oh, go away!" That is Tom Brown, he is taking me to lunch. Monday was my birthday and he is taking me down to the TQ. I think he will be talking to you next...

I just hope I've contributed something to the Observatory. If I haven't, then I am sorry. But you know, you would like when you are gone for people to say, "Oh yea, I remember her, C.C. Davis, she was good people."

Tom Brown

Well, C.C., Cecilia, and I are finished with lunch now, this is Tom Brown, **and I am a voice of McDonald Observatory**. I, too, am speaking to you from the library in the 82-inch dome. I was born in Ft. Davis. It was a home birth; the doctor then went from home to home. Our house was over there by the Evans' estate, right at the Y of Highways 118 and 117. You can still see the foundation of the house—it burned down several years after we moved to Marfa. I lived here until I was three, birth til three, then I went to school in Marfa. My mother worked for the Ft. Davis State Bank and Dad worked for the State Highway Department, with the engineering group before a lot of these highways up here were paved. They tell me stories about coming to the Observatory across dirt roads and things like that. I went to college at Sul Ross in Alpine and graduated there with a bachelor of science in industrial technology. I worked in the oil field for a while after that and did a little time in the Army. Then in 1981 I had an opportunity to come back to Ft. Davis—I saw an ad in the Marfa paper and knew George Grubb, the physical plant manager, so I contacted him and twenty years later, I am still here.

Physical Plant as a career at an observatory

One of the things you may be interested in is the different careers that are available at an astronomical observatory. Here in Physical Plant, our job is mainly taking care of the mechanical ends of things and some of the electrical—anything over 110 volts falls into our department. But, we take care of the infrastructure, the water, the wastewater, and the buildings. We make the domes rotate and the shutters open. We assist in working on the telescopes and we remove the heavy mirrors and things from the telescopes for aluminizing. We also maintain the thirty-two houses up here, everything from dripping faucets to new roofs on the houses. Physical Plant is kind of like being the "city office" I guess, of the town—we take care of everybody on the mountain.

There are fifteen of us in Physical Plant and four of us live on the mountain so we can respond to night calls and emergencies. I am also the fire chief up here and EMS. We have a little volunteer fire department and that's to the University's advantage—Ft. Davis has a fire department but it is seventeen miles away and a quick response sometimes is best. We are fortunate that we have, I think, fourteen volunteer fire fighters. We respond to not only structure fires but to wild land fires in this county or around. We help other fire departments so in the event we need help, they will come help us.

I am also deputy sheriff in Jeff Davis County. George was also. I have been in law enforcement for about seventeen years and George has been in now for twenty plus years—I think he will be talking to you next.

A typical day starts off with kind of a group meeting—Physical Plant group meeting. We get together, look at our night reports from each telescope observer, and decide if there are any problems that belong to our department that we need to go and work on. We look at requests for service from other groups; HET, or scientific support, or whatever, and requests for services from the residents. You know, if they have a broken front door or a broken window or whatever, then we assign someone to repair that. And, we work on projects, which vary from things like wiring the new storage unit up at HET to maintaining the new Visitors Center. Now that the Visitors Center is finished and property of the University of Texas, we maintain the building. We worked hand-in-hand with the building contractors during the building to learn how to maintain it. There is always plenty to do; we are busy eight hours a day.

We try to minimize the down time that the astronomers might experience for one reason or another—they just call us from the dome and we respond.

Really in the dark at McDonald

One night we had a contractor working in the dome in the 107-inch. He was putting in a computer floor and he wanted to work late. He went outside to his truck to get something but did not take a flashlight. The door of the dome closed behind him, he took several steps and realized, *man it's pitch black out here.* You know, we just don't have any street lights out here, obviously, being an observatory. But anyway, it was so dark that he couldn't find his truck, then he couldn't find the door to get back in the dome. He told us he wandered around in the parking lot or somewhere for a while and all he could hear were growls in the night, you know, coyotes in the distance. It was pretty spooky for him but then someone pulled down into the 107-inch parking lot with their parking lights on and he was able to find the door to get back in. Poor thing. People don't realize just how dark it does get up here. And that's good. That's the reason McDonald is where it is…dark skies.

We encourage people to use caution when moving around in the dark. We have adequate lighting. Not necessarily bright car lights and stuff like that, so when driving, slow down, turn your parking lights on, proceed with caution, make sure that you can see what's in front of you in case an astronomer is walking or whatever. They should have a light and should be swinging it, you know, the motion or movement of walking. We also just try to be observant. Know your neighbors, know their habits, know who should be at their house and who should not be and the types of vehicles they drive—just kind of a neighborhood watch.

One Saturday night at the Visitors Center there was a star party and this college boy laid down on the couch or something, somewhere in the Visitors Center. The star party ended, his group left without him, and the staff, not knowing he was in there, locked him in that night. He slept well until about five o'clock Sunday morning and when he got up and started moving around, the alarm system picked him up. I went down to investigate the alarm and as I pulled up in front of the building, I saw the window shade move and I knew we had a live one in there this time. It took a little while but we got his story straight. There is always a potential for a break-in but this time it was just a poor, lonesome college student getting locked in and spending the night.

One of the problems we have to deal with up here is the remoteness and the effect it has on people. We realized several years ago that some people were not cut out to live in this remote place, so on all job interviews we talk about these things—how remote it is, how do you think you would like it? How would your family like living out here? We also started bringing the spouse along on the job interview as well so they get a feel for just how "out in the country" we are. If you *need* to go to the shopping mall two or three times a week, well, maybe you don't want to live here. People who do live up here still get a little touch of cabin fever and have to go to the city for a "city fix." For most people, it kind of grows on them. They learn to like it and don't think anything about making a forty-mile trip to Alpine to go to a movie or grocery shop or whatever.

I hope I have affected the Observatory positively. There is an old saying, "A good Physical Plant is one that is not seen or heard of." I guess that means when you turn on the water tap, water should come out. When you flip the light switch, the light should come on. In our case, when the astronomer wants the dome to move or the shutter to open, that should happen. I am not sure what the percentage of *lost time* is, but it is minimal because of the preventive maintenance and things we do and keep scheduled in. If we see a potential problem, we try to go ahead a repair it rather than wait for a failure because, if it is going to fail, it will do it at midnight on Saturday night. So hopefully, when the astronomer comes out here to work and they have good skies and clear weather, well, they won't be bogged down by mechanical, electrical, instrument, or telescope problems.

Nothing has come up that we could not remedy. We can handle everything. I've got an excellent crew, a great bunch of guys working with me. If we can't machine the part or make the part, then we have to wait for delivery. That can slow us down. But most of the time we can jerry-rig it and find a temporary solution. Very seldom do we get caught to where we have to tell the astronomer, "We are just going to have to shut down for tonight, we can't repair it." I don't like to tell them that.

There are many aspects to McDonald Observatory. An image I would like to leave you with is one that I actually saw. One day I was up working in the C-Cass on the telescope and I looked down and saw a cattle drive going on. Bob Eppenauer, a neighbor of the Observatory, was down in the valley pushing his cows around. So when you come up on the mountain and take a self-guided tour, you can see this big scientific instrument over your shoulder, then look off down the hill, and see a cowboy on a horse pushing his cows around. At McDonald, you can see the past and the present. McDonald Observatory here in West Texas is different than anything else. Pretty neat.

George Grubb

Welcome to the Jeff Davis County Courthouse. Just now, the church bells are ringing eleven o'clock and I seem to be a bit late. Sorry, there is no air conditioning in here but with the windows open we can hear the birds singing just outside the window. Today is August 9, 2001, **my name is George E. Grubb, and I am a voice of the McDonald Observatory.** I was born in Jeff Davis County. We were living at the upper ranch but my mother did make it to the Alpine hospital with me. My father was a rancher, and then right after the fifties drought he got out of the cattle business and started coaching and teaching high school science…physics, chemistry, and biology. He did that up until the time he retired, although we got back in the ranching business on the side and then back out of the ranching business. Both Mother and Father graduated from Sul Ross. Me too. Mother was a 2nd grade teacher for twenty-five years or so.

Part time machinist and tour guide

Basically I started to work at McDonald in 1962 as a part time machinist and tour guide. Typically we would have somewhere around twenty-five people. We gave one tour a day at 1:30 in the afternoon and only on Saturday and Sunday. Then, of course, we had the Wednesday night program. One night a month on a Wednesday, visitors would come up and we would show them through the 82-inch. Basically we would have somewhere between 75 and 120 people on that night. At that time the stairway rotated around on the inside of the dome in the 82-inch so our limit was 120 people. Admission was free but you had to be one of the first 120 people to get in. We tried to treat everybody the same; it was first come, first serve.

Marlyn Krebs makes George a foreman

And then, lets see, I am poor on dates but sometime in around 1964 Marlyn Krebs was the superintendent at the Observatory, and he made me what we called at that time, Foreman. I basically ran the crews and in those days, the superintendent helped out a lot. Marlyn was a very mechanically adept person and I learned a lot. He taught me a lot about telescopes; he taught me a lot in the machine shop. Marlyn was an expert machinist. He had worked for the Elgin Watch Factory Tool and Die Company and he was a very meticulous machinist. The clock in this courthouse, he maintained it. He also maintained the scoreboards at the school. When Marlyn left, he willed me these jobs or "job opportunities," I am not sure which, but he told me that when he left he was putting me in charge of the clock work, the scoreboard work and the Free Fast Freight Service—he will talk about that in a following section of your book. He was also a happy guy and a lot of fun to be around.

One of my favorite stories is about Marlyn; he is such a super guy. And Marlyn was a prankster. One time up in the 82-inch, he took dry ice and ground it up real fine. He put it in the bowl of the toilet and put a little fan there so it was boiling up and blowing all of this smoke. Then he hollers at the janitor, "We got a fire, we got a fire in the bathroom!" The janitor runs over, snatches off the fire extinguisher, goes in and blasts the commode. Course it's CO_2, so it just makes more and more smoke coming up. We are all just dying laughing. He was always doing that. He may not tell you this, so I will. One time Dr. Chandrasekhar was there and wrecked his Volkswagen. It was all tore up on top and he had to leave right away but could not get it somewhere to be fixed. So what Marlyn and Tommy Hartnett did was plaster the top of his car with cement so it wouldn't leak while he was going down the road. Marlyn was always doing something.

When I went to work at the Observatory, we were under the University of Chicago. I worked for the University of Chicago for two years and then it came over to the University of Texas. W.W. Morgan was the director then and when the University took it over, Harlan J. Smith became the director. Then we started building the TQ and the 107-inch.

We had a standing joke about that time. You saw Baeza's grocery store on the way into town? Well, it wasn't here in the beginning, but the senior Baeza had a little beer store down there and that's all he sold, just beer. The Allison Steel Company from Phoenix, Arizona, was the fabricator on the 107-inch project and the construction crew, of course, were all steel workers—and they put away a lot of beer. So we had a standing joke with LeRoy Baeza in that the Allison Steel Company built the Baeza grocery store, just from beer sales.

Superintendent

Marlyn left and went to Nashville to the Arthur J. Dyer Observatory and so I was acting superintendent for about two years. Then they hired John Weiss, and then Curt Laughlin. The duties were divided a little bit and the physical plant side went under the physical plant at UT. So my title then was supervisor of maintenance and repair shop. But anyway, I continued to run the shops and Curt went more around on the optical and scientific side. About that same time, the University decided that we needed a fire department so we went to A&M and got fire training. The University also bought us an old fire truck that was from the city of Hamilton.

It was an army surplus, 1939 GMC, and we drove it from Austin to McDonald. Oh, it was treacherous; it was quite a trip. Marlyn had moved to Nashville, but Dickey Krebs, his son, stayed and was working for me in the shop so I took Dickey to Austin. That's a funny story in that we were coming back in this old open-cab fire truck and Dickey's ears were getting blistered, so we stopped in Dripping Springs and he bought himself a western hat. We took turns driving the truck because it vibrated, it was hot and windy, and we got tired. Well, when we came out at Iraan on I-10, Dickey was pulling onto the freeway but the mirrors vibrated so bad he couldn't see in them, so he stood up to look behind him. When he did, his hat blew off and at the same time a diesel truck was passing him. The last time I saw his hat, it was stuck on the radiator of that diesel truck and I guess that hat went to California.

Then, about 1973, the University decided that we needed some security up there. They wanted me to go to UT police school and get my certification but the sheriff here said, "That's a good idea but wait a minute; if you will let him go to the sheriff's training academy to get his basic, then I will commission him under the county and that way he can help out all over the county instead of just at McDonald." So that started my sheriff's office career. Of course, we were on call 24 hours a day at McDonald seven days a week and that gave me two sort-of-on-call jobs. Sometimes I had to juggle a little bit, but we had an understanding that if McDonald was on the critical list, I stayed there no matter what. So that worked out pretty well.

Right about that time we started building new houses at the bottom of the hill. We built fifteen new houses. About that same time we remodeled all of the houses at the top of the hill too. We actually went in and put in new walls because a lot of the old houses up there just had canvass over the boards, no sheetrock, and when the wind would blow, the canvass would stand out inside the house. That was not an uncommon construction practice in West Texas in the thirties mainly because materials weren't real plentiful in the thirties and forties. The War effort had taken a lot of material. Just prior to that we remodeled the 82-inch and we completely rewired it. It was all the old cloth-type wire.

At one time, all of the residents got together and built a tennis court down at the bottom of the hill and we had a little swimming pool in the garden tank. Let me explain that. Early on we all had little plots of land down at the bottom of the hill; you could grow tomatoes and chili peppers and whatever you wanted on your plot of ground, and we used the water in the tank to water the gardens. The tank was a little rock tank and is from our old water system. The water system required us to pump water up to the top of the hill from a well that is at the bottom of the mountain. It's right there in the housing area. You might have seen it; it is a silver derrick thing setting off over there. When they put in the water system in the thirties, they dug all of that pipeline all the way up the hill by hand so in a lot of places it's not buried very deep. Anyway, we are lifting water 500 feet to the top of the mountain and you have a lot of pressure on the pump, and in order to get the pump to start, we would have to drain the line back down the hill. So what we'd do is just drain what was in the line into the garden tank. Then each day people could water whatever they were growing. We've never had yards up at McDonald because there's been, not a shortage of water, but a guarded supply of water. But when we built all the new houses, that was too much on the water supply. Also, there were very few garden spots available because it's on the mountainside so we kind of just did away from that and made the garden tank into a swimming pool so the kids could go and have a little fun. It's still there but it's got an apple tree growing in it now. It's right at the end of the tennis court. When we built the new swimming pool, we tried to do a little bit of decorating or landscaping you might say, so we filled the garden tank full of dirt and planted an apple tree in it.

People

Then we built the TQ and right after that we built the 30-inch telescope, a swimming pool, a firehouse and a Visitors Center. And in between all of those, we built a trailer city down there, because by that time we started to grow. It was a stopgap measure until we could get the houses together.

Some of the early astronomers like Kuiper and Dr. Jose were very active in the community. Dr. Kuiper had all his certain people that every time he came on an observing run he went and visited all these people. Of course, his family had gone to school a long time here. Dr. Jose is another one. He was superintendent at the Observatory for a long time and his kids went to school here in Ft. Davis. He would come down to the schools and do star parties for the kids. He was a physicist so he left and went to White Sands for a while. Later he retired back here to Ft. Davis. He has since passed away, and his wife. He lived here until his death. Super guy. His daughter still lives here in his house.

Then there was Dr. van Biesbroeck. He really looked the part of the scientist and always wore a white lab coat. He liked to wait for a tourist to peek into the window of the Observatory. Then he would pop up in the window with his long flowing white beard and typical mad scientist lab coat.

The shooting of the 107-inch mirror

Probably one of the most famous stories at the Observatory is about the night the 107-inch mirror was shot up. I had gone to bed but was woken up by a noise but didn't exactly associate it with the dome. Then my phone rang and it was Eddie, the night assistant in the 107. He told me the other night assistant, Jay [not his real name], was up there with a gun. I didn't think too much about it because at that time we were a pretty lax community; people were amateur gunsmiths and they would go up and use the drill press if they needed to mount a scope on their hunting rifle and stuff. So I got up, stuck my pistol in my belt, and started up there. Nobody was around on the first floor, so I went up to the observing floor, walked in, and when I opened the elevator doors, Jay was there. He stuck his pistol under my nose and said, *"What are you doing up here."* And I said, "Well, I'm just making the rounds." Which I did a lot. I just went around checking on domes and stuff, not unusual for me to do that, but he didn't buy it. He said, *"They called you. Get on the elevator and go back down!"* So I just reached over and punched 1 on the elevator. I thought, I gotta get me some help, so I decided to stop at the aluminizing room and on the way down I punched 3 and got off. There was a phone right there and I intended to use it and why I didn't I don't know, I went through the coudé and on around to the dark room and used the phone in there. I called the sheriff's office (my uncle was the sheriff) and said, "I need some help and I need it pronto." "OK," he said.

About that time, while I was talking to the sheriff on the phone, Jay had seen me stop on 3. He took the elevator down to 3, opened the doors, fired three shots, shut it, and went back up to 5. He had Maurice Marin up there. He was making him bring the telescope down to the service position—that is, down low. Then I called Fred Harvey and said, "Bring your pistol, I need some help." So Fred showed up and then we heard some more gunshots. So I decide I am going to force him to come down the back stairs and I went in and shut the elevator off. We snuck up the back stairs and Derek Wills had gotten loose and came down through the back stairs. He was very excited and I don't blame him. So then we went back down the stairs and turned on the elevator but Jay had already called it. Of course, I wouldn't run so Fred and I hid behind a couple of machines with our guns. When the elevator came down, it was empty so I turned it off again. I told Fred, "You want the back stairs or you want the front stairs?" He said, "I'll take the back stairs." So I started up the front stairs, the visitor center stairs that go up to the visitor gallery. I met Jay coming down and I pointed my pistol at him and hollered at him, "Put the gun down Jay." I still didn't know what had happened upstairs and he said, "No, I'm not going to. If you want, just go ahead and shoot me. Just go ahead." He was holding his gun in a way that I could see it was empty. So I told him, "Jay, come on down." He came down and when he got down to the stairs, he kind of stopped, so I stuck my pistol back in my belt and reached over to get his pistol. Just then, he hit me with a flashlight. I didn't know anything about law enforcement then. I hadn't been anything but a court bailiff for my uncle at that time; it probably would have been different today. Then he ran down the stairs. Ed Barker was coming up the stairs, saw him coming, and went over and hid behind a Coke machine. Jay ran outside, but while I was waiting for Fred to come up, I had gone out and disconnected, pulled the coil wire out of Jay's pickup. So when he ran out and got in his pickup, it wouldn't start. He tried to start it twice and it didn't start so he said, "Somebody has been messing with my pickup." Well, Fred and I ran out there just about that time and Jay jumped out of his truck, jumped over that rail right by the 107-inch, ran down in front of the shop and started running down the road. Ed Barker had come out and we were chasing him down the road on foot. We were gaining but he got down there by my house, and that's when I was really trying to catch him. I didn't want him to go in my house. But the sheriff drove up about that time and saw us running down the road so he just pulled crosswise down the road, and got out. He said, *"Jay, give me that gun."* Jay gave it to him and he handcuffed him and brought him into jail.

He didn't effectively do anything but about one percent damage and he did most of that damage with a hammer, not with the gun. He shot it seven times I think it was, but all of the shots were in the shadow of the baffle tubes so it didn't really matter, it didn't change anything. We found glass from the mirror embedded in the wall. He had brought the telescope down into the service position, walked right down the tube and shot the mirror. There was glass and pieces of bullet fragment embedded in the wall but he didn't have a scratch on him. How all that stuff coming back out that tube missed him I don't know but he didn't get a scratch. Exactly, why he did that I don't know, but mostly I think the whole thing was over some frustration.

Then we found out that he shot at Maurice. He shot a hole that went through his jacket but nobody got hurt over the whole deal. That was a miracle, especially the more I learn about law enforcement and armed suspects, I realize we made a lot of mistakes that night. But we came out pretty well—it could have been a lot worse than it was.

The telescope was down for about three months while we repaired the mirrors and got them back into service. Bob Tull came up, worked eighteen-hour days; he was just one of those kind of guys. He will tell you something about that day in his section later in this book.

Another time, at the 36-inch, a student astronomer let the big hydraulic platform down on his toe and cut his toe right off. Al Krebs was a paramedic and he was also the night assistant that night. He called me and he said, "He let the platform down and he cut his toe off. I've got his shoe off, I've got the blood stopped and I've got his toe in ice and I want to use the suburban and take him to the hospital." I said, "That's fine, I'll be right up." So I ran up and got the suburban and made sure it had gas. He had already called the hospital and had doctors and everything standing by. He knew what to do; he is a paramedic so he got all that done. I said, "Do you want me to go with you?" And he said, "No," so we just put him in the back seat and he took off. They sewed his toe back on but it didn't work—these country hospitals, they try. When he came back up the next day and he said, "Dad-gum you. You sent me in the wrong vehicle last night." I said, "What? That suburban is the best vehicle we got. What happened? Did it break down?" He said, "Oh no, it runs fine, but I should have taken a toe truck." Al…bad joke.

What is the evidence that George Grubb was here? Well, it's like I told my guys when I told them I'm gonna retire. I want you guys to go on and run this, you know, take good care of this place. Me leaving is like a pencil in a glass of water. When you pull it out, it doesn't even leave a hole. But, there are things up there that got a part of me in them. All the way from the 30-inch dome to the Visitors Center. I got to know a lot of people, most of them I have treasured and still do very dearly. I enjoyed the work at McDonald because every day was different.

I stayed retired for about six months, then I had to do something and decided to run for Justice of the Peace. My job philosophy for Justice of the Peace is to keep everything fair regardless of race, creed, color, or religion. Everybody pays the same fine for the same offense. And as much as I strive to do that very conscientiously, it is not always completely possible because of the system. But that is my goal. In my office, I have a plaque that says, *"Justice tempered with Mercy is an attribute of every human heart. But the difficulty is to determine just where should be the dividing line so that the law – which should be sacred – is satisfied yet not too harshly applied."*

Marlyn Krebs
Today is March 12, 2001, and I am a voice of the McDonald Observatory. I am Marlyn Krebs and I hear some people have already been talking about me, but I have some more stories.

Growing up at Yerkes Observatory
My father was superintendent of the Yerkes Observatory in Williams Bay, Wisconsin, at the University of Chicago for, oh, forty some years. So I grew up at the Yerkes Observatory. It was during the depression era, the early thirties, and I was only ten or eleven years old. I was called on to mow all the lawns, which were many acres. Twenty plus acres of lawns and what not. So I'd start mowing on Monday morning and finishing Saturday noon and start right over again.

You may have heard of Dr. Struve. He was director at the Yerkes Observatory at that time and at the end of the summer, my father asked Dr. Struve if they could pay me forty dollars for the summer's work. He said, "No, there isn't any money in the budget. It will have to be written-off as a good experience." So that was my start at observatories, and I was going to hear "there isn't any money in the budget" many times.

The 12-inch site survey telescope

Yerkes had a terrific instrument maker, Karl Ridell, who was from Czechoslovakia and actually built many of the instruments for McDonald in the Yerkes shops. I probably was not more than twelve or thirteen years old when I started working with him in the shop. I was one of the few young people around, Edwin, the son of Dr. von Biesbroeck whom you've certainly heard of, and myself. Edwin is three days older than I am and we were raised at the Observatory, but he wasn't at all interested in machine work. So anyway, I worked the entire summer of 1938 in the instrument shop restoring the 12-inch telescope. The 12-inch had been returned from McDonald after it performed a site survey—testing the night sky for lights, which there certainly weren't any around there. But the telescope had spent a year sitting out in the open on a little area in front of Houses A and B, which was referred to as Benedict's Bench. Dr. Benedict was chancellor of the University of Texas then and they named this little bit of flat area, "Benedict's Bench."

There was no dome for the 12-inch; it was just covered with a tarp and was pretty well weather beaten. Mr. Ridell hired me to tear it down completely and restore the whole thing, which I did. It was not used again and I believe that instrument now is in the Museum of Science and Industry in Chicago. So that was my introduction to Yerkes and the instrument business.

Elgin Watch Factory

I graduated from high school in 1940 and I had been accepted to an apprenticeship program at Fairbanks Morris at Beloit, Wisconsin. Fairbanks is large machinery, locomotives and submarine engines, all very large work which I really wasn't particularly interested in. But, a week before I was to go to Beloit, I got a phone call from the head of the engineering and apprentice school at the Elgin Watch Factory. He asked if there was any way he could visit with me on that Sunday afternoon. I told him certainly. So Sunday afternoon I went over to his home and he told me what his position was, what he did, and asked if I might be interested in coming to Elgin to serve in an apprenticeship with the Elgin Watch Factory in fine instrument work, and co-op with Lewis Institute in Chicago. I certainly did—it was exactly what I wanted to do.

I was fortunate that I was deferred for a while in World War II. I was allowed to complete my apprentice course so I didn't go to the military service until early May of 1944. Arlene and I were married the year before in 1943 and I returned from service in 1946. I immediately went back to work for Elgin in the engineering department. It was sometime, probably in early 1950, I came home from work one day and my parents were there. Elgin was sixty-five miles from Williams Bay and that was a long ways for them to be coming in the middle of the week. Dad told me they were planning to re-aluminize the 82-inch mirror at McDonald and it would be the first time the mirror was ever out of the telescope. Dr. Hiltner, of Yerkes, was going to supervise and run the job and they had asked Dad to go down and help them. Dad just wondered if I might be interested, get some time off, and go down with him.

First visit to McDonald Observatory

Well, I managed it. When we arrived at McDonald we found out there was no resident astronomer. There wasn't a superintendent. In fact, I think I was the first one that was designated a superintendent of the Observatory. But anyway, "Would I be interested in a position down there?!"—I told them that after months at Camp Fannin in Tyler, Texas, creeping and crawling through the rose bushes, I really had *no* love for Texas. I didn't really want to. But for some reason, we were all sort of fascinated with the place. It was nice. I hadn't been informed of the problems they had getting help and keeping help. In fact, before we arrived there, one "would be" superintendent and his wife arrived in the evening and left the next morning.

Anyway, we returned from the aluminizing job and Dr. Chandrasekhar, who was acting director of Yerkes at this time (because Struve had gone to Berkley in California), and I thought it over and decided yes, I would go down to Texas. The agreement was that they move our household possessions and furnish the house and utilities and $400 a month—which was a cut from what I was getting from Elgin at the time. But anyway we agreed to go... partly because we knew that Dr. Strömgren was coming from Denmark to be Director of Yerkes and he would be over McDonald as well. I had known him for many years and he was just a wonderful person. And Dr. Strömgren had written me a personal letter and asked if I might consider going down there, that he would really appreciate it, etc., so those were part of the things that led up to me taking the job.

Gone to Texas

We owned a three-apartment house in Elgin and we finally sold it. There was no instrument maker at Yerkes during that time—Mr. Ridell had retired—so I went up there, stayed with my parents and ran the instrument shop for a few months. Then one day, Arlene called me and said, "A truck has appeared with McDonald Observatory on the side of it. It is just a flat bed truck with Joe Rodriguez and his son Joe Jr. in it, and they say they are to move us to Texas!" They just showed up, no warning.

Dr. Hiltner had sent this truck up from Texas—no sideboards on it—just a flat bed truck. So I immediately drove down to Elgin to see what was going on. I then had Joe Rodriguez bring that truck up to Yerkes where my father and I built some sideboards on it. We didn't have a lot of things but we did have five rooms of furniture to stack on that truck. We managed to stack on all the furniture very carefully, but just covered the top of it with a linoleum rug that was in our kitchen. Joe Rodriguez and his son left for McDonald in the truck with our stuff and Arlene and I left the next day. We went on the southern route through Little Rock, Arkansas. We had torrential rains for four days—just downpours—and poor Arlene was about sick. She just knew all of our furniture on the truck would be ruined. But, fortunately, Joe Rodriguez and our furniture got lost and went a northern route. He ended up going through Tulsa and Oklahoma City and had nothing but sunshine all the way. Didn't see a drop of rain.

So after all, we arrived at McDonald before he did on the 15th of November and the temperature on the mountain was *fifteen degrees*. There was *nothing* ready for us. They knew we were coming. They had called ahead to tell them we were coming but there was no house ready. Finally, they were convinced we were going to stay so they gave us keys to House B, which…oh, it was dirty and cold and no heat turned on. Anyway, we unpacked our possessions and the groceries we bought in Ft. Davis.

Harold Johnson needs help

We had no more than unpacked our personal possessions when Harold Johnson was knocking at the door wanting to know how soon I could get up to the 82-inch dome—the telescope hadn't been in operation for three days and there was nobody there to fix it. Well, I knew Harold well because I had built a photometer for him at Yerkes and I really liked him a lot. So I found out how to light those little open butane burners—which we'd never seen before—left Arlene and the two children (Dick was about four years old and Tommy was eighteen months old), and I went on up to the dome and went to work. I found that the focus

64

mechanism for the 82-inch had jammed and hadn't worked for two or three days. Harold was just waiting for me to get there. So we worked *way* into the night—ten or eleven o'clock that night. When I finally got it back in operation and went back to the house, the gas burners had gone out and Arlene and the two boys were sitting on the couch wrapped in blankets. It *wasn't* a *real* nice reception, but I think they saw we were probably just ornery enough to stay.

Travel to McDonald Observatory and flagging a train

At that time at McDonald, we had the 82-inch telescope, we had a 10-inch telescope on loan from the University of Pennsylvania, and we had a 13-inch telescope and, of course, Yerkes was providing all of the research staff. They would alternate between Yerkes and McDonald. They'd come down for observing runs of two to four weeks. There were a number of them, Dr. Hiltner, Dr. Kuiper, they were probably the two senior ones, W.W. Morgan didn't come down very often; however, he was the backbone and a strong person at Yerkes. He had been my Cub Scout leader, so I'd known him for a long time. I'd known all these people for many, many years.

At first the astronomers would come down by train—come to Pecos. There was one train a day from the East that arrived at Pecos at 6:15 in the evening. That's ninety miles from the Observatory so I'd drive over to Pecos, meet the train and bring them back. The same when leaving; the train left Pecos at 6:15 in the morning. So that means we had to leave the Observatory by 4:00 in the morning. So the astronomers would get up and Arlene would have them all for breakfast, whoever they might be. This was before the TQ and Arlene would cook for the visiting astronomers. I think they started paying her a dollar or a dollar twenty cents a meal, or something like that. Then I would drive them to Pecos and be back in time to take the children school at Ft. Davis. We drove sixty-eight miles a day *just* to take the kids to school in Ft. Davis.

Now sometimes, we would just go to Kent, which is about fifty miles from the Observatory, and have them flag the train down. First I had to call Van Horn and say, "Now look, I have an astronomer on the eight forty-two to Pecos but we gotta get him off in Kent." And they would tell the engineer when the train came through Van Horn, "There is going to be somebody flagging you down in Kent, *so stop*." So we went to Kent, they would stand out there with a searchlight, and as soon as they saw the train, they started waving the light. Then the train would stop and let the people off. Well, you hoped they stopped anyway.

Sometimes, it worked a little different, especially when we wanted to get that astronomer back on the train. The train was due in Pecos at six o'clock in the morning and came through Van Horn a little after four o'clock. I'd try to call ahead to Van Horn to tell them I needed to flag the train but there was never anybody in the depot from midnight until six a.m. So I had a big lantern and I learned to do the washout signal. It was a motion across the front of your body and that was the way to notify the engineer that the track had washed out and he had better stop. So when I saw the train—and I could nearly see from Kent to Van Horn—I would get out in the middle of track with this lantern and start waving. And boy, when they would apply the brakes the sparks would fly and, *oh*, the engineer would be furious because when they stop the train this way, they often get flat spots on the wheels from the sliding. I have been there when they slid right on through Kent and went to the next town. Then I would have to get back in the car with the astronomer and drive like crazy to catch the train up there and put him on it.

Then in later years, most of them when not driving down themselves—which was then a *four-day* drive from Yerkes—would fly to El Paso. Well, El Paso is 200 miles from the Observatory. The plane they liked to take would arrive in El Paso at eleven o'clock at night their time, which was twelve o'clock midnight our time at the Observatory. So I'd work all day, then at eight o'clock drive 200 miles to El Paso and pick them up. It would be four o'clock in the morning before we got back to the Observatory. I'd jump in bed for an hour and a half, get up, get the men started and the children to school, and go on with a day's work while the astronomers coming in could sleep all day. They didn't work till night. It was a bit hectic for a long, long time.

Now, after Texas took over the operation of the Observatory, I believe Fritz Kahl would meet them at the Midland-Odessa airport and fly them to Marfa or pick them up in Austin in the plane. I talked to Fritz on the phone the other night. I used to fly around with him a good bit. He says he still flies a little, but he'll be eighty in September and it's too hard to remember all the things that you must remember when flying an airplane. Oh, he's a terrific pilot. He was a flight instructor at the Marfa Air Base during World War II. Fritz is coming up in the book soon and he will tell you all about the Marfa Shuttle.

Improving Observatory life

And, of course, when Texas took over they built nice residences, which were needed. One of the first things I did was to go in to all of the dwellings and insulate them and put sheet rock on the walls and put in thermostat controls and gas fired central heat. That made things a lot more livable. We didn't need air conditioning up there fortunately.

You know there are 600 and some acres of land at the Observatory and there was always a concern of range fires. Every summer it was dry and there was an extreme drought for several years. Lightning would start fires and the immigrants from Mexico coming across and heading to Pecos to the fields to work would start campfires that got out of hand. It was a serious situation. And there we were on the mountain with no protection whatsoever. If a fire started, what could we do? So I discussed it with Dr. Strömgren and decided that I should buy some cattle to keep the grass down, and the danger of fire. So I bought a few cows. I think at one time I had as many as twenty-five of them. Some of the astronomers were not happy about them. They said this is an observatory, not a ranch. But, in raising the cattle, we had our own beef.

Tom and Eloisa Hartnett, they lived at the bottom of the mountain and were great, wonderful people. Anyway, we built a chicken coop and a yard down there and I bought a hundred chickens and Eloisa raised them for the eggs and then we would divide them, butcher them, and put them in the freezers. After that, I bought a milk cow because there was no fresh milk available out there at all. Lalo Granado, a Mexican man that lived down at the bottom of the mountain, would milk the cow. We gave him half the milk for milking the cow during the week. On weekends the Granados would go to their home in Ft. Davis and I would milk the cow. So now we had fresh milk for all the people there.

So anyway, we were raising our own beef and chickens and having our own milk cow, so we decided to have a big garden at the bottom of the mountain—down where the fire hall is now where they keep the fire trucks and what not. And, it was just for anybody at the Observatory who wanted to plant a garden, which we all did. We grew and froze our own produce, which we almost had to do out there. There were two small grocery stores in Ft. Davis, but they really were limited on fresh vegetables and things of that nature. Alpine and Marfa were forty some miles away. So by doing these things ourselves, we had fresh groceries that we needed and Arlene was more than happy to feed the astronomers for a long time.

Now I need to tell you about the Ft. Davis Free Fast Freight Line because George Grubb promised I would. Well, everything came by freight; even dry ice for the photoelectric cells came by freight in cardboard boxes. But there was no truck line running out to Ft. Davis so twice a week somebody had to go to Alpine and pick it up. Since I was there at least two times a week, I picked up all of Ft. Davis' dry cleaning and whatever else there was at the freight lines and hauled it all back to Ft. Davis to the drugstore, which is now a bed and breakfast place, and left it there for everyone to come and pick up. Now, one time I was away, I think out to the Lick Observatory in California, and when I got back there was a letter for me from the citizens complaining that the Ft. Davis Free Fast Freight line hadn't operated while I was gone and they demanded their money back or some silly thing. It was just a joke thing and the letter was pretty funny.

The letter read:

To: Marlyn Krebs, You Haul It for Others Service, Ft. Davis, TX.
February 5th, 1960
4 cents postage

Dear Mr. Krebs,

Since the government pays us for not raising hogs, we feel it only fair that you pay us for not delivering our needs from Alpine to Ft. Davis. This service has been disrupted due to your absence and the undersigned feel that it only fair and fitting that you reimburse each of us for not delivering our supplies from Alpine, free of charge of course. A fair and just appraisal of the amount due each of the undersigned will be made as soon as the number of days this service has been denied us can be ascertained.

Respectfully yours,
The Dead Beat Generation

It is signed Margie Grubb, Carlos Turner, the superintendent of the school; D.C. Bouche from the hardware store; Bill Friar from the drug store; and Pansey Espey. These are the ones who convened at the drug store for coffee every morning and must have gotten together and wrote it. It must have been quite a chore for them, too. We did not have word processors then but this is typed and everything.

Cleaning the mirror
One of the jobs we had to do occasionally was clean the mirror. We'd lay the telescope over horizontal so that the mirror inside the telescope was standing vertical and then we'd walk right down inside the telescope to the mirror. We had made a trough that fit underneath the mirror with a hose coming out of it that would carry the water off to buckets setting down below. In washing mirrors, you never rub them because there's a danger of scratching that reflective coating which is very thin. We would mix this aerosol soap solution and puddle it, just puddle it, and then rinse it with distilled water. We would do this until it was clean. Then for the final rinse, we would spray alcohol on it. And of course, it would mix with the water and dry it off. We never could dry the mirror with a cloth; there was the danger of scratching it. So it was a job that had to be done periodically—more often in the spring when we would have the sand and dust storms. But you try not to do it too often because it's a big job to re-aluminize. Now, I understand that they have

some group opticians come in and re-aluminize the mirrors very regularly—every couple of years or something like that. But we had to do all that ourselves. That is why the big vacuum chamber is up in the dome.

Hiltner designed the new vacuum chamber. The old vacuum chamber, the original one that was there from the time of construction, had the mirror laid flat in the vacuum chamber. The coils holding the aluminum and chromium were right above the mirror and if something would break, it would drop right on the mirror and damage it. So with the new vacuum chamber, the mirror stood vertical and all of the coils holding the aluminum and chromium were facing the mirror. So if one of them should break, it would fall down and not damage the mirror at all. Well, the new vacuum chamber was built up in Chicago and had to be shipped in to Kent out on Highway 80. We were fortunate enough to get a big crane from Midland/Odessa to come and offload it onto a big truck and bring it up to the Observatory, raise it and put it through the shutters. We were not always that fortunate.

Warner Brothers movie crane lifts new mirror cell

You might have heard the story about when the new mirror cell for the bottom of the telescope arrived in a flatcar in Kent and we had to go over, unload it from this flatcar onto the Observatory truck, and haul it to the Observatory. Then it was a problem of getting the cell into the dome. This was the time when they were filming the movie "Giant" over south of Marfa. We were able to get someone from the movie rigging crew to bring their big crane up to the Observatory.

It was very illegal to put that kind of a crane on the road, so we decided to do it early one morning and I went over to Marfa to meet them. Bringing it to the Observatory we didn't break down the boom, the big arm that sticks out on the front of the crane; we left it in one piece and laid it out horizontal. I drove in front of them. There was some problem getting it around the curves in the road so when we'd get to the curves, they'd raise the boom up and get it around the curves that way.

We got up there in a hurry and it didn't take too long to pick up the mirror cell and put it through the shutters in the dome. But by the time we got that done, the telephone rang. It was a friend in Ft. Davis telling me the State Highway Patrol was sitting down in Ft. Davis—they heard we had this big crane up at the Observatory. One of the troubles they were concerned about were cattle guards built in the highway, but we had gone over all the cattle guards days before to make certain they were capable of carrying the weight for the crane. But it was still not licensed to go on this highway—it was way, way over sized, over length, and over weight for anything that should be on this highway. Anyway, he told me

69

the Highway Patrol was waiting down in Ft. Davis for us. They had come in to Louie's Cafe to drink coffee and were discussing it, so they overheard. To go back to Marfa, the movie crew broke the boom down in sections. We loaded the sections on the Observatory truck, and I went ahead of them on the back road this time—the scenic route.

Movie crane lifts new mirror cell up into the 82-inch dome through the slit. The men on the catwalk, left to right, are Eddie Webster, Tom Hartnett, and Lialo Granado; Joe Rodriguez is standing on the ground next to the truck. McDonald Observatory archive photo.

When I came back through Ft. Davis, of course, they recognized the Observatory truck and they stopped me. They wanted to know where the crane was and what it was doing. I said, "I don't know…there was no crane at the Observatory…none whatsoever." Anyway, they didn't believe me and followed me to the Observatory. Of course, when we got there, there was no crane, so they left. They knew we had done something but they didn't know what…we got by with it anyway.

A-s-s-ending Mt. Locke

I don't know if you knew this but one time Lady Bird Johnson was supposed to come to visit the Observatory with her whole safari. We had been warned ahead of time, so we had everything just spit and polished. There was an old sign down at the bottom of the hill near where the Visitors Center is and the State Department was notified that we needed that sign changed—it was in pretty bad shape. I had gone to Marfa early that morning and when I was returning and approached that flat road coming up by the Visitors Center, I could see a sign up there. I thought, Lord, the Highway Department had been here already! I looked at that sign and *my heavens*, I backed up, got out, and took a picture of it. I went on up to the Observatory and called the State Highway Department in Ft. Davis. I said, "I see you put a new sign up." They said, "Yes, we went out there early and put it up." And I said, "Well, please come and take it down." She asked why and I said, "It's misspelled." She said, "It is not, I was there with them myself." And I said, "It *is* misspelled. It's got 'a-s-s-ending Mt. Locke.'" But, she insisted it was right so I called the district office in Alpine and told them. They said, "Thank you, Marlyn. It will be down." And I swear, within an hour that sign was down. So altogether that sign probably was not up more than two hours.

This sign appeared briefly on the road up to Mt. Locke. Photo by Marlyn Krebs, McDonald Observatory.

Dr. van Biesbroeck

I would like to say a little bit about Dr. van Biesbroeck. He was like a second father to me, really. They lived right near our family at Yerkes. Dr. van B was just a tremendous person. Very quiet, unassuming, went on about his own business. He had a white beard, distinguished looking, small stature. He slept less than any astronomer I have ever known, and how he could do it I don't know, but every afternoon he would walk down the mountain, way down to the Eppenauer Ranch and walk back up the mountain. I don't know how many times he's walked to the bottom of the Grand Canyon. That was just him. When he got up, wherever we were working, I don't care what we were doing, Dr. van B would show up. He just loved to be around us. And, of course, he did the original site surveys for McDonald. He had a lot of interest in the people in the community and everyone who knew him thought the world of him.

van B's Knoll is on the way to Ft. Davis from the Observatory. Just before you get to that field of solar panels on the same side of the road and back toward the Observatory on the left hand side, there's a small mountain, a hill. That's van B's Knoll. I think it got its name dating back to the site survey days when they were looking for the Observatory location—we just always called it van B's Knoll. You will have to look for that when you drive home.

The U Up and U Down Ranch

The U Up and U Down Ranch down there was owned by Dr. and Mrs. McIvor. He was a very famous surgeon from Concord, New Hampshire. Mrs. McIvor had inherited the ranch from her family, then she married Dr. McIvor, and they went to live in Concord. They were wonderful people. They would come out during round-up time in the fall. He would always have us down, he and Mrs. McIvor, for dinner when they were there. We got to be quite good friends. I talked their son, Don McIvor, into taking my place on the school board when I left the Observatory. I know Don quite well. I remember when he was a student in school and he would come home in the summer. He will talk to you soon, too.

I saw Bit Miller at the dedication of the 107-inch and visited with her. Her husband and I were great friends. Keesey was just a terrific man. And Keesey's parents owned the old Limpia Hotel, and that's where van Biesbroeck and all the astronomers stayed during the site survey times. Way back then.

Dangerous work at the Observatory

One of the more unfortunate things that happened to me was when I lost a major part of my hearing. We were blasting the area down where the 36-inch is located and I was setting all the dynamite myself. Tommy Hartnett was helping me bring it in. We had to be very, very careful so that we didn't set charges off so big that it would damage the 82-inch right above it. It was in the summertime and very hot. When we had something like nineteen sticks of dynamite set, we would go out to where the garage for House A is. Joe Rodriguez was sitting over near House B with the detonator. We would signal to him and he would hit the detonator and set off the dynamite. I had just finished the last of the nineteen sticks of dynamite and Tommy Hartnett was walking out ahead of me. I had walked possibly fifteen or twenty feet from the charges and Tommy took off his hat and wiped his brow. Joe Rodriguez saw him do that and thinking that was the signal, he hit the detonator. I was close enough so that the small rocks went over me and the big rocks didn't hit me either, but I got a terrific concussion and it knocked me down. I had a nosebleed and what not. I had a terrible headache and I think we laid off blasting for a couple of days. Anyway, Susan, our daughter, was just a baby, and Arlene said to me in the morning, "Didn't you hear Susan cry last night?" "No, no I didn't hear her." And she said, "You didn't hear the astronomers rap on the door last night either, did you?" I said, "No, I didn't hear them rap." Anyway, we decided there was something wrong. After a visit to the doctor at Ft. Davis, many visits to doctors in Tennessee, surgery, a long, long time with vertigo, and more surgery, my souvenir of the 36-inch is about forty percent hearing in this ear and five percent hearing in the other. It could have been worse though.

Construction of the 36-inch dome, checking the pier. Dr. van Biesbroeck is on the left, Ernest Krebs and Tommy Hartnett are on the right. Photo courtesy of Marlyn Krebs, McDonald Observatory.

Hand-chiseled 36-inch telescope dome
    The 36-inch dome project was a challenge, but it was fun. We had to blast off that side of the mountain to prepare the site. Dr. Hiltner

picked that site. Those of us who had to work there said it was the most difficult site he could find in the area, but I know he wanted the dome protected. They wanted a southeast view for observing and they wanted to protect it from the winds from the west and north and what not. The rock bricks for that dome came from the U Up and U Down Ranch. We quarried it all by hand, brought it back to the Observatory and stacked it all up by where the fire hall is now. We spent the whole winter in the cold with chisels and hammers squaring up all those rocks—by hand, every bit of it. There is a picture of the dome here, but you can go right up and see it yourself.

Then it was decided to put a hydraulic platform in the dome. I wasn't sure what to do, so I bought a filling station grease rack hydraulic cylinder, jack hammered a hole in the rock ground, and put the cylinder down in it. That's the only thing I could think to do at that time. It turned out it was a great idea and it is still there and working.

The pier for the telescope, that's a story. I built the forms in the shop and carried them down there and waited for weeks for somebody who was supposed to come and check that I had it positioned true north on the pier. Nobody showed up and it was getting that time of year when we had to get all that cement poured and get on with it. So I rechecked it myself again and I said, "That's as good as it's going to be. We've got to go on." Well, the week after we had it poured, Dr. van Biesbroeck and my father came down. It was just divine guidance or something that it turned out perfect.

One time I broke my knee up there. Fred Pearson, the optician at Yerkes, actually made five 36-inch mirrors. One for McDonald, one for the University of Wisconsin, and I forget where the other three went. But I drove the Observatory truck to Yerkes and hauled these five mirrors all the way back to McDonald to aluminize them. We didn't have a device to get them up in the dome, they were in crates and quite heavy. I used two-wheel dollies to get them up the stairs to the hallway, make a ninety-degree turn and then up the final stairs to the dome. The mirrors are thirty-six inches so the crates were at least forty-eight inches across and probably eighteen inches wide. We had to turn them to get them in the doorway to start up the stairs. Tommy Hartnett was down on his *hands and knees* trying to pull the dolly, trying to get it squared around in the stairway and all of us saw the mirror start to tip. Tommy's head was right between the mirror box and the doorframe. I just took my foot, pushed Tommy, I actually kicked him in the head, but just pushed him back, and when I did, the crate tipped over and caught me on this knee. I have a big scar, but that *would* have been Tommy's head.

About ten years ago I had total knee replacement, and I guess I have sacrificed some parts of my body for that place. Well you know, those are the would-be *good*-old-days but you had to do with what you had. We just had no money to work with. Every time we wanted something, there wasn't money for it. It's not in the budget. But the jobs had to be done so we got them done. We were real fortunate and it was interesting.

The astronomers

I knew Dr. Elvey. He lived with my parents for many years and married my 8th grade schoolteacher. He was just like a big brother to me. Just a great guy. Gerard de Vaucouleurs and his wife, Antoinette, were astronomers and were together all the time. They came out from Austin and stayed very much to themselves. They were a very hard-working couple. They would be up in that office, both of them, working like crazy. They would be gone for a couple of hours and be back and work all night. They did a lot of observing at McDonald right after Texas took it over. I knew Jesse Greenstein, when I was a child. Henyey, Hynek, and Greenstein were all at Yerkes. I was really quite young then, but I remember them. The Burbidges were wonderful people, absolutely wonderful. Margaret was really the astronomer, Geoff the physicist. I have nothing but the kindest thoughts of those two; they are really great people.

I know that Bob Tull, another Texas astronomer, will tell you some stories on me. Bob was a hard worker and just a terrific young fellow. I don't know of anything I could tell about Bob. It would all be good… and I hate to say something good about him.

I also knew Sergei Gaposchkin, but as before, I was only a young fellow at Yerkes. It's difficult to imagine the Observatory now; it's come such a long way. When I think back and knowing all these people for the last seventy or so years, it is interesting to see how far astronomy has come—in my lifetime. I remember when a group of astronauts came out to McDonald—the original group. They were out in the Big Bend area doing some would-be practice of moonwalking and all of this sort of thing. They showed up at the Observatory pretty much unannounced. We were living on the hill then and I took Tom and Dick up. Since then, Alan Bean sent photographs of all of them, autographed, and I have given them to Dick, our oldest son. That was the start of the space program. I remember when the first satellite, unmanned, I'm sure, went over McDonald. Dr. van Biesbroeck was there and he could calculate exactly when it should be over. It was in the evening and he was down at House C for dinner and we went out on the patio and watched it going over. It just looked like Venus going across.

Right now, at Tennessee State University here in Nashville, I am finishing a spectrograph for a new telescope on Mt. Washington in Arizona. It is completely remote controlled. To think of a telescope being two thousand miles from here, computer controlled without ever seeing it, is really awesome. It is awesome to see the strides astronomy has made. And just a whole lot of them are due to the space program. Just a lot of it. That, plus, for a number of years now I've done prototype instrument work for cancer research. Building precision radiation measurement devices for K&S Radiologist Associates here in town. That's just fun. My wife keeps asking me when I'm going to retire and I told her when it quits being fun. When it starts being work, I'm gonna quit.

You might like to talk to one of my boys, you know, get the perspective of a youngster growing up on the mountain. The oldest one, Dick, did more with me at the Observatory and was inclined to giving visitors lectures.

Dick Krebs

Thanks, Dad. This is Dick Krebs and I am a voice of McDonald Observatory. Probably the first thing I remember was going to the post office in Ft. Davis. There was no postman to deliver mail and people went to the post office twice a day. Probably still do. That was the big activity in Ft. Davis. When we were there several years ago, my wife and I stayed at the Limpia Hotel. She had never been to Ft. Davis before and we were sitting out on the porch one morning when all these cars come driving up about nine o'clock. She said, "What's going on?" Because in about fifteen minutes the cars were all gone. And I said, "Well, that's the post office, everybody comes to the post office; they get their mail and leave. Then they come back in the afternoon and do the same thing."

From the Observatory, we used to go to Ft. Davis twice a day for the mail. Daddy had a school bus, or I think it was just the station wagon, and that is how we got to school. We picked kids up on the way. There were two other families. Let's see, there was the Grubb family who lived just below the Observatory on the U Up and U Down Ranch, and then just down the road from them before you get to Prude Ranch, we'd pick up more kids. Then in the afternoon we rode back, dropped them off, and went back home. There were at the most six kids in the car. Now sometimes there were kids that the astronomers had brought with them to the Observatory and if they were going to be there for a while to observe, then the kids would go to school with us. There were the Kuipers' kids, the Strömgrens' kids and the Hiltners' kids. I particularly remember Roy Strömgren. He joined the band as soon as he got to Ft. Davis and they gave him the tuba. He sat in the back of the station wagon every day holding that blamed tuba all the way, seventeen miles from the Observatory to Ft. Davis and seventeen miles back.

Hand-crank phones to the first video phone

I remember we had a crank telephone; it was huge and I remember lightning knocked that thing off the wall one time. There were maybe eight of them on the mountain; every house didn't have a phone. Dad said that toward the end of our stay everyone did have a phone and a dry-celled battery-operated buzzer system. I remember the dry cells and the little buttons. The secretary would answer the phone in her office and then each house had a code—so many dots or dashes—and she could buzz the particular house for whomever the call was for. I remember the line came down from the 82-inch, past House A to the Prude Ranch. Then at the Prude Ranch, the line went over behind the Indian Lodge, over the mountain, and came out right near Bit Miller's house. That line was in when we got there but it was in terrible shape. It was a little noisy but it worked.

I have to tell you about the telephone operator in town, in Ft. Davis. She would answer, "Well, who do you want to talk to?" and then plug in the phone call on her board. That office is still there; it is next to the Limpia Hotel. Daddy said that office was really handy because there were windows all around and if you wanted to know where anybody was, you'd just call from the Observatory and ask the operator, "Have you seen Marlyn? Has he picked up the school kids yet? Has the Observatory car come through yet?" The operator could look out the windows, see the bank, the post office, the grocery store, and the drug store. She could see it all and she knew it all, too; she knew where everybody and everything was in town. If you called and wanted to talk to Odie Grubb, well, she would tell you, "He is not here, I just saw him walk across the street to the bank so call back in a little while." Or she would holler at him going down the street, "Marlyn's looking for you, call him." I guess you would call that the first video phone—pretty high tech.

I remember going to kindergarten at the old Fort. Three of the houses and the officers' quarters had been restored and we went to kindergarten in one of them. There were six of us kindergarteners. Well, five were cousins and then there was me. We all graduated together from high school, except for one, Earl Grubb, who moved to New Mexico.

Ponies and entertainments growing up on the mountain

My little brother, Tommy, and I had a couple of ponies that Dad got for us when we were five or six years old. On his way back from Austin one time, Daddy saw a sign near Junction that said they had ponies. He stopped there just for a break and found out that this place raised ponies for the Ringling Brothers Barnum and Bailey Circus. Anyway, they had a corral full of thirty or forty ponies and he got to looking at them. This fellow came up and wanted to know where Daddy got the trailer he was hauling and Daddy told him he had built it. The fellow said, "Boy, I'd sure love to have it. I need a trailer so bad." So Daddy traded him the trailer for two ponies.

One of them was real gentle, mine, his name was Smokey. And the other one was Scout and he was a little wild. But Smokey was real gentle, so Tommy and I would go up the hill in the afternoon on Saturday or Sunday when there were visitors around waiting to go into the 82-inch dome. They'd have all the kids with them and Tommy and I would put the kids on the pony and lead them a couple of times around the turn around. I think we charged them ten cents. You know, it gave them something to do and we made a little spending money. Wasn't much to spend it on though.

Another way Tommy and I would keep busy and make a little money was we'd go dig up barrel cactus and sit down there in the parking lot and sell barrel cactus to people. We had them in one pound coffee cans that my mom saved. She was in on the enterprise, too.

Once in a while we'd ride the ponies up on Flattop almost to Eppenauer—out past there sometimes—or go down the other way to Dead Man's Curve and ride around there. We had a Cocker Spaniel dog named Chiquita, and she would follow us down the mountain to near where the Visitors Center is now. But there was a cattle guard across the road so she would get under this big gray oak tree and wait. She knew we had to come back that way. Then at noon, Daddy would come down the mountain in the truck, pick us up, and take us up to lunch. Then after lunch he would take us back down again. Sometimes we just rolled rocks off the side of the mountain back down by the 36-inch. There was always something to do, you know, we'd just go out and find it. It was a wonderful life.

When Tommy and I were older, we used to take the visitor groups through the Observatory on Saturday and Sunday. We would do this as soon as I was old enough to drive anyway, which was probably twelve or thirteen. I still have the little magazine where my picture was taken as I took the groups through the Observatory. I gave the lectures and Tommy would work the front door, let them in and out. He counted so many in and then so many out. It was a thirty-minute thing. I had a speech all down and then we would take questions. It seemed like the most common question was, "What is that big gray thing?" Well, after they put the big orange vacuum chamber in, there was the old gray one that just sat there for years and everybody wanted to know what that was. I would tell them about how they would aluminize the mirrors and all that sort of thing.

When Tommy and I were finally able to *legally* drive, Dad bought us a car. He put around 50,000 miles a year on a car, about a thousand miles a week, and had to trade every year. He was always putting on new tires and new brakes, too.

One time, Jean Texereau (he was an optician from France) came over to the Observatory to work on the mirrors. He was driving out here in his Mercedes—I guess they shipped it over—and he was broke down in Uvalde. Daddy came down to the garage and told me to go get this guy. So I left, drove down there and picked him up. Nobody stocks Mercedes parts out in Uvalde, Texas, I guarantee you, so the guys at the gas station had ground down a rotor cap for his distributor. We started back and had gone, I don't know, several miles and the thing quit running again. We had to leave his car out there and drive back to the Observatory in my car. Then probably on Monday he had the car towed to Alpine. We were very near and dear to him after I came out there in the middle of the night and brought him to the Observatory.

I observed a lot on the 82-inch telescope with Antoinette and Gerard de Vaucouleurs; they were some of the first astronomers to come out from Austin. They observed at the prime focus on the telescope, out in the dome, and it was *cold*. She was always trying to get me to go in and get some coffee or hot chocolate, but I wouldn't. I would stay with them all night. They worked together and worked a lot.

I remember when we had the one Wednesday night of the month for the public to come up and look through the 82-inch. They were fortunate people because they don't do that anymore. We had to limit it to 200 people; you had to mail in your reservation, and we would send you a confirmation. There was a dime telescope out in front of the 82-inch; you put a dime in and could look through it. I think it is a quarter now. We took them to the prime focus where the Burbidges were observing— take them up on the bridge. It was free too. Each night it was always free. Even the weekend things were free.

In the summertime they had problems with the cars vapor locking, overheating coming up the mountain. So they kept two of the maintenance men down in the shop just working on cars on visitors' night. The mechanic in Alpine told us about wrapping aluminum foil around the fuel line and reflecting the heat off. So they would get the cars going, and before they started back they would wrap their fuel lines with aluminum foil. They kept a supply of fan belts, radiator hoses, and foil on hand. That was all free too.

You know the chickens Dad told you about that he bought for the residents at the mountain for eggs and freezing? Well, they'd buy baby chickens; it seemed like to me there were about a thousand of them, but I guess it was really just about a hundred or two. Anyway, everything came in the mail, even the baby chickens. They'd come in cardboard boxes and we could hear them peep, peep, peeping in the mail.

One of the things we could do at night was ride up and down the road and shoot jackrabbits. It was all right because the land around there was mostly for cattle and the game warden said that three rabbits will eat as much as one cow, so the ranchers didn't mind as long as you weren't shooting the cows. So we'd ride up and down the road at night and spotlight jackrabbits.

One time I did get in trouble with the sheriff but that went away. Daddy was the deputy for a while but this was a different time. When we were older we'd go to Marfa or Alpine on dates or stuff and we'd find somebody to buy us some beer. We'd bring it back home and hang around the gas station at Crawford's. But then about eleven o'clock, Wilber, the sheriff, would get up, get in his car, drive *across* the street to us and say, " OK, it's time for ya'll to go home now." And everybody just went home. We didn't get in trouble the way they do today; there wasn't any DUI that I knew of, or drugs, or anything like that.

A third-generation experience

My wife and I sent our youngest boy to Prude Ranch. Let's see, he was probably twelve and he had no earthly idea where he was going. He had grown up here in Nashville. The kids fly from wherever they live to Odessa and they pick them up on a bus and take them out to Ft. Davis to the Prude Ranch. Before he leaves he is wanting to know, well, is there a mall, or is there a this or a that, and what am I gonna do, how much money do I need to take? Well, I told him, "There is no mall and there is no this or that or anything. And five bucks is all the money you will need, trust me." The first thing they do when they get there is they give each kid a horse, they give him a stall, and they give him a shovel and a rake. The kid has gotta take care of this animal for two weeks. He had a hard time the first week, but then he worked into it. Most of the kids that go there are from Texas and not a whole lot of city kids go there. He had an earring; he was in the earring stage. I told him, "Don't you wear that earring out there." And I guess he lost the earring about two hours after they got there because the guide, Chipper Prude, said, "Boy you better get that earring out of your ear or somebody is going to whip your butt."

I got a phone call from the boy on one Sunday and I said, "Are you at the mall?" And he said, "No man, I am at 'Bye-yay-zees' store." I said, "You mean Mr. Baeza's store?" He said, "I guess." But he had a good time anyway because he went back. He made two years down there. I tried to talk him into going back when he was a freshman and sophomore in high school, just to go and work as a counselor, but he didn't like it that much. He did not continue to wear the earring though.

Apollo astronauts. Left to right, back: Edward White, John Young, Charles Conrad, Neil Armstrong, James Lovell, James McDivitt, Elliot See, Frank Borman, Tom Stafford, front: Gordon Cooper, Gus Grissom, Scott Carpenter, Wally Schirra, John Glenn Jr., Allan Shepard and Deke Slayton; all astronauts autographed the original photo. Used with permission of Alan L. Bean, Marlyn Krebs, and Dick Krebs.

I have that picture Daddy was talking about—the one with the original Apollo astronauts. From what I understand, they came to the Big Bend to do some survival training out there. Then they came to the Observatory. They were there several days it seemed like. They did some observing and navigation stuff and Daddy took us out there, Tommy and I, to meet these guys more than once. I know one thing they were doing, taking turns going and looking through the telescope and making star charts from memory. After seeing a certain area of sky through the telescope, they'd go back down to the library, one at a time, and make a star chart just from their memory. Later on, Daddy got a letter from Alan Bean, and a picture. I have it framed now and in my den at home.

Letter from Alan Bean to Marlyn Krebs. Reproduced with permission of Marlyn Krebs, Dick Krebs, and Alan L. Bean.

While I was little, I used to carry Daddy's toolboxes around at the Observatory and what not. We just spent a lot of time together. Then in the summertime when I was older I helped him build the sidewalks that are out there now, and the sand and gravel we used for them we got from a creek on the Alpine road. I was like Daddy's helper or something.

Daddy left the Observatory in 1965 and I left the Observatory in 1966. It was a good life.

Pat Olivas
I am Pat Olivas, and I am a voice of McDonald Observatory. Way back in August of 1969, I was out on the farm working on the tractors and my uncle came out to visit. He said to me, "Why don't you go out and try to get a job at the Observatory?" I said, "What am I going to be doing?" He said, "Well, probably just about everything. Just go out and try." So I came out one day and applied; I filled out a few sheets of paper and was hired right on the spot. They were looking for a night assistant at the time.

From tractor to experienced tour guide in one day

The first day I came on board, well, I had no idea what I was going to do. I was fresh out of high school, just a teenager, and they gave me a sheet of paper and said, "About nine o'clock, you will have a bunch of tourists come up, so go give them a tour." I said, "What am I going to tell them? I don't know anything about this. I just came on board." They said, "Here is a sheet of paper, just read it off and if they have any questions, answer them to the best of your ability and lie about the rest." Five or ten people came up. We went up to the 82-inch telescope and I read them the sheet of paper. I had no idea how to move the telescope or anything. I wasn't instructed on that yet, and I said, "Well if you have any questions, direct them to me and I will see what I can do about it." So I got by that first day—it was pretty neat, but I had no idea I was going to be a tour guide the first day. After that, they started teaching me how to operate the telescopes.

Getting to know the astronomers

I met a lot of people, a lot of astronomers. The astronomers, you gotta watch out for them because they are really something. Most of them you could get along with, some you couldn't get along with, but they were pretty nice people, no different from anybody else. They just had their unique way of doing things.

The first year I was here I met most of the old timers; Dr. de Vaucouleurs, Dr. Harlan Smith. Dr. Smith, he was very interesting to work with. He was a real particular kind of guy, real strict in the way he did things, and very professional. I liked working with him because he taught me a lot of things about astronomy. He mainly got me interested in astronomy because it was just a curiosity that didn't develop in me until I was working with him. He had an impression on me. I met Dr. David Evans, Dr. Ed Nather, Dr. Robinson, Tom Moffit, Reinhard Beer.

I always loved it when Reinhard and Dr. Tom Barnes came out because they were cigar-smoking dudes. When they would both get together, they would work until a certain hour, measure about a hundred stars, and then they said, "All right, let's cut her down. Let's go have a beer, smoke a cigar, and play poker." I would sit down there with them and it was a *smoke-off* because they would have the whole TQ full of smoke after a while!

Sometimes, after Dr. Barnes stopped working, I said, "Well, it is kind of early, can I leave it, the telescope, open, and just look around?" He said, "Yeah, go ahead." So I would have fun with the 82-inch. We had that old Teletype computer with the ticker tape and I would just type up anything that I would like to see and had a blast the rest of the night. The 82-inch was the best one to look through for viewing.

After that first year, I got drafted. The government told me, "If you volunteer for one more year and make it three years, you won't have to go to Vietnam." So, I did. I was in a company of about 600 people; 296 people went to Vietnam, and the others went to Germany. I was number 287 and went to Vietnam anyway. So, what can you do? But it was OK. I didn't have too much of a hazardous duty and didn't have to shoot or kill anybody, which was good on my part. I didn't want to do that. It was rather frustrating, aggravating, and annoying for me to think of having to be involved in the War. That was probably one of the saddest parts of my life.

After a year and a half, I came back and did my regular tour. I returned to the Observatory and asked them, "Well, can I have my job back?" And they said, "Yeah, you can come back here." I said, "Good, I planned on being here."

I was here when the 107-inch was shot up. George tells the story but I can add that after it was all over, I went to the TQ and had a cup of coffee. Maurice Marin was there and when he went for his cigarettes, he finds a hole in his jacket. He is looking at it and wondering what it is and I said, "Maurice, I think that's a bullet hole." He kind of went bananas for a little while because he came that close to getting shot. I think he went through that whole pack of cigarettes in about half an hour.

That bullet hole was still visible in the wall for a while. I guess it missed Maurice by just a fraction. I think I was the one who patched it up, put a little plaster of Paris on there or something. It is surprising how the guy did not get killed because shooting something flat, the mirror, at no more than twenty feet distance with a 9 millimeter, it would just ricochet right back to you. The bullets have nowhere to go; they are in a steel tube. It is really surprising that he didn't get killed. Then after that, he threw a sledgehammer at the mirror. He didn't do anything with the 9 millimeter and he wanted to break that thing in half.

You always see something new

My favorite thing about McDonald Observatory is the height, the altitude. It kind of gives you a rush. You are just able to look forever when you are here. If you live out here, you always see something new, whether it is another road down there cut across the mountain or you see some mountain lions going across. The other day I was by the Millimeter Wave, just sitting there at coffee break and about ten feet from me, here comes a little fox. He didn't know I was there so I just whispered at him and he looked around like, who the heck said that? He just looked at me like, come on, I know you are there…just move so I can see you. Then, he just went away. You can tell a normal, healthy fox, because it is real pretty to look at and they will usually shy away from you.

Jimmy Welborn

My name is Jimmy Welborn and I am a voice of the McDonald Observatory. This might surprise you but I have only been out to the Observatory probably less than a dozen times. Twenty some years ago I was hired as the scientific instrument maker for the McDonald Observatory. Just one of the ways you can be a part of the Observatory and not be an astronomer. I started working at the Bee Caves site near Austin. I worked there for three or four years with Jack Easton, another instrument maker. My first project was a flip cage for the 107-inch, which is still in use. Shortly after that, we moved the shop into the 17th floor of the RLM building here on the University of Texas campus. We have been here for about twenty years.

We've built many things for the Observatory. Flip cage, focal reducer, Cassegrain camera, photometers, parts, and modifications, and lately I have been involved in CCD work; I get something different every day. For weeks, it may just be little rectangular parts and then for weeks it may be big, round rings. You just never know. We just have to be able to build anything they can dream up. Usually these things go through an engineering process before it gets to me. Engineering draws things up on blueprints, then the blueprints and a chunk of aluminum come to me, and I build whatever they are asking for. You can't just order things from a telescope company; you have to build things especially for the telescopes at the Observatory.

I get a lot of odd things in the shop. I built a part for Phil McQueen that was a cold-finger housing. This part started out as a 20-pound chunk of stainless steel and when I finished the part it weighed something like 2 pounds. I had to remove a lot of material to get to that part. It's kind of hard to describe what these parts look like. Basically, there is a rectangular part that is about 3 inches long. It had a flange on one side that was probably 3 inches by 5 inches, and in the middle of that it had a rectangular arm that came out of it. I had to remove all that unnecessary material—pretty crazy part.

Sometimes I will do the designing myself. Occasionally someone will come in with an idea off the top of their head and I will build something for them. Maybe make up a sketch, or something like that. Or they will come in with something that is not quite right. It's not exactly what they want, and we'll modify it. That sort of thing. One time one of the astronomer's wives came in with her daughter and they wanted me to build something to inject catsup into french fries. I did that for her but I don't know if anything came of it.

I can usually take a look at something, make it absolutely perfect, and make it work. It doesn't have to be brought back or redone and it doesn't have to be thrown away either. I just make it so it absolutely works.

China

Ed Nather sent me to China to do some work at an Observatory there. Ed Nather, one of our professors, had given the design for his photometer to the Chinese and they started to work on it. They got the basic box built and that's as far as they got. A lot of it is pretty complicated and they just didn't have the talent at their shop to do it. So that photometer went on the shelf. Then a student here at UT, Scott Kleinman, was in China and just happened to see that photometer sitting on the shelf. They decided they wanted to get it going so they sent it back to the United States, to Austin, and one of their graduate students from China came along with it. I was assigned the task of working with him and finishing up the photometer. Over the summer we rebuilt it using some spare parts that Ed had lying around. We had to redo a few things. They put a real good paint job on the photometer so we had to have that stripped off. We finished the photometer and they are using it.

While I was in China, I also taught some classes to their technicians. We were going to buy some equipment for their shop, but the money fell through so what we did was just try and fix up the equipment they had—get it running and teach them how to use it. Basically they had a milling machine, a lathe, a drill press, and a few hand tools. Their technicians were basically night attendants. They took care of the telescopes but they weren't machinists. But they were interested in learning how to do some of those things so that they could make repairs. The money wasn't there for new machines, so we patched up the old equipment and I taught them how to sharpen tools, how to design tools for turning, how to set the lathe up, and that sort of thing. They caught on. While I was there one of the astronomers came in with a job. He said he needed to have it bored out. The technicians took it in with their machine and did the job for them. Left a lot of confidence in them. They know how to operate the machines now. I think I made a difference in the way they do things, and hopefully, their future will be okay.

We had to do some modification on the 107-inch mirror cell at McDonald for the radial supports, so we did this while the mirror was being aluminized—while it was off the telescope and sitting on a rack on the mezzanine floor. These supports are some pneumatic pads that went all the way around the perimeter of the mirror to keep it from sagging. We had to put several hole patterns in the mirror cell and in each hole pattern there was at least five or six holes and one of those holes was 1-inch in diameter. The back of the mirror cell was, I believe, 5 or 6 inches thick so we had to drill through 6 inches of steel while the mirror cell was in the cage. Now this mirror is not in a friendly position, we had to get underneath the mirror cell and drill up through it. We had a magnetic-based drill press. It's a small drill press about 18 inches tall and it has a big magnetic base on it so you can just stick it to a piece of steel and drill holes in it. What we had to do was take the head off the drill press and turn it upside down so it would point up. We took a metal table, put it underneath the mirror cell, and stuck the magnetic base to it. Then we could get under the mirror cell and drill up through the cell, through 5 or 6 inches of steel. It wasn't any fun. We were basically on our hands and knees working on this. We bought some kneepads and it helped a lot. But still, it was quite a chore.

We were working late one evening on this project at the Observatory and a storm came in. It had been pretty nice all day, but the storm came in and it got real cold and started to sleet and snow and ice. We worked a couple of hours into the evening anyway and when we finished up and went to get in the truck, it was frozen to the road. In just a couple of hours it had froze the truck to the ground. It wasn't going anywhere so we had to walk to the TQ, and it felt like I was going into hypothermia by the time I got there. In the morning the storm passed and it started to thaw so we were able to chip the truck loose. But that's West Texas. The weather changes pretty quick from one day to the next.

Looking back and some advice

I've been a machinist all my life. I didn't have to go to college, I was too smart. Metal work is all I've ever done. Out of high school it just sort of evolved. I was raised in Lubbock and moved to Austin in my early twenties. I had several jobs in Austin, all in machine shops, and I just moved from one job to the next and found a home here at the

Astronomy Department. I've got my hand in a lot of the instruments out at McDonald Observatory, and some of the instruments that I have built have already been retired. I don't know what makes me interested in doing this. It's just something that kind of happened. My grandfather was a blacksmith. Something about it interested me, so I just started doing metal work, and I just stuck with it. I think I'm pretty good at it. I think I do have some intuition; I don't know about genius. I'm pretty much self-taught with on-the-job experience. If it's something you think you want to do, then get after it.

Fritz Kahl

It's cloudy today at the Observatory, but we are in the director's house, House A, and the view is beautiful anyway. I was invited up here to talk to you about myself, this place, and how we have affected each other. **I am Fritz Kahl and I am a voice of your McDonald Observatory.** I was born in the town of Radcliff, Iowa, in the very central part of the state, in 1921. I attended high school in the town of Nevada, then went on a baseball scholarship to the University of Iowa. And thank the Lord because it was in the depths of the depression— tuition was fifty dollars a semester but it was waived—plus I worked in the equipment room of the athletic department.

The impact of Pearl Harbor on young men
Then Uncle Sam and I entered a partnership. On December 7th, late, late, late at night, all of us boys were in the fraternity house listening to a football game when the announcement came that Pearl Harbor had been bombed. With that, we all looked at one another, and by the next morning, there were three people in the fraternity house: the housemother, the janitor, and the cook. The rest of us went down and signed up.

We were appointed aviation cadets for the swearing in and our first station was in Williams Field, Arizona. We were not issued army clothes; we were sent to Santa Anna, California, to do our basic training…in civilian clothes. From there, we went to Visalia, California, for primary training; Merced, California, for basic training; Stockton, California, for advanced flight training. Then when we graduated we were assigned to Mather Field in Sacramento, California. Fourteen of us were then assigned to Marfa, Texas.

Training pilots
We arrived a year after Pearl Harbor and Marfa had been active one month. We got there in time to do the night-flying training. We did

blind instrument take-offs in the desert out here. Blind instrument flying is accomplished by using green glass on the windshield and wearing red goggles. You can't see anything but the instrumentation. The fluorescents in the lights make the difference. It was really an experience. Looking back on it now, it probably saved our lives and helped save lots of other lives, so I see it as a very, very worthwhile experience as far as training and survival is concerned.

You know, we have a rule in the FAA that you fly three hours with a student before you solo him at night, before he can fly at night by himself. The regulation also says ten landings and three hours. And Visitor, in a light airplane, you could shoot ten landings in an hour to an hour and a half. What are you going to do with that other hour and a half? I used to split those up into two flights, forty-five minutes each: one where you had a full Moon, one where you had total darkness. This is the darkest place on the North American continent and it is *bad* dark here, especially when the Moon is not up.

We, amongst us out here in 1943, when we critique ourselves and our training program, we knew damn well that we were not doing right by these guys at night. It just wasn't enough time in the dark. When you go off the end of the runway, in 30 seconds you can kill yourself. You know, upsetting spatial disorientation, the little hairs in your inner ear fall down and you don't know whether you are standing or falling, if you are going forward or backward. I never knew anybody who didn't give every student he had ten complete instrument take-offs before they flew at night. Most of my students got four hours of nighttime, instead of three. All FAA regulations are based on minimums. Well, do you like minimums? I don't, not in airplanes. Nobody, no place.

I stayed at Marfa for, well, until 1946 and went from there to Hobbs, New Mexico, for B-17 transition training, and stayed there and instructed instruments in B-17. Then I was separated from the service, got out of the service from Roswell, New Mexico, where I had only two or three flights in a B-29, the super 4. I just had enough time to not like the airplane. The separation took place at Omaha, Nebraska; then I went back to school at the University of Iowa.

Transition to civilian aviation, West Texas style

Georgie Lee, my wife, and I were in school when her father became quite ill. He had substantial ranch holdings around this part of the country, Ft. Davis, and he phoned us, sort of begging for help because help was hard to get. We decided to honor his request and come back here to live. I went to work and have been here ever since. I was not involved in aviation for about ten years and then an opportunity came up that got me flying airplanes again. We had a lot of ranchers here who had holdings in other places, mainly Mexico. They needed transportation back and forth and transportation being what it was in Mexico, we bought surplus Army airplanes to fly the ranchers to and from their holdings. So I was back again into the same old niche and having a great time in Mexico flying airplanes that I knew something about. This lasted for several years. I was a flight instructor as well and we had a charter service. We did anything that is required of airplanes because we had a full-blown shop with mechanics and everything that goes with it. We were able to do major repairs such as major overhauls. That is about the story, but now we are getting into involvement with McDonald Observatory.

Neil Armstrong subbing for Nixon

Actually, soaring and McDonald started about the same time. Do you know what soaring is? It is gliders and this is an ideal place for gliders, just wonderful. We even had an International Soaring Championship here. This was an international function so it was protocol to invite the President. Nixon very graciously declined and said, "Who would you most like to have?" And of course some of our guys who were bright in the aviation business said, "Neil Armstrong!" Well, we all knew him. He had flown out here and did some gliding before he went into the astronaut program. So Nixon says, "I can take care of that!" About a week after, I got a call from Neil Armstrong. He said, "Fritz, I understand I am going to be President Nixon at your house for about eight days. Would you please hide me? You don't know what I am talking about, but when I get there, you will."

My wife's aunt was going to be in Europe for about six weeks and we asked her if Neil Armstrong could stay in her house. Well, she sat straight up in her chair, and said, "Well, I don't know if I am going to Europe if Neil Armstrong is coming to my house!" But she did. Her property had a long entranceway where we could hide his glider. And I will say this to you about Neil Armstrong: there is not a more delightful person in the world.

OK, I am off track a little bit here. By this time McDonald was barely in motion on the total rebuilding phase at the end of the Yerkes-Chicago deal when we started the service to fly the astronomers. Browning Aviation contacted me for the shuttle service. They programmed their operation schedule on three trips a week, or on an "as needed" basis. And believe me, they needed it and they used it.

Jake Jacobson, an aviator's aviator

The real giant in this whole operation was a man named Ingvar Jacobson, Jake Jacobson. Bowlegged Jake. If I am qualified to pass judgment on anyone, it is on aviators and there is nobody like Jake: a perfectionist to the nth degree. He is the reason, the real reason, for the success of this shuttle operation. The astronomers were afraid of him; they respected him because he did not let them change anything in or out of the airplane. The astronomers would be real concerned about their luggage and would ask, "Jake, where did you put my luggage?" Jake would say, "You darn Ph.D.s, keep your hands off that luggage. It's mine for this trip. It isn't yours, it's mine now." What he was referring to was he wanted the airplane to be in balance. Just because it was a big box did not mean it was heavy, and just because it was a small box didn't mean it was light. So Jake did not want them moving anything around in the plane to make it go off balance. Jake, well, I just can't say enough for that guy. He was the main man, and rightfully so, captain of the ship. We don't have a lot of weather out here, but when we do have, it is not very good. This is where Jake was a master—very, very few aviators can measure up to Jake.

On occasion I would fly with Jake to Austin. There would be two loads of people and luggage down there. There was another Aztec airplane there and I would fly it. If they had one or two, too many people, I would take them in my airplane. Or if Dr. Smith wanted to go west or north or east, not southeast, I'd take the flights. So I became personally acquainted with everyone who flew. We developed a routine that was set. Without fail we had fresh coffee and doughnuts for the people going to Austin. The people going to Austin from the Observatory were more often than not astronomers. They were sleepy, but they had not had anything to eat. So a doughnut and a cup of coffee and you were off to the big city. And those coming this way, to the Observatory, were trying to kind of sleep their way into a schedule for that night because they were going to work. This thing lasted for six years, with a little bit more perhaps. You know, it was ragged to start with and ragged quitting, but it was unique in aviation, I can honestly say, and I think it is a credit to aviation

David Evans delivers his po-em about Jake

One of my best friends is Dr. David Evans, at the University. This year at the Board of Visitors meeting, down under one of the big tents set up for the visitors, he said, "Let's tell Jake stories!" Well, he and I sat and visited; my wife and his wife, Betty, sat and listened. I guess we told Jake stories for thirty to forty-five minutes. That man said in his best-exaggerated accent, "Have you ever *ha-yad*, my *po*-em about Jake?" And I said, "By God, no!" He said, "Would you like to *he'ah* it?" I said, "I certainly would." And just like a schoolboy, he sat just straight in that chair and read this *po*-em.

"We flew out to Mahr-fah through thunder and ga-ale,
All the visiting firemen were shaken and pale.
But the rest of us knew, with no chance of mistake,
With our own special pilot, it would all be just *Jake!*"

I said, "Would you write this down for me?" He said, "Oh, most *suh*-tun-lay."

I have never seen such dedication as astronomers. They are crazy people because they work at night, you know; their days are our nights and our nights are their days. But they are dedicated and they are friendly. They don't go out of their way to make trouble. So I have a lot of affection for these people that we flew…Jake, me, and everybody else.

Frank Bash, the BoV and lighting ordinances

I am an early and current resident, and I am also a Board of Visitors member for the McDonald Observatory. The reason I became a BoV member is because, well, because Frank Bash asked me to be. I would do damn near anything for him. Dr. Bash is coming up and will tell you about the organization, but we as members, support the Observatory in whatever way we best can. I do what I can. I am mayor of the little town of Marfa. We may be forty miles away, but with all of our commercial and private lighting, we are close enough to make a difference in the quality of observing at McDonald. Remember when we talked about the student pilot's forty-five minutes' flying in the dark with no Moon to make up for *minimums*? Well, in the dark—no Moon nights—I would fly them around the Observatory and say, "OK, look, this is dark over here on your left, totally dark. But look over yonder, towards Marfa." There we could see the city lights and if we could see that, the astronomers at McDonald are seeing that. So we passed a lighting ordinance; Alpine did too. You can pass all the ordinances you want to, but if you don't enforce them, they're not worth the powder to blow them up.

So right now we are about through with our budget time and I have a date with Bill Wren at the Observatory. As soon as that budget is passed, he and I and somebody from Alpine, maybe somebody from Pecos, maybe even somebody from Ft. Stockton, are going to get together and put down some things to do to make that lighting ordinance *effective*. So it is a thing with me, Visitor, and it is about all I have to offer to McDonald Observatory. I don't have ten million dollars, but there has got to be some housekeepers.

An amazing place and a good ride

It was interesting to fly over this place and look at it and see how those houses were each placed on the mountain without disturbing trees or rocks. Now that was an amazing feat of planning if you think about putting the plumbing in around all those trees and rocks and all the water lines and stuff. And power lines…there are no power lines above ground out there. Isn't this an amazing place? And the people, I think it is a good mix, and a healthy one. You go to these BoV meetings once a year out here and see these astronomers like Dr. Kormendy. What a guy. You can't help but like that man. They are human beings that just like to work at night.

To sum up Fritz Kahl, if there were a song or a *po*-em about me, the title would be, "It's been a good ride." It has. Lord o'mercy, you won't run into many old boys who have had a better ride than I have had. I did what I wanted to do for twenty-five years, plus the army experience. I kind of wonder sometimes if I would have been better off to stay in the air force because I like to fly airplanes. But everything has been good to me. So good that I'll never be able to give it all back.

David Doss

I am a fifth-generation Texan. My great-great-great grandfather is buried up at a little place called Salt Creek Baptist Church in Brown County. **I am David Doss and my voice of McDonald Observatory comes to you from the 107-inch dome control room.** One of my heroes, next to my dad, was my scoutmaster when I was a kid. My scoutmaster told us the legend about Andromeda, Cassiopeia, and Perseus. Stories of the constellations, to me, I found quite fascinating; that was my introduction to astronomy. I must not have been more than ten years old when we looked at Saturn through a small amateur telescope. I thought it looked real neat. I mean, it didn't have any more of a deep meaning than that. I liked it because it was pretty.

Amateur astronomy to McDonald Observatory

Now, how I came to the Observatory. I started school at Sul Ross in 1968. I had an interest in astronomy, just purely on the amateur level, so I took their astronomy course. Me and the old professor, a neat old guy, got along real well so I took his second semester class the next year and ended up helping him teach labs. When it came up time for graduation, the professor said they were wanting to hire night assistants with college degrees at McDonald Observatory. He knew Chuck Cobb, head of the night assistant group, and through that connection, I got an interview for a night assistant position. I got the job, and when I graduated in December of 1970, I started to work up here January One, of 1971. I have been here ever since.

Back in the old days when I started to work here, we had enough telescope assistants that there was one on the 107-inch and the 82-inch, twenty-four hours a day. The daytime assistants took care of instrument changes; that is, taking the outgoing astronomer's instrument off the telescope and then putting the incoming astronomer's instrument on the telescope. At night, the evening shift assistants, I think they started at three o'clock and they worked until midnight. Then one would come in from midnight until 8:00 a.m. So there were lots of people around. Then budget cuts came and it was changed to a night assistant would come on this telescope, and he would generally just work from the start of observing, a little after sundown, until sunup. The twelve hour shifts can get to be real difficult. The night assistants, what they did was they took care of moving the telescope and the dome. Now we have computers that do that and *they* are not very friendly. They can be very unfriendly at times.

This is not an eight to five job for me; fortunately, my schedule is a little flexible. The day starts for me on days like today; I got up a little after 7:00 a.m. to make an instrument change. This morning we changed the telescope from coudé to F9 Cass so that required us to change the secondary mirror on the telescope as well. Then we mounted the instrument that the astronomer is using tonight. It's called IGI. We put it together and checked it out a little bit to make sure it is working. Then we helped the astronomer with the set up. That's the sort of routine thing I do.

Hopefully tomorrow if there are no changes, maybe a little after 8:00 I will get up and be here about 9:00. It's a nice day, there is no clock punching. Things are generally fairly relaxed unless we have scheduled stuff that has to be taken care of. I generally stay here until 5:30 or 6:00, then I'll come up and spend half an hour to an hour at night basically just checking in with the observers, seeing how they are doing, if they need anything…just saying hi, letting them know that there is someone around if they need something. We don't have the night assistants now and sometimes, other than myself, the only other people an observer might see during the whole run is just the TQ staff. I just want them to know if they have a problem, I always tell them they can call me. I may not be able to fix the problem, but I can usually direct them to somebody who can.

If something breaks, the astronomer calls me and if it looks like it's something that can be fixed pretty quick, then we try to do it. If it looks like it's gonna take a long time, we have to tell them sorry, and start working on it the next morning. Generally, to me, the reason for me living here on the mountain is to be able to try to get them back operational and as quick as we can. That is very important.

Cleaning the telescope mirrors

One of the standard things I do is I clean the mirrors and check their reflectivity. Now we are using CO_2 to clean the mirrors. It's basically like taking a fire extinguisher and just opening it up on the mirror and blowing it off. We used to do a soapy water wash. You blow off the mirror, get the dirt off first and then you would literally rinse it down with soapy water, dry it, then you would rinse it with the distilled water and dry it again. Now, supposedly the CO_2 particles, the snow in the CO_2, helps blow off the dust. It certainly does some but I don't think it does quite as good as a water wash. The problem with these mirrors is the surface coating is very thin. It is about 900 Ångstroms thick and it's very soft and so literally, with a fingernail you can scrape through it. So you have to be very careful. Just about any time you touch a mirror, you are going to hurt it a little bit. Hopefully we improve it more than we hurt it each time. CO_2ing is supposedly a little less damaging to the mirrors than the water wash and we do a CO_2 cleaning every month. The water wash we would generally do about this time a year and then we maybe wouldn't do another one until after the dust storms in the spring.

You can certainly do both. A lot of observatories went over to the CO_2 cleaning and I think now some of them are going back to the water wash. The dust adheres to the mirror if it sits on it very long. Maybe you really need to CO_2 it once a day to keep the dust from adhering. This 107-inch mirror was recoated in June and now, only two months later, I can already see that there is a light dusting that won't come off with the CO_2.

The 82-inch, an old friend

There are things about every one of the telescopes that I like and there are things about every one of them that I hate. The 82-inch, I love it; it's just a neat old telescope. There are some awful things about it. Like, we are having problems with the track now. We can't figure out what the heck it's doing. This 107-inch, it's neat; it tracks very nice and a lot of the stuff on it is very easy to do like balancing it. Just the work on it is a lot easier than the 82-inch, but it also, it just doesn't have the feel of the 82-inch. The 82-inch is just like a nice old friend. This telescope, the 107, it's a friend, but it's not an old friend. It's just not as old.

A story that I heard when I first started working here was one about Gerard de Vaucouleurs. He used the prism spectrograph, and to use it you have to pull part of the platform floor out of the 82-inch dome. Well, apparently he was working one night and fell through the hole. So from then on he required the Observatory to buy him some big foam mattresses that he always had stuck underneath that hole in the floor when they were observing with that spectrograph. You always have to be very careful in the domes. You can't use any lights to see, so you have to know where everything is at all times.

The 82-inch prepared for work as twilight settles in the Davis Mountains. Photo from McDonald Observatory Archives.

Mountain weather and cloudy night entertainment
We get a lot of weather out here and like Fritz Kahl said, it's bad. Wind is a real drawback in this area; you get very tired of it. Quite often in the spring it will start blowing in late February and really won't quit blowing until maybe May. It affects observing certainly if it gets high enough and have to close the domes, and generally we have a dust storm associated with it

Another part of our weather is snow, but it is really not a problem. We get, on the average, maybe three or four little snows a year of an inch or so; big snows maybe three inches. The biggest snow I have seen here was I guess maybe ten to eleven inches. That's been years and years ago.   Certainly the last few years, we haven't had lots of snow. Generally, I don't know that we haven't had a winter when we didn't have at least a couple of little dustings—an inch or so. The snow is great here. You get a snow and then usually within three days it's gone. None of this stuff where it hangs around for weeks or months at a time.

There is an old, old post card that shows where the clouds came up from the valley to just below House A, just below the 36-inch dome. In a year it probably happens three or four times. It's neat. It's neat to get out and look at it. Sometimes it looks like you can just step out on it. Sometimes it looks like an ocean and we are just the island sticking up out of it. Generally the clouds don't get any higher and the astronomers can still observe. It's generally not a summer thing; it's a fall or winter thing.

On cloudy nights in the old days the astronomers would read, play games, or work on their data and that was about it. There were no computer terminals or Internet to be interested in. Apparently Harlan had indicated that he did not want a TV in the TQ and they didn't get one until the first Apollo landing. The NASA people came out here because of the lunar laser stuff going on here, which Pete Shelus will tell you about, and apparently the NASA people brought in a bunch of TVs to be used out here. When they left, they left one TV for the TQ. We could pick up maybe two TV stations and generally they went off the air about midnight, so after midnight they had to find other things to do.

In the years, a few times, we have had a lot of rain. We had, in 1985, we had 12 inches of rain in two weeks and in every crevice in every mountain in this area there were little waterfalls. It was beautiful. We were sort of in the fog for two weeks solid and almost a constant light rain. It was great. It is hard to imagine that today. The largest amount of rain I think we ever had was about 35 inches in one year. The lowest rainfall we ever had was a little over 8 inches and that was in the droughts in the 1950s. Two years ago, we had the second lowest rainfall we ever recorded, that was about 10 inches. Our average rainfall is between nineteen and twenty inches. And the weather changes very quickly and you can experience many types of weather in one day if a cold front comes in.

Jake weather

I have a great "Jake Jacobsen and the weather" story for you. I think Fritz Kahl talked about him, too. He was a neat guy, I never really talked with him that much because he was the driver, the pilot, and I was the passenger and usually I sit in the back. I don't recall ever riding in the front seat. I remember one very exciting trip; we were flying out of Austin, coming back here. The weather was certainly not great. There were little thunderclouds all over the place, real hazy like it is there in Austin. We took off and we flew right into a thunderstorm. And it was bumpy; it was the bumpiest ride I ever had in my life. The guy that was up in the front, later he told me that the turbos on the engines stalled, almost lost power, and apparently the tower had known about this storm that was out to the west of San Antonio, but failed to tell Jake. He was apparently rather angry about the whole situation. That was a very interesting ride.

I remember another time when Jake and I were landing in Marfa. We had come back from Austin late and the runway lights were out. They were redoing them or something so there were not going to be any runway lights. So Fritz Kahl and somebody else got their cars and they each sat at each end of the runway with their headlights on and Jake landed right on the runway in their headlights. That was very interesting.

We used to have some fairly decent parties up here. Somehow they were always on Sunday nights or Monday evenings. At the TQ they cooked steaks on Sunday night and they had wine with the steaks. That is where things got started and degenerated from there. I saw one of the astronomers one night in a sombrero with a bottle of tequila. That was a rather interesting party. Has anyone told you about Karl Ponca yet? He ran the TQ back in the early days. He and his wife, Barbara, were the first TQ managers. Karl was an Osage Indian. I think he was half Osage or something like that. Karl was a rather interesting character, very friendly, and he liked to party. He was the one that initiated a lot of the Sunday evening parties.

Also, back in the old days they had a school bus for the kids and you could order stuff at the grocery store, or wherever in town, and then usually Marlyn Krebs would take the school bus and make the rounds before picking up the kids. Then they would bring the groceries and the kids home. So we had sort of a delivery service. So we could order, you know, a gallon of milk, pound of hamburger, or whatever. Baeza's doesn't do that anymore. If you are an old-timer you can still have a charge account, but they are not letting out new charge accounts.

Plagues, the Marfa Lights, and other natural phenomena

People talk about the plagues that we have here. In the summertime we have plagues of ants. The first good showers we have, ants swarm and the sides of the domes just literally get covered with flying ants. I guess these colonies, once there is a little moisture in the air, the queens leave, the new queens, and they go out and kind of start new colonies. When the ground gets a little bit wet, they can dig into the dirt a lot easier than when it is parched dry.

Then we have the infestation of the ladybugs. Every year we get ladybugs but not like we used to. Back in the early seventies we had a year when the bottom of the 82-inch was red with ladybugs. There were so many of them that they sent the janitors up with vacuum cleaners to vacuum them off. Once they vacuumed them, they sprayed bug killer into it. Ever since then, we haven't had near as many. I don't know if that was the cause of it, but it was certainly interesting. Ladybugs don't taste very good. They have a very peculiar taste. I say that because when they are flying all over the place it's kind of difficult *not* to suck one in.

On night we had a spider crawling across the window of a CCD. I have a picture of that frame. We just got a nice flat field image with this little shadow of a spider on it.

Arachnid (aka little spider) on the window of a CCD chip. Image by David Doss, McDonald Observatory.

A lot of people ask me about the Marfa Lights. Well, I think they are real. I think there is really something there. I am inclined to believe that it's a geologic phenomenon. The area has a lot of fault areas and so you get this Piezo-electric effect that produces charges and you get things that look sort of like ball lighting. I've never seen them. Ninety-nine percent of the people out here, I think, have just seen the lights on the Presidio Highway. And people that say they see Marfa Lights from up here at the Observatory and I would say 100 percent of those are just highway lights, car lights. The only lights I have heard described that sound like the real Marfa Lights are when the people say these things appear very close to them, about 100 yards and they bounce around and do weird things. These people who say they see a light way off in the distance, I don't think those are the real Marfa Lights.

People ask me about that weather balloon; you can see in the west. Well, that's not a weather balloon, that's the Aerostat. It's looking for drug smugglers and the Feds run it. That's my definition of high-tech welfare. It is my understanding that they've never busted anybody with that thing. It's got radar on it and the idea was to be able to spot planes coming out of Mexico. Apparently, the drug smugglers have found ways to evade them; the high percentage of the time there is a good wind coming through and they have to take the thing down. I think they are on their third balloon now. They had one of them disintegrate at high altitude—the radio traffic that night was rather interesting to listen to. The other one they lost came apart on the ground. They can see stuff on the ground as well. They can see vehicles coming up on the roads out of Mexico, but if they were walking I don't think you could find them with the balloon. They have got a whole slew of those things all across the southern United States.

How big do you think that thing is? I've been told it's about 300 feet long. It's a big balloon. It's very low pressure. From what I heard in the early days, you could actually shoot a hole in it and it wouldn't fall. It doesn't lose its helium very fast.

Human technology, respect, and a few words of advice

We've got some Indian artifacts in the area. There must have been some settlements or at least some Indians passing through. There was a cache of points found at some cliff shelters below Mt. Livermore—the mountain over to the west of us. They call the points the Livermore Point, because of the mountain name. That cache of points they found is in a collection over at Sul Ross in the museum. The Livermore Point apparently is a fairly late point and it is very delicate—not strong. It's weird; the older the point, the better they are. You notice now that when we have a new technology, like a microwave, the really old ones lasted a long time and the newer ones don't seem to. Well, I guess human technology hasn't changed much. We learn how to do something and the more we do it, the worse it gets.

Visitor, when you come to the Observatory, I hope you always have fun and learn something. I hope you gain a respect for astronomy. I hope you gain respect, and not the other way. I also hope that when you read this book you learn that astronomy at the telescope is just a small part of what astronomers do. I used to think astronomers just look through the telescope. The telescope is certainly an important part, but it's not the only part to the astronomers here. You must know that the data reduction is the real work—it is the creative part of understanding what the information from the telescope means. And with that, the instruments are important, too.

When I look up into the dark skies, I think about some of the same things humans always have. I wonder who else is up there looking down at us, or up at us, or whatever. I am sure there is something else out there, someone else out there. It would be neat for me to know that for sure before I die. I would like to see, in my lifetime, life detected somewhere else and I would like it to be more than a bug. I would like to know it was something intelligent.

If I had not come to McDonald I might have been a farmer like my ancestors. I might have had a pansy or a tomato farm out here. I told my kids every morning when they went to school, "Study hard, play hard and have fun." I don't think it did them any good to hear that but it made me feel better. My life has certainly been fun, for the most part. This observatory is part of me. I hate the thought of retirement.

What am I going to do now? Well, it is 5:30 in the early evening. I'll probably go down and check my email, make sure there is nothing urgent or semi-urgent in it. Then I'll go home and feed the dogs and the cats. Then I will wait and see if anybody shows up before I get real hungry, and if they do we'll fix supper, and if they don't I'll fix me some supper and watch some of the Olympics tonight. Then I will come up on rounds about 9:30 or 10:00, then head home, and hopefully, get to bed about midnight or so. What are you going to do?

30-inch telescope exposed during dome rotation on a rare cloudy night. Photo by Karen S. WInget

Chapter 6 Scientist Administrators

Ed Barker

I was an undergraduate physics major at New Mexico State in late 1959 and I started thinking, what will I do instead of building bombs? I was from Santa Fe, I had connections to Los Alamos and at that time, physics was really into atomic energy. I might have become a chemical engineer building reactors, but I had a chance to work at the Planetary Research Center in Las Cruces. Clyde Tombaugh was the head of that, and I got started in planetary astronomy by working for Clyde for a couple of years. I had no prior astronomy background and Clyde recommended I go to Kansas for a basic graduate program in astronomy. Later on, I would have the chance to show Clyde Pluto through the 82-inch telescope at McDonald. He was thrilled because at that time, it was the largest telescope he had seen Pluto in. **I am Ed Barker and I am a voice of McDonald Observatory.**

Currently, I am assistant director for McDonald Observatory. I have been associated with McDonald Observatory since 1965 when I came to the University of Texas as a graduate student working in planetary astronomy. Initially, I worked for Bob Tull on spectrographs and had a research assistantship with him in 1965 and 1966. I then got a NASA traineeship for my dissertation work and received my Ph.D. in 1969. I had a combination of Ph.D. advisors: Harlan Smith was my UT Advisor, and Ron Schorn, from the Jet Propulsion Lab, was doing Mars work and was my outside advisor.

Mars

Gerard de Vaucouleurs was also on my Ph.D. committee because he had written the basic textbook on Mars. Ron and I did spectroscopy on the 82-inch looking at Mars' atmosphere to determine what it was composed of. Everybody thought Mars had nitrogen in the atmosphere and at that time, we determined it was primarily a carbon dioxide atmosphere. We could also see that the carbon dioxide abundance changed dramatically as Mars rotated. Because the image of Mars was so small we didn't know much about the surface of Mars. We didn't know about the massive canyons and we didn't even know Olympus Mons, the Texas-sized shield volcano, was there. We found that the amount of carbon dioxide was directly related to the atmospheric pressure, and when we saw less carbon dioxide we were looking on the top of high mountain ridges. When we saw more carbon dioxide, this meant we were looking in the low lands—sea level of Mars. At this sea level, liquid water can exist. The first couple of high-resolution spectra of Mars were taken in 1964, which showed water lines in the atmosphere of Mars. We now have thirty-five to forty years of data on Mars in terms of the behavior of water vapor in the atmosphere of Mars as seen from the ground.

In the early seventies, the NASA planetary program developed and we worked through the solar system: Mars, Venus, Mercury, Jupiter and Saturn. As the detectors got a little better, we went further out and did Pluto and various satellites. Now we have been doing Kuiper Belt objects, so we've done a survey of the entire solar system from ground-based astronomy.

I really don't know if Mars is a place we want to develop in the sense of permanently living there. However, in terms of exploration of Mars, I think that is a good idea because in a hundred years from now, things may be different. The Earth is going to be so heavily populated, maybe we would want to populate Mars. It's going to be difficult because there is not much water. The atmosphere is primarily carbon dioxide, which is not conducive to humans, but there is oxygen. That was one of the early-on discoveries of the NASA planetary program—to discover molecular oxygen in the atmosphere of Mars.

Life on Mars

Was there life on Mars in the past? All of the indicators are there. Water is there; probably salty brine was there in aquifers underneath the surface. I just reviewed a StarDate script today saying we will have spacecraft on the way to Mars hopefully by the end of May (as of today we have Mars Express and MER(1) on the way). We have had two spacecraft in orbit around Mars taking pictures and making atmospheric thermal measurements for the past four years. So, we are really busy on Mars. There are a half a dozen pictures released to the Web each week out of the hundreds taken of Mars every week. It's a geologist's paradise now. I think Mars is going to be the only habitable place for humans. Some of the outer satellites of Jupiter might be, but probably not. Mars is the only one. Venus' atmosphere is just like Dante's Hell.

I think that there has been life on Mars, microbial, cellular life of some type. I think the full story on the Martian Meteorite is still out as to whether it really shows life or structures that had to come from life forming processes. I think there is a lot of evidence in both directions. A lot of careful work has been going on. The meteorite is definitely from Mars because we have evidence of argon, an inert gas, in the isotope ratios that say the meteorite is non-terrestrial, and the only other place in the solar system we know that there is argon, in that particular abundance ratio, is on Mars.

Harlan

Harlan Smith arrived at UT two years prior to when I came to Austin. He was very definitely the go-getter entrepreneur and was building the Astronomy Department at that time. Harlan was an observer. There are probably tales of his wanting everyone to be observing, even if it was cloudy. But Harlan felt that it was better to practice making the observation, even under the marginal conditions. So in retrospect, he got a reputation of observing in pretty poor conditions. But there was really a value to that practice that I have taken on. You go practice and practice and then you do it right when you have the right weather conditions.

I have to tell this Harlan story. We were driving back to Austin on those smaller roads between Austin and McDonald, before I-10 was completed. We had left Junction coming to Fredericksburg and I had to ask Harlan why, at three o'clock in the morning, was he was driving right down the middle of the road? He said, "Well, because there are deer on both sides of the road and it increases my probability of being able to avoid them by driving down the middle rather than driving down one side."

He always had a positive outlook. I don't think I ever saw him in a negative mode. There were numerous times that he would catch us leaving the department at five o'clock and he would say, "What's going on?" An hour later you might get to go home.

He would routinely walk from the ground floor of the building to the 15th floor. He would catch us at the elevator coming up and say, "Come on, walk up the stairs with me." This wouldn't be too bad in that day and age when we were all younger and it was easier to do. But, he would again say, "What is going on, what are you doing?" So you'd end up having to talk all the way up the stairs while he would just walk up. You could really get into an oxygen debt a lot quicker by talking and climbing instead of just climbing.

Superintendent of McDonald Observatory

As a mentor, as a thesis advisor, and then just as a friend, Harlan was a wonderful inspiration. Harlan and Tom Barnes came up to me one day in 1988 and said, "We have a challenge for you. Would you be interested in taking over the superintendent's job at the Observatory?" Very hesitantly, I said, "Yes...I think so." I hadn't worked in a management position before so this was a turning point in my astronomical career. I lived at the Observatory for the five years as superintendent. Actually, I had lived out there from 1970 to 1977 as well, heading the planetary research program. We would observe with the 107-inch twenty-four hours a day, for two weeks out of each month. Daytime was prime time to do Venus and Mars and even as late as last year, I used the 107-inch telescope to do Mars in the daytime.

Work at NASA

After five years as superintendent of McDonald Observatory, I moved to Washington D.C., and worked at NASA. That was a contrast. Instead of walking the road from House B at McDonald with its beautiful views and solitude, up and around to the 82-inch dome to go to work, I would walk to the Metro stop, the subway, and ride the Metro to downtown D.C. to go to work just off the Mall. It was a change. I was doing grant management for the ground-based planetary astronomy program in the Solar System Exploration Division of the Office of Space Science. This was in the time period we had the Shoemaker/Levy9 comet event come along, and I had responsibilities for coordinating the NASA and NSF efforts to observe it. We really didn't know what was going to happen but we had a comet; it was broken apart, it was strung out, and we thought it was going to hit Jupiter. It was one of those unknowns, but we had just enough funding available to support most of the worldwide ground-based astronomy programs that were available.

We observed Shoemaker/Levy in a lot of different ways. At McDonald, we had people doing imaging, in special filters, and in the infrared, because at that time we didn't know what we were going to see. We were also doing spectroscopy of the impact zones. We went from having a pristine southern equatorial region to having seventeen individual impact events encircling the planet. These impacts left basically black eyes, black scars in the atmosphere of Jupiter. That was a scientific bonanza and we learned lots of things. We learned about comets in the sense of their tensile strength, what binds them together, and about their breakup processes. We learned that the comet got just close enough to Jupiter during its previous orbital pass-by to get ripped apart but had enough energy to keep going on its orbit. The next time around, it was actually destined to hit the planet, and it did.

We got to witness the impact dynamics. Although the impact was not like cratering on a surface, it created a shaft down into the atmosphere. It created a very hot, rarefied gas, and then it exploded and came right back out the shaft. That is what we were seeing. We didn't know how long the flumes—the soot that came out of the gas shaft— would hang around in the upper atmosphere. The southern equatorial zone of Jupiter, which is a significant portion of the disc, had remnants of the scars for a year and a half.

Toward the end of my time at NASA, comet Hale-Bopp was discovered and we started planning for a worldwide ground-based astronomy campaign. I left just about the time we started the observing sessions around the world for Hale-Bopp. I came back to the Astronomy Department at UT and studied Hale-Bopp, other comets, and did some Jupiter work with Larry Trafton. Then, Tom Barnes asked me to take on another challenge—to start helping him schedule the telescopes while he concentrated on getting the HET into operation. I eventually took over part of Tom's associate director's job, which evolved into being responsible for all of the scientific scheduling at the Observatory.

Telescope scheduling at McDonald Observatory

To schedule the telescopes, we break the year up in to three periods, four months long. I'll just give an example of what we've just been through here. The first of February, proposals were due for all the telescopes. Proposals are submitted by staff members, faculty members, graduate students, and outside astronomers as well. We have a Telescope Allocation Committee (TAC), which consists of six people—a chairman and five other people who are either faculty or research staff. It's a peer review process but you cannot review your own proposal, that of your spouse, or that of a close collaborator. The TAC personnel review the proposals and send me their rankings. The TAC actually does the decision making, and I facilitate by making sure the rules are followed and then work out the schedule.

There are a couple of observing courses offered in the summer for undergraduates and we have time on the telescopes for them. In addition to the regular public night once a month on the 107-inch, we have the 82-inch program now where we grant visitors time on the telescope. The Visitors Center gets two, maybe four, nights a month on the 82-inch for amateurs to spend a night at the telescope. I fit those nights into the schedule after all of the science needs are met. The Visitors Center advertises the nights as public viewing nights and people apply through the Visitors Center. There is a reasonable charge for half a night on the telescope. They have a good eyepiece system and they just go out and enjoy the sights of the night sky. I wish I could have time just to do that sometime.

Atmospheric acoustic sounding

Backing up a little bit, back into the eighties, Harlan had the idea of building the 300-inch telescope and he wanted to find the ideal spot for the telescope. You want to have an observatory where there is as little turbulent air as possible. He asked me, "How would you like to become our expert on atmospheric acoustic sounding to select an observatory site?" I said, "Yes, I've heard a little bit about it, but not much." He said, "Well, day after tomorrow you are going to Hawaii to meet the experts on top of Mauna Kea to learn all about acoustic sounding." So I went out and started learning all about Echosonde, or SODAR, which is like underwater SONAR but it is atmospheric instead of under water. The process told us about the temperature structure in the lower part of the atmosphere. Actually, the commercial aspects evolved into Doppler radar for looking at thunderstorms and wind shear.

In a couple of months, I got two Echosondes running around the Observatory, one on a trailer and one on Mt. Livermore, the 2nd highest peak in Texas. The turbulence around the top of Mt. Livermore was really bad, so we decided that would not be the place for the 300-inch. Then we did detailed studies between Mount Locke and Mount Fowlkes. Harlan and I published a couple of papers back in the mid-eighties saying the site seeing on Mount Fowlkes was good and it may be slightly better than the Millimeter site on Mt. Locke. That's why we ended up putting the HET where it is.

As part of this whole picture of atmospheric turbulence, we've been using another set of telescopes at the mountain, which are called DIMMs, Differential Image Motion Monitor. They are 12-inch Meade telescopes and masked down with two, 2-inch apertures. With a prism mounted in one aperture, we form a picture of a single star, but two images, on one CCD chip. We measure the relative motion caused by turbulence in the atmosphere between those two apertures. If you have a real stable atmosphere, then you've got two points that are just sitting there solid, side-by-side. If the atmosphere is unstable, then those points are moving, kind of bouncing around with respect to each other. We can determine the intrinsic seeing from these relative motions. This is the best seeing you can expect with respect to the atmospheric conditions on that particular night. The seeing we measure at the foci of the large telescopes inside enclosures is a combination of the atmospheric seeing and the turbulence inside the dome. We have some control over the dome seeing. We monitor the atmospheric seeing in real time on a display at the console of the HET and open or close the louvers to keep the telescope and the dome in thermal equilibrium.

Future efforts

We just brought ROTSE (Robotic Optical Transit Experiment) into operation, which is a collaborative effort. This is the second generation of these telescopes; the first generation has now been retired. The second generation will consist of four telescopes: one at McDonald; one already has been installed and is just coming into operation in Australia; there will be one in Namibia; and a fourth telescope is scheduled to go in southern Turkey. The ROTSE telescope is primarily used for gamma-ray burst follow-up. The HETE, High Energy Telescope Experiment, is a satellite that looks for gamma rays. The satellite detects a gamma-ray burst and sends the information to the University of Michigan. They alert the ground-based telescopes to do optical follow-up within a few minutes. This is being run remotely at McDonald with little or no interaction with the McDonald staff. The telescope here is a 0.4-meter, which tries to image the optical counterpart of the gamma-ray burst.

Yale is implementing another robotic effort on the 36-inch telescope to do quasar spectroscopy and imagery.

Another collaboration coming along is the MONET telescope. It is a German effort, which will put the MONET North telescope at McDonald, and the MONET South telescope in South Africa. They are in the design and early construction stages and we haven't decided exactly where at McDonald it will go, but probably near the Millimeter site on Mount Locke. Basically, they are going to do several different monitoring type efforts, light curves, and supernovae. It has a particular aspect in that forty percent of the time this telescope will be used remotely by German school students as teaching telescopes. They will submit their projects via the Web and can sit down in the classroom to perform them. These will be 1.2-meter telescopes and will be the largest robotics telescopes around for some time.

I hope I have given you an idea of some of the things we are doing at McDonald Observatory. Anita and Bill Cochran are coming up and they will tell you more of the science we are doing. Oh, there is one more story, about the McDonald flag. Do you know about the McDonald flag? It is an unofficial, yet inspired, flag and has flown on a couple of continents including a total solar eclipse expedition to Mauritania, Africa. Ron Schorn was really the person who created McDonald Flag in about 1966. He was a history buff and was studying military flags at the time. We were spending a lot of time with cloudy nights at the Observatory and came up with this flag idea. It shows a Coors beer can, crossed pool cues and balls, Saturn, a star, and a cloud. This was before the TQ was built and we had a kitchen up in the 82-inch dome on the second floor. It was sort of the rec room or ready room. There was a little pool table there, sort of like bumper pool, and a lot of billiard games were played on that. That's where the crossed pool cues came from. Coors beer, at that time, was the only good beer. That is where the Coors can came from. The Saturn and the star were on it because that is what we did at the time, planets and stars. Then, the small cloud stood for the nemesis of all observers and it was cloudy a good part of the time. Harlan did not like the cloud at all. Initially, he didn't allow the flag to be flown, but later relented and a flagpole was installed at the TQ. (Taking pictures of McDonald with clouds in the shot was also frowned upon by Harlan.)

Tom Barnes

I came to the University of Texas in October 1970 as the W. J. McDonald post-doc fellow and spent two years on that fellowship. After that, I was six years on the faculty as an assistant professor, including one stint as a part-time dean at UT. Then I went into management working with Harlan Smith in 1978. I had a variety of positions with Harlan, starting as assistant to the director and then associate director. When Harlan retired as director and Frank Bash became director, I stayed on as associate director until August, 2001, when I left that position and became a senior research scientist. After working in management, which I enjoyed tremendously, I am now doing research and hope to find some time to teach, both of which I enjoy. **I am Tom Barnes and I am a voice of McDonald Observatory**.

Variable stars and the distance scale of the universe

Most of my research now is focused on the distance scale of variable stars, particularly Cepheid stars. Using the Hobby-Eberly Telescope, I am looking at individual Cepheid stars in our local group of galaxies, the nearest of the big galaxies being M31, which is the Andromeda Galaxy, and M33. I will also use the Hubble Space Telescope to look at fairly nearby-in-our-own-galaxy Cepheids. The current Cepheid distance scale is not directly calibrated by geometry. It's an indirect calibration so there is always the little nagging worry that maybe something jumped the tracks in this indirect calibration. We really want to pin it down to geometry, to trigonometric parallaxes.

I work on these stars because they are the *coolest* stars there are. No, no, I don't mean cool temperature; I mean cool really interesting. Even though they are very distant, they are extremely luminous—bright, so you can see them and, they draw attention to themselves because they go on and off, so to speak, with a period of about anywhere from a few days to a few months. They are a wonderful yardstick to measure distances in astronomy.

I got here in 1970, just after the 2.7-meter telescope was commissioned. My research led me into a wholly new direction because of the brand new nature of the 2.7-meter (107-inch). I also fell into a collaboration with David Lambert and Reinhard Beer, of the Jet Propulsion Lab. Reinhard created a Fourier-transform spectrometer—a device for measuring the spectra of stars in the infrared. There was no other instrument in the world that could do that. We were working on the third largest telescope in the world, and we were having a ball doing stuff nobody else in the world could do. It's a great feeling. During that time, we were the first team to detect deuterium off the planet Earth. It had not been seen, and we found it. That was pretty fascinating.

In 1976 David Evans wandered into my office with a puzzle that led to a beautiful new way of determining variable star distances, which we have worked on intermittently ever since. I call it the Surface Brightness method, because it's a method based on the surface brightness of the star. Some people in literature call it the Barnes-Evans relation, which makes David immensely happy.

Transition to management, working with Harlan

In 1977 I didn't get tenure, which was one of those awful occurrences that turn out to be wonderful for one's life. In some ways, it's kind of like a divorce that turns in to a great marriage later because it let me discover that I could do management very well and I enjoyed it. So in early 1978 I accepted the job with Harlan Smith in management. I just had a great time. It was fun. For a few years I was kind of aide-de-camp to Harlan. Harlan is one of these people who ran the show. He didn't delegate real well. He really *ran* the show. In fact Paul Vanden Bout once laughingly said, "Tom Barnes, he's like the guy in the parade who follows the elephants around with the shovel and the bucket—he follows the director around and takes care of problems." It wasn't always difficult. Harlan gained confidence in me, I gained experience, and it went very well. I got in on the ground floor with the "Eye of Texas"—the 300-inch telescope project, then the SST, the Spectroscopic Survey Telescope, which turned in to the Hobby-Eberly Telescope. It was a fun time.

Frank's style

Then there was a change to working with Frank. Working with Frank was very different; Frank is terribly easy to work with. An illustration is early on when Frank was director we had a command performance in the University president's office in the Stark Library to present our case for why we should be allowed to continue with the SST as opposed to having this thing flushed. This is a big deal, because if the SST went down the tubes then we might not have a big project to work on, and then inevitably McDonald Observatory would go down the drain as well. Inevitable. So this was really a big, important thing. So he and I and Al Mitchell, who was then the project engineer on it, and several others, were gathered together by Frank to work on the presentation. I will compare the two directors. If we were working with Harlan, we would have been up for a week working until 8:00, 9:00, 10:00 at night, polishing every sentence, rewriting paragraphs, going over the viewgraphs, because Harlan used his team as a blackboard to clarify his thoughts. He oftentimes would come into my office and say, "Tom, I need you to be a blackboard for a little while." And he'd just talk something through and I would interact with him, giving him my advice, my thoughts, my view of it. And it was his way of doing the sorting out in his head. But with Frank, we worked a few hours a day and then it got to be Friday and the meeting was on Tuesday. I was expecting we would work on the weekend and Frank said, "Look, I'm going to go up to see my dad because he's not doing too well. We'll be back on Monday and we'll present on Tuesday. See you." I about fell out of my chair. What, we don't have to work the weekend? We don't have to work until ten o'clock every night? Frank had confidence that what the team had put together, with his polish on it, was fine. Frank and Harlan's ways were both successful—it is just a difference in style.

The HET, cigars and strategic planning

When Frank and I really focused on the HET, starting about 1991, it really consumed our time. I can remember sitting on the deck of my house with Frank one afternoon. Frank and I would do these things that we both thoroughly enjoyed—we'd have cigar talks. We're both cigar smokers so we would go away someplace where we could smoke cigars and talk for hours as a way of getting ourselves marching in the same direction. I would smoke only one cigar because there were consequences in smoking too many. But anyway, we laid out a map of how we wanted it to go. We just laid it out and it actually happened just that way.

In 1997, Frank asked me to be the commissioning manager for the HET. But at that time, the project team was disbanding because we were out of money. So we were going to have to finish the telescope using the operating budget and a legislative descendent of the Border Bonds because the Border Bonds had been spent on construction. The operating budget and Border Bonds are the two ways the legislature put funding into the telescope. The operating budget partly came from the legislature through the Line Item called "The Center for Advance Studies in Astronomy", which was created during the 1990s era to support the Hobby-Eberly Telescope. Border Bonds are issued to improve the State infrastructure in the counties bordering Mexico. Jeff Davis County, if you look at it, is shaped a bit like a horizontally, elongated diamond and the western-most point touches the border—tah-dah—we got access to Border Bonds, which gave us, I think, one or two million dollars. That evolved into the main source of funds for us to support the operation of the telescope, our Texas share of the operating budget.

The next two years were spent just making the telescope work, and the HET was finally commissioned in the fall of 1999, and began science operations. In the late fall of 2001, we had good science coming out of two instruments: the Low-Resolution Spectrometer and the High-

Resolution Spectrometer.

A return to science

In August of 2001, I resigned as associate director, and Frank gave me a wonderful golden parachute. I got a five-year appointment as a senior research scientist, which I was delighted with. I get five years to transition to being a self-supporting research scientist, or five years to wrap up my career, whichever way it turns out. Either way, it's fine.

A Harlan story, the role of director

One of my favorite stories illustrates something that directors do and it is a Harlan story as well. A director's job is to keep every telescope open as much as possible, because that is the way you get papers out, which is the way you get a reputation. When I came here, I was a photometrist, which is to say, the kind of research I did at McDonald generally used the smaller telescopes, and it required *pristine* weather—total absence of any cloud in the sky whatsoever during the observing. One time the weather was not great and we—another photometrist that was working on the other small telescope and me—couldn't work. The two big telescopes were doing spectroscopy just fine without the pristine weather—they could work in thin clouds; they could work if clouds came and went. So they were working and we were sitting in the TQ drinking coffee, shooting the bull, waiting for the clouds to clear. Harlan walked in the door and looked at us and he said, "Why aren't *you* observing?" We said, "Well, it's not photometric; we can't do good photometry." He looked at us and said, "Well, get out there and do bad photometry." So yes sir, and we went to the telescopes, piddled around for a while, then went back to the TQ, because there really wasn't any more we could do. To this day I don't know if he was kidding or not. You couldn't always tell if Harlan was kidding.

Observing at McDonald, then, now, and in the future

In the seventies and eighties, I enjoyed going to McDonald a lot. I spent a lot of time there and it was great fun. The chemistry amongst the observers was good. If it was cloudy, I'd play bridge with David Evans. There were numerous poker parties—you know—nickel, dime, or quarter poker. There were numerous games with the graduate students playing Risk. Just a lot of interactive time with other observers on cloudy nights and that was really very enjoyable.

Now if you go out to McDonald, you don't see people sitting around playing games on a cloudy night. They're all at their computer terminals, they are on line, working on doing something and they are doing it in their domes, not the TQ. Going to the Observatory now is lonelier than it was then. I remember one time in the late seventies I realized I had now spent more than half of my Christmases at McDonald Observatory working.

Eventually, going to the Observatory will end. I had a graduate student candidate here last week who said she loved doing observing. I told her, "Enjoy it while you can because in fifteen years, maximum twenty years, nobody will be doing it." It will be done the way I get data now from the Hobby-Eberly Telescope—remotely. I come in to my office on campus or at home and I log on to my computer; it says, "You have data." I don't actually go to the HET. The only people who do observing are the people hired specifically to live at the Observatory and do observing. I create the science program, I create the observing program, then I get the data. I reduce the data, I interpret the data and I write the paper. But I don't go for a walk around the catwalk at three o'clock in the morning and enjoy the stars. So I told her that's going away unless you are one of those people who work in an observatory. So her career will be completely different as an observer. That's a big change that has happened over the last ten or fifteen years—this phasing out of the need to go to the telescope.

An old favorite, the 36-inch

One of my favorite telescopes is the 36-inch—it's a hands-on telescope. The telescope dome is small, and everything was done from within the dome, not from the control room, and the computer controls were set up on the dome floor. We used a NOVA 210 and the only ones now are in museums. We were also out in the ambient temperature a lot of the time, which was very cold. So we'd go take a break in the TQ, warm up, have something to eat, and get some coffee. I remember one of those nights I brought a Styrofoam cup full of coffee back with me to the dome. I set it down and then we got busy. We got so busy that we worked from one in the morning until dawn without a stop. At the end of the night, my cup of coffee was frozen solid to the bottom.

It was cold and uncomfortable in the 36-inch, but it was enormously satisfying because I was right there with the telescope, and I was right there with the stars, and I was right there with the outdoors. It was great fun. The 82-inch is a little bit like that except that it's bigger. It doesn't move as fast, and it's operated out of a control room so you are constantly running from the control room to the dome, dome to the control room. But it's still a hands-on telescope. And it still makes those telescope noises when it moves; you know, the clank-clanking of gears. I felt connected to the telescope and to the sky.

Alphabetical David and scheduling telescope time

I worked with David Evans a lot; he is a grand old man of astronomy. He's a remarkable guy. He's one of those people who loves and craves the limelight, but he insists on alphabetical listing of names on all papers. 'Evans' is early, but it's not first so he always insisted I went first on our papers. I know people in astronomy who insist on going first all the time on papers because it is referenced with the first person's name, Jones et al., David doesn't do that. Every paper is alphabetical.

I can remember one night Reinhard took David, me, and our wives out to dinner. We all ate too much and we all drank too much. We were riding back, six of us in his car, and we're all singing to the top of our lungs, because David just loves to sing. He would always sing. He came into the office and you could hear him singing down the hallway.

When I first got here, Harlan Smith created the telescope schedules. Since we didn't have computers, he did it using a huge poster board that had graph paper taped to it. On the graph paper he had the telescopes listed going down the left side, and across the top he had a calendar. In those days we just asked Harlan for time. We went in and said, "Harlan, I'd like some 82-inch time to do this." And he'd say, "Great, how would you like this?"—and he'd get the pencil out and pencil it in on the graph paper. Oh the pencil, that was very dangerous. I can remember I was at McDonald one time on a telescope—I think it was the 2.7-meter and I had been out there almost two weeks. He rang me up one afternoon and said, "Tom, there's been a change in the schedule." You're on another week. I was out there three weeks, and three weeks at McDonald, especially if the weather's bad, you just go stir crazy. You never really knew what was happening on the schedule. The only way you'd really know what the schedule was, was if you sort of slipped into Harlan's office and looked at it.

Well, by sometime in the mid-seventies, we'd grown enough and there were enough of us, there was true competition for telescope time, and the graph paper and pencil were not satisfactory anymore. So at some point in there, David Evans, as associate director for research, got assigned the job of creating telescope time. He did it by requesting written proposals on a schedule. Then he would sit down and decide from the proposals who got what and when. Then Rob Robinson was assigned the task, or volunteered the task, to assist David in creating the schedule and the two of them would decide.

Once it was decided, David posted the schedule sort of like Harlan did, with the telescopes going down the y-axis and the calendar going across the x-axis. But he had a very clever scheme. He had a pegboard, with holes in it, mounted on his secretary's office wall, and he used

114

color-coded golf tees and you wrote on the head of the tee. Some of the heads would say an instrument and some of the heads would have an observer's initials, like TB, Tom Barnes. So he would put pegs in holes to show which dates, on which instrument was Tom Barnes. And under my name would then go what instrument Tom Barnes is using, with golf tees pegged into the holes below my name for the telescope. This schedule was prepared for three months at a time. It was very, very clever.

When Excel spreadsheets became possible, they got published. Then a little later it was decided that we needed a more formal mechanism yet, and a Telescope Allocation Committee (TAC) was formed that took over from David and Rob and the schedule was printed out and posted on the wall. Now it is posted on the computer.

Public outreach at McDonald

I have gone over the events that affected me, particularly, but I think there is something else that has changed a lot. It's unique to McDonald and should be in our history. That is the Public Information Office and the public outreach effort. It is completely unique to us. There is no other program that does anything near the quality and quantity that this program does. None of them have StarDate, a radio program that hits millions of people every day. It's incredible. It's won awards, it's informative, it's entertaining. And then there's the StarDate magazine, which is a very good thing. All this comes out of Harlan Smith. He saw the talent and nurtured it. It is directly an outgrowth of Harlan Smith and the later support of Frank Bash.

Public outreach was so important to Harlan. I heard him say, "At night, other observatories lock their gates, we throw ours open." He meant it. He didn't mean it in the sense that we want you to stroll into the observing room while I'm doing my observing program; that would be disruptive. But, rather in the sense that we want visitors at the Observatory at night seeing the sky because it will enthuse them about astronomy, and it's their tax dollars that pay for astronomy. It is our moral responsibility to make sure that the public sees what they are getting for it. If we don't tell the public about astronomy, we haven't done our job. To add to that, Frank's view is that public outreach enables us to get the kids. By getting the kids, we enthuse a generation about science and technology and we do a significant part in creating technologically and scientifically competent citizens. It is directly an outgrowth of Harlan Smith and the later support of Frank Bash and to Debbie Bird, who wrote the first radio programs, and to Sandi Preston, who made it survive, grow, and prosper. And Damon Benningfield, who now writes the radio program. If we had a professional astronomer writing those scripts, that program would be dead in a year because we don't have the talent Damon has. What fascinates professional astronomers is something else. So Debbie Bird, first, and then Damon, speak to the interest of the amateur.

On the Mountain with our future President and First Lady

Now, one more favorite story. It was in August of 1997, when President Bush was Governor. President George W. Bush and the First Lady came out for a tour of McDonald and I got the job of giving the tour. They came out late one afternoon, spent the night in House A, and left late the next morning. I have given lots of politicians tours of McDonald; it is one of those obligatory stops when they are out. I won't speak about the politicians that caused me to say this, but the difference in giving President Bush and the First Lady a tour was it didn't feel like giving a politician a tour. He has tremendous one-on-one charisma. He just was one of the guys; he made jokes and just talked with me about stuff. It was obvious that Laura had an interest in science. After dinner, I was all set to give them a tour through the 36-inch telescope. When it got dark enough I had an observer set up to run the telescope and we had programmed what we'd look at. We were all set. After dinner we visited for a while, and it was getting dark. But President Bush said, "Oh, I think I'm going to bed." So okay, all right, everybody goes to bed.

His staff was all staying at the TQ with us, and so I'm sitting, BS-ing with one of the observers and people came walking up the stairways talking on telephones. They say, "Tom, Laura wants to see something with the telescope." Okay. We went out to the telescope and gave her a tour of the sky. She was fascinated, asked questions and was very interested. President Bush didn't show up. The morning after, we are sitting at breakfast just chatting, and President Bush said something like, "Now what was that bright light that I viewed from the patio last night?" I looked at him curiously because he had not come to the dome last night. He said, "Oh, I got up in the middle of the night and was looking out. What was that light?" So, he did go out and look.

The President is just like a regular guy. The first afternoon of their visit we were walking around the ring road of the Observatory and up to the summit. There was a bunch of us. There were the Texas DPS guards, there was me, there was George and Laura, a couple of staff security persons, and Mark Adams, our mountain superintendent. The bunch of us was walking up the street and a couple of tourists are walking down to their car. We pass them and the tourist kind of looks at President Bush like, I know that guy…and President Bush just stops on a dime, goes over, shakes hands, introduces himself, greets the wife, introduces himself to her, chats a little bit, comes back and as he catches up with me, he grins at me and says, "*That's* the part of this job I just love!"

The main thing I drew out of his visit was he is just one of the guys. Speaking to some politicians is very stressful because you don't really know who you are talking to. It is kind of like talking to a mask. That's not the case of George W. Bush. Speaking to him is speaking to the person. Either that or he's really, really good with the mask—but I don't think so.

Your ever-changing McDonald Observatory

I would like to say to all our visitors that you should enjoy your time visiting one of the great observatories in the world. You should take pride that you support it and take credit in what's done here. I think you should know it's good to come back again because the Observatory changes. The exhibits change, we get new telescopes. Last time it was cloudy, this time may be clear. Maybe the first time you saw Jupiter in the telescope, this time you might see Saturn. You will have totally different experiences. But there is another reason you should come back. Almost all of us live in cities: we're surrounded by buildings, we're surrounded by cars, we're surrounded by roads, and we're surrounded by people. But you know, there are places you can stand at McDonald Observatory, and you can look to the horizon, and without much trouble, you can pretty much see West Texas the way it was before people were there. So come back, come back in the summer, come back in the winter, see different things.

Frank Bash

I was born in Medford, Oregon, in 1937, so I was a young kid when the Second World War started. The Japanese were putting incendiary bombs on balloons and sending them across the Pacific Ocean by the prevailing winds in an attempt to set our forests on fire. They were not very successful, but as kids, we were warned not to ever touch anything like that. My father was an air raid warden and we had helmets, fire extinguishers, and that sort of thing in our basement. These were pretty strong memories. Outside of town there was a military base that was very active during the Second World War, and after the War they turned it into a Veteran's Hospital. While I was in junior high school, I was chairman of an organization called the Junior Red Cross. I organized a program that we put on at the Veteran's Hospital every month. That was my early experience in management. **I am Frank Bash, current Director of the McDonald Observatory and I am a voice of McDonald Observatory.**

Besides my early organizational experience, I was always interested in mechanical things—never thought at that stage of being an astronomer. Probably my thoughts were in the direction of being an engineer, but I didn't have any specific thoughts. It was a time when I was pretty comfortable about my eventual career. I didn't ever worry about what I was going to be when I grew up, I just knew it would be something that I would be perfectly happy doing.

I went to college in Salem, Oregon, called the Willamette University. It is a small private liberal arts college with a fairly strong science program. I graduated with a physics degree and a minor in art history; it was an interesting combination and I found it very helpful later on. In my senior year, I started thinking about where this physics degree was going to lead because initially I was going to be an engineer. One of the first classes you had to take as a budding engineer was a course in mechanical drawing. I had this small, very primitive, instrument that was two pieces of metal with a little screw that could make these two pieces of metal farther apart or closer together. In between these two pieces of metal was a drop of India ink and I drew with this thing on paper. But, if you weren't really careful, this thing would go bloop, and the whole drop if India ink would fall on the paper and ruin your drawing. Of course, you could work on this for hours and then ruin it at the very end. I was so inept at this, this was such a pain, that I decided on the spot that I didn't want to be an engineer, so I became a physics major.

It was just fortunately true that Willamette had hired a new, young faculty member to teach physics and he had an interest in astronomy. He had a telescope, we started talking, and occasionally we would go out and look at the sky with his telescope. I thought this was really neat. Willamette subscribed to the Astrophysical Journal, I think primarily for me, and I started reading this thing and also got some textbooks. I never had a course in astronomy at all as an undergraduate, but I just did it on my own. It was fun.

When I started thinking about what my career would be like as a physicist, I started thinking about the way a physicist sees nature. This was probably partly influenced by the fact I had lived through the invention of the atomic bomb and seen what it could do. I thought the relationship of a physicist to nature is often a controlling relationship, restricting nature sufficiently so that you can fit a portion of it in your laboratory and believe that you have some control. That wasn't interesting to me. I have, and I think astronomers in general have, more of a feeling about nature like a forest ranger feels about a forest. Sort of awed by it all and affected by all kinds of external things. If you are an astronomer and it's cloudy, you can't observe; it's just part of the business. You are not in the corner of a warm little laboratory with a corner of it where you are controlling nature, but you are subject to the whims of weather and all kinds of things. And in astronomy, astonishing new discoveries are made almost weekly, discoveries of things you never even knew about before. I liked that. I liked that relationship to nature. An astronomer also has a very broad set of varied interests. And that's the way I decided to become one.

My first job in astronomy was working for Frank Drake, who is famous now for searching for radio signals from extraterrestrial life. That was a real break for me, because at this stage I had a master's degree and I didn't know what to do with it. So I applied for a job at Green Bank, West Virginia, and Susan, my wife, and our little girl, Katy, and I—in our Volkswagen—drove in the fall to Green Bank, West Virginia. The car was completely loaded with this little baby in the back seat that you could barely see because of the mountains of stuff all around her. We got to West Virginia and it was cold. I mean the weather was very cold, in the teens and sort of wintry West Virginia weather. There were no houses available on the compound of the Observatory, so we rented a house about fifteen miles away, down on a farm.

I worked at Green Bank in the early days, 1962, with Frank Drake and did all kinds of radio astronomy stuff. After Willamette I went as a graduate student to Harvard in radio astronomy. These were interesting days because the place was very new, doing all kinds of interesting stuff, and seemed to have tremendous amounts of money. The 300-foot telescope had just been put into operation—the one that later collapsed. Frank Drake was doing some of the early work listening to radio signals coming from, supposedly, planets around nearby stars. What I did was mostly work on planetary radio astronomy, which was Frank's interest, as his research assistant and later as a collaborator.

Radio astronomy had been discovered by an amateur astronomer named Karl Jansky, who discovered that radio waves are coming from objects in the sky. But the professional astronomers, all being optical astronomers, were completely uninterested in his result. Grote Reber, who is a radio engineer and amateur astronomer, followed up the result. He looked around the sky with his homemade radio telescope and noticed objects in the sky that gave out radio waves and sent a paper off to the Astrophysical Journal (ApJ). Well, the ApJ got this paper from this guy they had never heard of on this bizarre stuff, and it probably took an executive decision to publish the paper. But they did publish it and it is a famous beginning paper on radio astronomy.

Eventually Green Bank hired Frank Low, who is the famous infrared astronomer and one of the pioneers in infrared astronomy, to come and start an infrared astronomy program. I worked with Frank

Low for a while, and I finally decided this was sufficiently fun and I really did want to do astronomy. I decided I wanted to go ahead and get a Ph.D. and the quickest, most convenient thing to do was enroll at the University of Virginia, because the scientific headquarters at Green Bank were being moved over to Charlottesville, Virginia, which is where the University of Virginia is. So we moved over to Charlottesville maybe a year ahead of the move of the headquarters of National Radio Astronomy Observatory, the NOAO, and I stayed on their payroll. I was paid to go to graduate school, which was great, so we could move, and now we had two kids. I ended up doing a dissertation in radio astronomy with the early interferometers. So that was just a lot of fun. I was fixing equipment all the time. Very pioneering kind of stuff. It was great.

Gone to Texas

To go back a little bit, when I was at Harvard as a graduate student, I had to go down to Yale to get some equipment and while I was there, I met Jim Douglas, who ended up on the faculty at the University of Texas. So at the time I finished my Ph.D. at Virginia, I started looking for jobs and saw that the University of Texas was building up its program. Harlan had been hired there, and I had met him before, and Jim Douglas was there. The radio astronomy program was getting started at Texas and it was an exciting opportunity. So I came down here and worked with Jim Douglas for some years building a radio telescope which we built with our own bare hands in the fields south of the highway between Marfa and Alpine.

We built it all ourselves with a small crew, more pioneering, dirty hands sort of stuff. It was a low-frequency observatory spread out over several miles around. We put the equipment in old semi-trailers, surplused, abandoned semi-trailers, and they were our buildings. We just hooked them all together in this sort of modular complex. It was kind of bizarre but the whole thing worked and it worked really pretty well. The telescope is no longer there; we dismantled it when it finished its work

We were living at the radio Observatory but occasionally I'd get up to McDonald to eat at the Observatory or pick up some equipment. I remember the first impression of coming up to McDonald was to see the 82-inch telescope, which was famous, and I had read all about it when I was a student and the work it had done. The remarkable thing was the concrete piers for the 107-inch telescope had been poured, but the dome wasn't there and the telescope wasn't there, so these huge pieces of concrete were sticking out of the ground and looked sort of like Easter Island or something.

Chairman to Director

Eventually, one thing lead to another, various promotions and so on, and I became the University of Texas Astronomy Department chairman after Paul Vanden Bout and Harlan. I served out my 4-year term as chairman and the end of that term about coincided with Harlan's retirement as director. So the search for the new director to follow Harlan was on and I was on the committee to chose Harlan's successor. After some time, Gerry Fonken called me up and said, "Frank, I want you to take the job." Initially it was an interim appointment for a year, to see if they liked me and if I liked the job, and it was made permanent after about a year.

My radio Observatory work with Jim Douglas had finished and I had started working on the Millimeter Wavelength Telescope, which still sits on the mountaintop at McDonald. Paul Vanden Bout was running it and he and I had started working on that, which involved my getting interested in star formation, a different topic than I had been working on before. So I was going to restart my research career after my chairmanship, but because I agreed to be director I had to give up that and my sabbatical—that was the only painful thing about it. That was in 1989 and I haven't had that sabbatical yet.

The astronomy program at the University of Texas

The astronomy program at Texas is organized in the historical, old-fashioned way, modeled the way Harvard, Chicago, and Princeton are organized. That is, there are two organizations involved—the academic department, with the department chairman that runs all the classes and pays the faculty and then separately, the Observatory. They each have a separate budget and separate director effectively in charge. The McDonald Observatory director is in charge of all the Observatory's operation and its budgets—essentially the research side of the house.

The health of the astronomy program depends on an intimate interconnection between the academic department of astronomy and the observatory. If they don't work well together, extremely seamlessly together, it's not going to work. So the first job of the Observatory director is to make sure I work as closely and productively as I can with the astronomers. The astronomers are typically either students or faculty members of the department. We are big enough, so we also have the privilege of having research scientists on the Observatory staff.

In terms of the job, I guess the first and most important thing is the program in astronomy depends on the quality of the people you can attract. So the director's job is to provide equipment, supporting facilities, places to sleep, places to eat at the Observatory, people to fix the roads, and all of the support facilities to attract the best astronomers.

They see something at the Observatory they want to use in their research so they want to come here. So my job is to make the place as attractive as I can to the best people you can hire. Period.

Important aspects of McDonald Observatory science

There are some things that I am very honored to have been a part of here at McDonald Observatory. I am proud that we started out with a very strong program in extragalactic astronomy, partly because of the earlier history of the Observatory, but we made it stronger by attracting a very interesting guy, Gerard de Vaucouleurs. He certainly was our leading astronomer and Texas was seen as a place where you could study galaxies, and that is why we could get one of the greatest experts in the world.

Then we started doing a broader set of studies in radio astronomy. We started attracting stellar spectroscopists like David Lambert and Chris Sneden. In the early stages, David Evans, and Ed Nather started working on stellar variability—Ed Nather still does. So what I'm really proud of now is a very strong program in stellar spectroscopy, that is the analysis of the composition of stars. And work done here at Texas is the best work done anywhere in the world on that topic. Then with Brian Warner in the early days with Ed Nather and then Don Winget, the modern study of high-speed stellar variability really took off.

I think rather than specific little individual discoveries, these kinds of major themes are more interesting. It is interesting, too, that in the modern times, our emphasis here on spectroscopy and stellar variability is not terribly fashionable around the world in astronomy these days. The fashionable thing is to be doing extragalactic astronomy, not stellar astronomy, and we are a little bit at odds with the rest of the world. It is somewhat uncomfortable, but it is true. The Hobby-Eberly Telescope is capable of doing interesting work on galaxies and we have recently attracted John Kormendy and Karl Gebhardt to come here in a conscious effort to build up that capability of the Observatory and the telescope, which I think is going to lead to some really interesting and nice work.

Funding the Observatory.

The State of Texas funds the University of Texas in a giant lump of money. And by State law, the legislature can't get inside the state budget and eliminate the Philosophy Department or something like that. But, at the end of the State budget that funds the University, there are these things called Special Line Items. And McDonald Observatory is partially funded by two of the Special Line Items. One is called McDonald Observatory and one called The Center for Advanced Studies in Astronomy. Those provide the bulk of the operating money for the

Observatory. Now, unlike the bulk of the University of Texas budget, these individual Special Line Items *can be vetoed*. They can be raised, lowered, or vetoed independent of the rest of the University budget. So, McDonald Observatory is much more politically exposed than say the Philosophy Department is.

This year we have $14 million to run the McDonald Observatory. Just to put $14 million into perspective, to run the Observatory it takes: $1,166,666.67 a month, $269,230.77 a week, $38,329.91 a day, $1,597.08 an hour, or 44 cents a second. So one dollar is good for 2.25 seconds.

We get money from the State of Texas to the amount of about $5.4 million a year. We have contributions from our partners in the Hobby-Eberly Telescope, people pay for their housing at the Observatory and such things, to the amount of about $2.2 million a year. The Public Information Office brings in money through the sales of merchandise at the Visitors Center and subscribers to the magazine, and grants, and so on and that brings in about $1.7 million a year. The astronomers here attract research grants from NASA and NSF predominantly, at about $4.7 million a year. So the whole operation, if you take all this together, is about $14 million a year. McDonald has one hundred fourteen full-time equivalent employees—fifty-two in Austin and sixty-two in West Texas. That's everybody on the McDonald payroll. It's a fairly big operation. It's one of the bigger observatories in the world.

If the Governor draws a line through us, we would have to close the Observatory. We would have to close it and fire all the people. Then, if two years later when the legislature next meets and they decided to fund it again, you've got those people you fired but presumably wouldn't be able to hire back because they've got other jobs now and so you'd have to hire new people and retrain them. We have experts at the Observatory who have been out there working for us for more than 30 years that know every nook and cranny of the place. It would be very hard to replace them. People like David Doss.

The consequences are hard; it would be pretty bad. Science would lose rather a lot I think because the amount of science we do here is really amazing. It would devastate the astronomy program because one of the reasons a student wants to come to the University of Texas Astronomy Department to study and get a Ph.D. is because he or she has access to the facilities at McDonald Observatory. Also, McDonald frequently funds equipment that the students build as part of their dissertation work. If those funds are gone, then that opportunity wouldn't be there either. It would wipe the whole astronomy program.

Texans can influence the legislature

Well, I think the set of people in the State of Texas who are supporters of McDonald Observatory is a very large set, and although this is a theoretical possibility, we can talk about here. I have never, never had the slightest worry that it was actually going to happen because anytime something like this is threatened, the amount of support that surfaces is truly astonishing. But, it *has* to be there. I've had legislators comment to me that when McDonald Observatory was threatened, the number of letters and telephone calls and telegrams they received was just astonishing. That is how the public can help, with letters and phone calls supporting the Observatory.

And if you need something to say in your letter, phone call or telegram, some of the things you can mention are: consider the families coming to the Observatory and the Visitors Center. Consider the young kids and their excitement about the Observatory and about learning what's going on in the sky. Consider the pride Texans feel that their state has one of the major observatories in the world. Consider the educational programs McDonald Observatory offers to help Texas teachers use astronomy in Texas schools. Consider the young people learning, not just about becoming astronomers, but their excitement about learning to become engineers, scientists, technicians, physicians, or health professionals because they have seen how important science and discovery is at McDonald Observatory. Most important to remember is these kids visiting and learning at McDonald Observatory are the future adults who will ultimately affect the future economy of the State of Texas. If you don't have kids in science and technology in this State, it is in big trouble. Astronomy is one of the vehicles we can use to get those kids excited. So these public outreach programs, which initially were just evangelistic, have grown specifically in the direction of education. This is what we need to say to a legislator. I think McDonald Observatory is doing a very effective job and I think that Texas will be better for this effort.

Board of Visitors

A zero in the Special Line Items was threatened one time. One of the previous Governors vetoed all the Special Line Items. But fortunately, his chief financial aide was a member of our Board of Visitors and told the Governor to please reconsider, and so he did.

The beginning of the Board of Visitors precedes my being director, but my understanding is that at the time, the president of the University, Norman Hackerman, a chemist and a fairly hard-driving, hard-charging guy, was very concerned that Harlan Smith needed advice from hard-headed business types about how to manage the Observatory.

Hackerman sort of forced a group of people on Harlan, like the president of Texas Instruments and people like that, who could tell Harlan how he ought to run the place. One of the first things they did was notice that McDonald Observatory had no fire hydrants and no fire system. So the board brought that to the Regents of the University and caused a whole set of fire hydrants to be installed out there. They raised money to build a swimming pool and various other quality-of-life issues for the staff.

By the time I became the director, I saw the Board of Visitors as a very important part of the place, but they had grown considerably. It seemed we had lost control of who the board was and what their function was. We started taking better control of the nominating process for board members and energized it so that the board now is composed of people who can directly help us, in a variety of different ways. There are members whose political influence is necessary to McDonald in the legislature. There are members who have entrees to corporations and who can go with me and introduce me to their friends, the CEOs of some big corporation, and I can talk to that person about their financial support. It includes people who are wealthy and can give us money. It includes people who know wealthy people and can give introductions. It consists of people who can be directly beneficial to McDonald Observatory. And they have been enormously helpful. It is the biggest board of any organization in the whole University System except for the M.D. Anderson Cancer Center Board.

The McDonald Observatory Board of Visitors is a group of brilliant people, who are extremely interested in what we are doing. Any time I propose a program for a Board of Visitors meeting that doesn't include enough science talks, they complain. There are people on the board who are working in various companies around the State of Texas who, I think, had their circumstances been different, would have been professional astronomers. It is very gratifying to know each and every one of them.

Something unique about each telescope.

First of all, the telescope I know best is the Millimeter Wave Telescope, which is now retired and we are in the process of seeing if a group in Mexico might take it. It has done some really pioneering work, especially in high-frequency radio astronomy.

The 36-inch telescope, the second oldest telescope on the mountain, is the one Harold Johnson did the UBV system with. Johnson was here on the faculty.

The 30-inch telescope was used earlier with an enormous electronographic camera. I always was impressed that little telescope was able to carry such a huge instrument. A student, Chuck Claver, and Phillip McQueen, a staff member, put a prime focus camera on it and have more recently modified it. When it was installed, the camera would hit the dome at a certain place. Gerry Fonken, who was the Provost and was then the guy I reported to, just said, "Well, I'll fix it Frank. I'll just buy you a bigger dome." So he did, and that solved that problem.

Of course, the famous elite 82-inch telescope, one of the most beautiful telescopes around, is the original telescope at McDonald: The Otto Struve telescope. Still being fairly intensively scheduled but when the Moon is full, it's not always scheduled. It's getting creaky like the director is. It's got leather bearings in it in places, and the leather is wearing out. It's one of those issues that to modernize it, it would probably cost more than it would to buy a whole new telescope of that same size.

The 107-inch telescope, which I saw the piers of when I first came to McDonald and reminded me of something on Easter Island, is distinguished by being one of the ugliest telescopes on the face of the Earth, in my opinion. And, it is the one whose mirror was shot by a deranged night assistant who wanted to prevent us from seeing God with it. But the telescope is distinguished, not so much by the telescope, but by the spectrograph attached to it. It's got a beautiful Bob Tull-designed spectrograph. We often get requests from people who want to use that telescope, not because the telescope is impressive, but because the spectrograph is. So we've done really beautiful work with that. David Lambert, Chris Sneden, and the stellar spectroscopists have made very, very effective use of it. And the collaboration of Bob Tull and the two astronomers has been one of the most effective and productive collaborations I've ever seen between instrumentalists and observers.

The Hobby-Eberly Telescope

We were talking a few minutes ago about what a director's job is, and I want you to look at that in a slightly different way. The director's job is the future of the Observatory. What is the Observatory going to be like five years from now, ten years from now. The people who work for the director are in charge of what's going to happen tomorrow, what's going to happen tonight, or what happens if the telescope breaks, and so on. But the director's job is to worry about the future of the Observatory. Period.

I became director twenty years or so after the 107-inch telescope had gone into operation. This was a time when Harlan had proposed to build a 300-inch telescope, which he had always wanted to do. Harlan was a dear friend and really, one of the most sincere and devoted astronomical evangelists that the world has ever seen. He was enthusiastic to the core of his bones. So he launched off on this effort and was hoping to put the telescope on Mount Fowlkes, the adjoining mountain a mile away from Mount Locke. But, about that time the economy turned sour, and in the face of a worsening economy this just didn't look like it was going to happen.

I was department chairman at that time and had gone to an American Astronomical Society meeting in Baltimore. I met with Dan Weedman, who started here the same year I did in 1967, but who went on to Vanderbilt and then to Penn State. Dan had said that he and Larry Ramsey had this crazy idea to build a telescope. They were going to make the mirrors out of Pyrex, they were going to figure the mirrors by having graduate students grind them in the basement of the physics department of Penn State, and they were going to cover it with a grain silo. He said they could do this whole project for 6 million bucks. It was novel kind of design and I brought this idea back to Harlan. Harlan seemed to be interested, but he was having a very hard time letting go of the 300-inch telescope project.

That was about the state of things when he retired and I became director. I saw the reality of a 300-inch telescope was not going to be affordable, although the Japanese built it and it is called the Subaru—they used the design we produced and the telescope cost a fortune. I knew we had to do something because McDonald was beginning to start a decline. We were no longer terribly competitive for the best talent, so we had to start a project. Thus we started the Hobby-Eberly Telescope project; it was an affordable option for us.

Penn State was very much interested in finding a partner for the telescope Dan had told me about. This partner would provide the place where the telescope would actually be built and some of the funding. University of Texas president Cunningham was intrigued by the idea and looked at the 6 million dollar cost and said, "Well, Texas should try to do half of that and I will put up a million and a half." He immediately put a million and a half dollars on the table. He really did that; it happened just like that.

If I could raise the other million and a half, that would result in a total of $3 million for half of a $6 million project. I started looking at Dan's project and I could tell in a matter of hours that A) this was not a $6 million project—it was certainly more than that; and B) there was no way I was going to get involved in project where the mirrors were going to be made out of Pyrex and ground in the basement by graduate students and be covered by a grain silo. It was an endearing idea, but there was no way I was going to do that. I actually had to build the thing, and I didn't want to waste six million dollars. So we rapidly started assembling a team of people to run this effort initially, to quickly look at the telescope design.

A quick look at the telescope design suggested that yes, it was

127

certainly going to be more than 6 million bucks and we had to do this professionally and get the confidence of the University administration to launch-off on this project. So we had to do enough of the effort with the people we already had to convince the administration that we knew what we were doing so they would allow us to hire somebody, a project manager who *actually* knew what they were doing. So we provided the designs, did it with local people, and eventually, we knew the cost to build this thing was approaching $10 million. I can remember the day I told president Cunningham that this was going to be a $10 million project. He made me go with him down to Lieutenant Governor Bill Hobby's office and made *me* tell Bill Hobby this. Of course, Bill was not one who suffered cost overruns gladly. This was not an overrun; this was just a lack of knowledge.

The Hobby-Eberly Telescope. Photo by David Reaves.

The key that finally got us the permission to proceed was when the University administration told Bill Hobby they wanted to honor him for all of his time as Lieutenant Governor. He said, "I don't want a statue or anything like that. I would like that telescope to be named for me, and I would like to go out and help Bash raise the money to build it." And so he did.

The costs still grew and we had to find additional partners. Greg Shields, astronomy professor at the University of Texas, had graduated from Stanford. He was able to interest Stanford in the project and eventually to join. We accreted the German partners through Rolf Kudritzki, who had been a candidate for the directorship and was very involved and aware of McDonald Observatory.

One thing led to another and the HET finally ended costing an official $13.5 million. But, we're still putting money in it. We've probably gone to $16 or $17 million now. Of course, compared to the competitive telescopes of similar size, it's still a heck of a bargain, so we are very proud of it.

The guy we hired to manage the project is Tom Sebring who had all kinds of experience. First he was a hippy n'er-do-well, operating a ski lift in a ski resort and stealing apples to live on. Fortunately, and eventually, he went to school and became an engineer. He worked for Eastman Kodak, then got involved in the whole government Star Wars thing. He was looking around for a job that would involve his optical engineering strengths and saw our ad in a national magazine and applied for the job. Instantly, when I talked to this guy, I said, this is the right guy to hire. Penn State agreed and we hired Tom Sebring. He was the key. We wouldn't have been able to do it without him.

And then, of course, one of the keys to keeping cost under control was to use commercial equipment. You can hire companies that only build telescopes, but they are frightfully expensive, so the Hobby-Eberly is made out of standard commercial equipment. Tom also understood that the Pyrex mirrors were going to be a major problem and he contacted Schott Glass Works in Germany. They had been trying to make an 8-meter diameter single mirror out of this material called Zerodur and the first three they made, broke. They had these huge broken pieces of mirror that were maybe two feet thick. So Schott had all of this spare material, out of which they could cut our small one-meter mirrors. We got the mirrors at bargain-basement prices.

The Hobby-Eberly Telescope has had its struggles. The Hobby-Eberly Telescope is tremendously promising and is beginning to realize the promise. We didn't have enough money, but now we have some money, we have some people, and we're really making some tracks now.

So that's a little blurb about each of the telescopes. Of course, we've also got the laser-ranging project, which has been running now for a very long time, probably about thirty years. And we're proud of the work they've done. Pete Shelus will tell you about it.

The future

There were many, many, many ups and downs. Many tough days. But, we eventually built the HET and, of course, went on to build another telescope, which is finishing up now in South Africa. I would love to do another telescope with Tom Sebring someday.

It was always clear to me that the Hobby-Eberly Telescope was what we needed to keep our position in astronomy from eroding and to keep us able to attract good talent. But the HET is not the final step. There is another step that needs to be taken and it is a little tougher. I earnestly feel that in the future, McDonald Observatory must get involved in another telescope project. I also feel that it will have to be built outside the borders of the State of Texas. And so the effect of that decision on our funding and on our State support, both financial support and other kinds of state support, are going to be something the new director will have to wrestle with.

Why does another telescope have to be outside of Texas?

The atmosphere. Although the skies are incredibly dark at McDonald Observatory, the mountain is just not high enough. It is understood that the atmosphere is the major problem in ground-based astronomy. Increasingly, the sites where we must put new telescopes are on taller and taller mountains. Mauna Kea, 14-thousand feet in Hawaii, is the current favored location. There is nothing at 14-thousand feet in the State of Texas. And, of course, future sites that are being seriously considered, one of which I am interested in, include 18-thousand foot mountaintops in northern Chile. So effectively what we will try to do is build a space telescope on the ground, with as little air between us and the stars as possible.

An interesting house and interesting people

House A

Well, one of the great perks of being director of McDonald Observatory is you have use of a house on the Observatory called House A. The original houses were designated by letters and so the director's is called House A. In the presence of the University president, I referred to *my* house at McDonald Observatory. And he said, "Frank, that's not *your* house, that's the University's house." And I said, "Thank God the Governor is not here."

It is a wonderful house built of native stone and built extremely substantially with big, wood beams and so on. It probably has the most beautiful view in the State of Texas, looking out south over the valley below. It's just been an absolute delight to have. We're, of course, not in it very much and when we're not in it, it's used by Board of Visitors, people and their families or other visitors or State officials or university VIPs and so it's become a really nice thing to share with people. It's also got a problem because people hear about it and I'll get a call from the So-And-So Association in Houston wanting to raffle off a week in House A as a prize to raise some money. I have to explain that I can't do that. I get a call from a medical school faculty member in Dallas and they say, "I hear the University has this wonderful vacation house that we can sign up for." So I have to stop it. And of course the family, Susan and I, have enjoyed very many wonderful times out there.

Harlan J. Smith

I could go on forever about Harlan. He was just an absolutely wonderful guy, an astronomical evangelist in the true sense of that word. He said on more than one occasion that he felt sorry for all the people who weren't astronomers because of all the fun they were missing. And he really meant it. But I think the other thing that people don't recognize is the atmosphere of this place. Harlan was such an open and wonderful guy and the atmosphere he created has never been allowed to degenerate into warring camps, as it often does in other places. McDonald maintains a really nice atmosphere, where people talk to each other and the doors are open. There are no cliques or in-fighting. We respect each other.

David Doss

There is a guy at the Observatory all of us know, David Doss. He has been at the Observatory for a long, long time. I've always said that one of my goals was to retire before David because I didn't know how we could run the Observatory without him. He is an expert on the telescopes, just a phenomenal guy who has never been interested in traveling, never been interested in leaving the mountain very much, and is just a terrific talent. Everyone at the Observatory knows David's value, but it is the most understated fact because we just have trouble finding the words.

Some popular questions from visitors:

Why don't we have a planetarium?

We specifically considered a planetarium in the new Visitors Center, but the staff and I rejected that for a reason that will give some insight into my peculiar personality. When you have skies that are so dark and you can look at the real sky, it's almost obscene to have a planetarium. I add to that the peculiar feeling I have: I worry that kids too often today, with television and the skill of computer animators, sometimes have a difficult time separating the virtual world from the real world. So I think it is very important for people to go outside and look at the real sky. Not some animator's version of the real sky, but the real sky. I think it is very important for there to be cloudy nights because that is real. I think it is very important when you are looking at a real image of the Sun taken right now, that a bird flies through the beam, because that is real. This view gives some insight into the personality of astronomers, who, as I say, have a forest ranger's view of the physics of the universe rather than a controlled view.

Is there life in space?

That is one of the great questions astronomers have been wrestling with. The fact that we have never discovered life in space is itself very interesting. It makes me wonder if we are looking properly. One of the big thrusts now in astronomy is finding planets circling around other stars and asking the question, "Is it possible there are living beings on this planet?" There are other planets around other stars that we haven't yet discovered for their living things. It is interesting.

Will the universe stop expanding?

"Will the universe stop expanding, *ever*?" That is one of the current great questions, too. Doesn't look like it. Or if it ever does stop expanding, it will be at time equals infinity.

Do you believe in God?

I was raised as an Episcopalian, and I think that the answer probably is yes, that I do, but it is not a literal belief of a person with a certain appearance in a painting. I do feel that one's belief in God is not at all in conflict with one's interest in doing science. If you take the Bible literally, conflict may exist. Astronomers talk about a thirteen billion-year-old universe and the Bible, if taken literally, implies a five thousand-year-old universe. So there is a conflict there, but I think if you read it with a broader view, there isn't really any conflict at all.

I believe that we can reconcile the "Big Bang" with creation and I very strongly believe there are all kinds of things that are unknowable to science, which is a whole set of experiences and thoughts people have that science is never going to be able to attack.

What is difficult about being an astronomer?

As you know, families who have a member heavily involved in a career have difficulties to put up with. Astronomers have the additional problem of having to travel frequently to go to meetings or observing, so they are physically out of town quite often. And for some reason, I don't know why it happens, but if anything is going to break around the house it always chooses to break when the astronomer is out observing—the water heater goes, or whatever.

The other thing that is difficult is that if you are an optical observer, you have to switch back and forth from a night schedule to a day schedule. If you have young kids that force you to be on a daytime schedule, you really have to switch rapidly back and forth between the two and you *have* to be effective while you are doing it.

I've always said to everybody who works for me that you've *got* to make your family one of your top priorities. It just has to be. And if I ever hear that the reason you can't do something is because you to have to go take care of something in the family, then that's *great*. You've got your priorities straight. If your goal in life is to make a lot of money and to have a fancy house and that kind of thing, astronomy is not particularly a lucrative choice to make.

I think most astronomers feel that the benefits vastly outweigh any of the difficulties—even for the spouse who's other half has a life like a vampire. Well, except for the hanging upside down part.

Retirement

The decision to retire is always personal, but, you know I'm sixty-five now, I'll be sixty-six this year. It's time. I've done my telescope, and I've done my Visitors Center and it's time for the next director to come along and do his thing. I think it's time for the University to recommit itself to the astronomy program and hiring a new director forces it to do so. My honeymoon has been long since over and it's time for a new person to come along and re-energize the whole thing. So that's really what it's all about. You have to retire at some point and this is the time for me to do it.

What does it mean for the Bash family? The biggest thing I've heard so far is the expression of regret that we can't go out and stay in House A anytime we feel like it. That's going to be painful. Otherwise, I don't think we have regrets. I am taking away a feeling of satisfaction that I have done a good job, and the investment of my time and energy in the directorship was as productive as it would have been if I had been concentrating on my own research. Because I hope that by Frank Bash's work as director of McDonald Observatory, I have enabled other people to do lots and lots of research. That really does satisfy me, because after all, research is the reason for doing all of this.

Especially from Dr. Frank Bash

Visitor, I want you to feel welcome here. Too often, I have seen observatories where their attitude to the visitor was, go away, you're bothering us; we don't want you to mess around with the place. In addition, they put barbed wire around it. That's absolutely not our attitude. I want you to feel welcome. I want you to feel free to ask a question and have the question answered. I want you to be treated with respect and feel welcome. That is the first and most important thing.

I think something that tends to be undervalued, because it's so hard to measure, is the effect astronomy has on the people who visit the Observatory. I look at parents here with their family and ask myself, Why did this person go so far out of his or her way to come to McDonald Observatory? I see in these people not only a genuine interest in astronomy, but a genuine interest in the *exploration* part of astronomy. I wonder if human beings aren't built with a need to explore, and since the surface of the Earth is pretty well explored, astronomers are their explorers.

Panoramic view of the McDonald Observatory Visitors Center at night. The domes of the Otto Struve and Harlan J. Smith telescopes are on the left. Photo by Bill Wren, McDonald Observatory

Chapter 7 The Board of Visitors

Don McIvor

Today, I drove up here to House A to talk to you. **My name is Don McIvor and I am a voice of the McDonald Observatory**. My ranch is the U Up and U Down and if you came to the Observatory from Ft. Davis, you passed the ranch on the way. It is called the U Up and U Down because after my great grandfather, G. Scott Locke, bought the land in 1882, he bought cattle with the U Up and U Down brand. The man was selling the cattle cheap because his daughter was going out with a "no-account army sergeant" and he wanted to leave the area. We never did find out if the girl eloped or how the brand originated. The cattle brand is a U in the up position and then a U in the down position. The brand stays on the cattle when they are sold so a lot of times a ranch will have two names, the owner's name and the cattle brand name. My mother was a Locke and the ranch is in the Locke Estate. It was called the Locke Ranch for a long time. When my mother married, it was the McIvor and McIvor and when my father died it was McIvor Ranch and so forth. It still carries the U Up and U Down name.

I was born and raised in Concord, New Hampshire, and as a small child I came down here in the summers. We had both the lower and the upper ranch and when I was old enough I was put to work on the upper ranch. I remember my mother talking about the Observatory. It was when Yerkes and the University of Chicago had it and it was just the 82-inch telescope then. My family was good friends with Dr. Elvey and a few of the old-timers that were up here and my mother was very, very glad that she could donate the mountaintop. They wanted to name the mountaintop after Mother's great grandfather, G. S. Locke. Her father, who was a physician, died when he was thirty-six of pneumonia, so her grandfather raised her. When he got too old, she took over the ranch. It was under the Locke Trust for many years until she died at the age of nincty-eight. After I went through college and the service, I went to work out in Arizona. My father was a doctor, a very fine doctor. He had a series of heart attacks and my mother couldn't come down here too much anymore. There was an eight-year drought that ended in 1957 and all the ranches were hurting. One day she said, "We are going to have to change; would you take over management?" So I said, sure. I had been out here as a child and been on the ranch a lot so I knew how to take care of it. I learned a little Spanish because my help spoke it, and I taught them some English. They were great people and it worked out really well.

When they ran out of water at the Observatory, we said, "We'll give you water." They had two pumps down below the Observatory and they were hauling water up to the top for a while. It was a chore. The Observatory said they wanted to lease it and I said, "No, I want to give it." They said, "Well that's complicated." I said, "Tough, we're going to give it to you." The Chancellor of the University Systems and I got together and chatted and they gave me some waterings off the line and we gave them the water. It was fun. We enjoyed that.

The Origin of the Board of Visitors

Then thirty some odd years ago, they started the McDonald Advisory Council, which is now called the Board of Visitors. There were eight of us originally. The McDonald Observatory wanted a Board because they had some problems and they wanted to have them addressed by professional, outside business people. I always laughed because they had Buddy Harris of Texas Instruments, and they had the manager of General Dynamics, all the biggies. I always felt like I was their token pheasant by law. But I remember there were just eight of us for several years, and I think now there are only two of us original members left. The rest have passed away. Pete Snelson, I think, was one of the originals and, of course, he is still around. He was a politician. We always had one politician in there.

It was interesting because at that time, eighty percent of the funding for McDonald Observatory was from NASA. We said, "No way!" I'll always remember sitting in that meeting with the Chancellor of the University using ten-dollar words, arguing with Board member, Buddy Harris, who was a good friend of mine. He was a rough diamond—he used words I understood. Buddy Harris said, "If you want us to help, we don't need all these people. You have some real problems and we'll solve them, but you've got to let us have free rein or we're out." Buddy won, and he was right. Then we sat down and went to work. The University was very good about getting politicians out here to see the complex and within four or five years, they had a Line Item in the Texas Legislature for funding. NASA became about twenty percent of the funding.

One of the first things we did was try and improve things for the people who had to live at the Observatory. While the houses were being built, they had everyone living in trailers. These trailers were ten feet apart and you could hear people flush toilets and talk and everything. It really got bad and they wanted to bring a psychiatrist up to settle everyone down. It was jammed living and isolated, and a lot of people aren't used to being that isolated. That's when we expanded the board and put in a swimming pool and a tennis court. We didn't want to isolate them from Ft. Davis, but they had to have some kind of recreation and diversions. When the houses were available, this sort of solved itself and they didn't need a psychiatrist.

Once a year, the board gets together out here at the Observatory. We get to have lots of food and visit with each other. I like to kid around. I used to act like an astronomer because I know the lingo. If they talked to me too long they'd find out I was just a layman and usually another board member would come over and say, "He's just a local rancher." That would blow my cover. It was fun. Several times, I didn't realize it but Secret Service had an armed group of people there because they had dignitaries from Russia and China. It was good for them to come out here because it crossed international boundaries and got them out of politics and into ping-pong and astronomy. I enjoyed those times very much.

I remember one time at the 107-inch, the astronomers were using spectroscopy which shows the elements of the object they are looking at. They were looking at Mars and got really excited because they thought they found phosphorous. They found out quick enough that someone was going outside and lighting a pipe with a kitchen match. Of course, he was embarrassed.

I like to joke around a lot and when McDonald started the laser program, I went up and told them they were going to give my cows pink-eye. That is a fascinating program with the laser and it is still going on. Not the pink-eye...that was a joke. I like to joke.

Dark skies in the Davis Mountains

Something that is most important to me, and my sisters, is the dark skies here. I want to be sure there are always dark skies for McDonald Observatory. That is critical. The complex up here is the last dark sky of any significance in all the Northern hemisphere. I knew many of the other observatories were having problems with light pollution and if I could sell some of the land with conservation easements attached, McDonald would be assured of dark skies in perpetuity. It took several years to accomplish but we did that. I'm still working to be sure that all the ranches surrounding here, as many as we can, have conservation easements so there will be no commercial building. We want to keep dark skies all around the domes.

The West Texas Utility, the electric company, is giving free shields to direct house lights down on the ground instead of up. They do that free. McDonald Observatory has a good crew working on the problem; you have to stay on top of it. I worked on a committee for the projected future of this area—all the little towns around here. I proposed the name of our publication, "Ft. Davis, A Progressive Little Town That's Always

In The Dark."

Fighting fires

I am a lifetime member of the fire department around here. Most of the fires get started by lightning. The upper ranch burned totally two or three times and I am sorry it happened, but it caused the forest department of Texas to give a lot of second-hand equipment to all these small towns for firefighting. It has helped considerably. It's not *if* we're going to have fires, it's *when*. Now, I'm really tired of beating fires and I am usually the first-aid machine going around with food and stuff for the firefighters. The worst fire was when about half of the upper ranch burned, about twenty thousand acres, and it burned for two weeks. We fought day and night and we were just about wiped out when the forestry department came in. We looked like Cox's army—just all wiped out and worn out. The forestry department had uniforms and special trucks and they all went like soldiers to fight. I'll always remember that feeling; they just took over and we were just exhausted.

Why support astronomy?

McDonald Observatory brought roads, electricity, and phones up here. It is a plus for us, otherwise the road here would still be dirt, and we would be out of the loop. The Interstate would just pass us by. I would like to say to the visitor that sometimes it is not clear how important astronomy education and the McDonald Observatory really are. Why should taxpayers pay money to support astronomy education? Well, I think one of the hardest things to get across to people is, it is pure science—it's ninety-five percent pure science, five percent practicality. It is that five percent practicality that counts. It's just like going to the Moon. Everyone said it's stupid, it's ridiculous. But you have to realize, it is the spin-offs of technology that came from the education we got from going to the Moon. It is the same with astronomy education, that five percent practicality we achieve with our exposure to the ninety-five percent pure science. It's worth every penny.

George Christian

George Christian was born and raised in Austin, Texas, and received a BA in Journalism at the University of Texas. He was a U.S. Marine and served in the Pacific and during the occupation of Japan in 1944 to 1946. He was press secretary to Governor John B. Connally from 1963 to 1966; Assistant to President Johnson and on the staff of the National Security Council at the White House in 1966. George Christian was a White House spokesman and at the center of Texas politics throughout his life. He passed away on November 27, 2002. I remember an eternal sparkle in his eye and a laugh that could make your side split.

I was born on the first day of 1927. I guess the first time I became aware of astronomy was when I was a very small boy and my mother and father purchased a one-volume encyclopedia called the Lincoln. It had a section on astronomy and I thought it was fascinating. This was shortly after Pluto was discovered as a planet and I was enthralled that someone was still discovering planets out there. Boyhood science fiction things like Buck Rogers and Flash Gordon cartoons probably added to my interest in space and the solar system. **I am George Christian and I am a voice of McDonald Observatory.**

My first real contact with an observatory was when my mother and sisters and I visited the McDonald Observatory in 1941. It was just a couple of years after it was dedicated and the University of Chicago was still running it. I can still remember standing up there on Mt. Locke looking out over the Davis Mountains, particularly Mt. Livermore which was near by, and going through the first dome, the 82-inch. I did not get to look through the telescope that time, only *at* it. But I thought, This has to be something pretty fabulous. And it was.

We've got a very diverse Board of Visitors. There are all kinds of people on it as you are finding out I'm sure. Some of them are former members of the legislature and are on the board because their representative districts were in the area and they just wanted to stay on after they left the legislature. We have a former Lieutenant Governor and his son both on the board. We have a few scientists; Dr. Hans Mark always tries to make the board meetings. Then we have some lawyers from some of the big firms, bankers, jewelers, members of large foundations. There is a tribe of them; I don't know of any Indian chiefs but we've got everything else. We are a diverse bunch and the only thing that holds us together is the glue of McDonald Observatory.

Catalyzing the Hobby-Eberly Telescope

Harlan Smith was the director at the time I came on the Board of Visitors. My first real challenge was when Harlan decided to go for outside funding to match the University's commitment for what became the Hobby-Eberly Telescope. The fund raising was pretty much languishing and it looked like we weren't going to make it. One day I got the notion that we've got to build this fundraising around somebody, somebody significant in order to get people interested in it. It struck me that we needed to name it for someone who had the reputation that would broaden our fundraising universe. I suggested Bill Hobby be the honoree and Harlan thought that was great.

So Bill Cunningham, who was then president of the University, and I went together to see Lieutenant Governor Bill Hobby. We asked him if he would be willing to lend his name to the telescope. He agreed and said he would be honored. He then became greatly interested in it and learned all about spectrum, spectroscopy...he could pronounce it; *I* can't. Anyway, he became greatly interested in it and was caught up in the design, the concept, and everything else. Hobby was obviously a great advocate of higher education and research, and I think he was the perfect choice. As it turned out, we were able to use his name, in effect, to raise money. We just blatantly used Hobby's name for a lot of it. Hobby had been a great Lieutenant Governor and people appreciated him.

The telescope was named Hobby-*Eberly* because the agreement was that the partner in the telescope, Penn State, would get to share in the naming. Robert Eberly, who had been one of their benefactors, also appears on the telescope. But without the Hobby connection, I don't think it ever would have come to pass.

I also helped raise money for the new Visitors Center. We failed to get money from the Highway Department that we thought we were going to get. But actually, it was somewhat easier to raise the money for the new Visitors Center, and I think the main reason is the Nowlins came through with their two million dollar contribution. They just came in off the street, practically, and gave—which wrapped it up.

How does the Observatory affect me? Well, I have to chuckle and say, "It keeps me working raising money!" Also, it excites me. I mean the fact that I've watched them over the years grow and become more important in the scientific community, and I've watched the Astronomy Department build itself from the ground up, really. We had no astronomy department at all when McDonald was built; we were just a player. Now I have seen our leaders in the Astronomy Department constantly looking at other avenues to advance the cause of science.

Just associating with the faculty members and astronomers has been a lot of fun. I don't have a scientific bent; I don't have a mechanical bent, or even use computers. I've got one sitting there but I never use it. But, it is the best computer in the world; I don't have to wait for something to print out or anything. I'm an old newspaperman. I'm always grateful Jake Pickle plucked me out of the newspaper business and asked me to go to Washington to work for Senator Daniel. That opened the door to the political world, which I have always enjoyed.

What would I say to the McDonald visitor? Don't expect to go up to the summit and look through the big one. It's not going to happen. Be willing to stand in line at the star party. It is worth it; sure it's worth it. My family and I go out often and we just enjoy the dickens out of it. We always stay at Indian Lodge. We always go to the Fort. We go down to the drugstore. We do all the things in Ft. Davis we enjoy doing. We go up to the mountain during the daytime and take pictures. We go to meetings up there and poke around. We always go to the Visitors Center, buy T-shirts and whatever else we want. It's just a nice little summer excursion for us.

In my life, my children have honored me, and my grandchildren. I am proud to have six kids and eleven grandchildren. I'm proud that I was able to play some role in the government of the State and the country. One of the members of the House asked me the other day, she said, "How old are you?" I said, "Well, this is my twenty-sixth legislature!" Counting my time as a political reporter in the Capitol and in the governor's office as a lobbyist, I have spent a lot of time around the Capitol. I love that place.

Deep down I am basically a historical preservationist and archeologist. My interests are varied and I'm glad astronomy is one of them. I'm not sure what is next for McDonald. It's pitiful that we have to fight to keep the doors open. It does take up too much attention. But whatever comes, I hope I'm part of it. It's going to be up to the guys, up to Frank and the folks in charge. I'll do whatever they suggest. I'm just a soldier in the ranks.

Clifton Caldwell

Today is February 23, 2001, and I will be sixty-eight years old next Friday. **I am Clifton Caldwell and I am a voice of the McDonald Observatory.** I was born in Abilene, Texas, but at the time of my birth, my parents were living about eight or nine miles the other side of McDonald Observatory on the Nunn Ranch, which is now the Caldwell Ranch. I was born and we immediately went back out there. In the thirties in the Model T or Model A my father had, it was about a six-hour drive from the ranch to Ft. Davis. It's only about an hour drive now. The roads then were single-lane gravel then. Today, you can look off the road and see some of the trucks that rolled off the road right below the Observatory. It used to be a mean road. You had to stop and put water in your car driving up there—they kept barrels on the side of the road full of water for your car. It was very common then along those long hills.

"Zervatory"

I remember driving by the Observatory when I was little and my mother has told me that "Zervatory" was my first word. I pronounced it with a "Z." "Zervatory, Zervatory," I shouted when we got near it. I remember going by there early on and the 82-inch mirror came in before the building was finished. I remember they had a well or a water storage tank in front of the dome and they kept the mirror in there to keep it a constant temperature until they finished building.

To this day, I look for the Observatory, no matter which direction I'm coming from. Whether I'm over between Marfa and Paisano Pass or whether I'm coming in from Marfa to Alpine or Marfa to Ft. Davis, I look across there and know exactly where to look. When I used to fly quite a bit, I'd always look for it to hone-in, because I could see the mountains over there and I knew exactly where I was. It has always been a landmark for me.

At our Nunn Ranch, the Caldwell Ranch, we hunted a lot and I would ride out with my parents and then take people deer hunting and such. But one Sunday in 1942, we were all having lunch in Abilene and my granddad said, "Everybody walk behind me and give me a swift kick. I just sold the Nunn Ranch. It was a mistake, I shouldn't have sold it, but this man kept telling me he wanted to buy it and he kept saying 'put a price on it, just put a price on it.'" My granddad said he paid seven or eight dollars an acre for it and so he decided to just put a price on it of fifteen dollars, and the old boy took him up on it. He said, "What am I going to do, I never go back on my word, so I sold it to him." It was about a thirty thousand acre ranch. We sold it for four hundred thousand dollars in 1942 and he sold it for ten million dollars just the other day.

Well, my other grandfather had a ranch and we still have it between Alpine and Ft. Davis, Mitre Peak Ranch.

Another story about the hill there at McDonald. When my parents bought new cars we'd see how far you could go up the hill without shifting gears. It was always interesting to see how far you could go and we were a braggadocios bunch, "My father's car can go up to within a tenth of a mile of the top of the hill before you have to shift gears!" Or something like that. As I said, it's been a landmark for me for various reasons, so when they asked me to become a Board of Visitors member, I fell right into it.

Harlan Smith

It was Harlan who asked me. Harlan was such a kind person. He was like a little kid about everything he did. He was very soft, but he was very enthusiastic. In the beginning as a Board of Visitor, I think I gave him the money to buy a PC-type computer. He needed a certain amount, not a big amount, two thousand dollars or so to start doing something specifically. I said OK and gave him a check. Every time something came up, I would get tapped on the shoulder and I gave him something. I just regret I can't give more. It's been kind of a love affair with McDonald Observatory. If I had a foundation or something, I would just give the money away and I'd love giving it to McDonald Observatory.

I am very much for the visitor coming to Texas. I want the visitor to have a good time anywhere he comes to in Texas; I want him leave Texas with a better feeling than when he came. I think the McDonald Observatory is a bright spot in that. It's a recreational thing for people to do. I've sat in those star parties at night and people are seeing the Milky Way for the first time. Some of them didn't even know it existed. They come from a city and say, "What's that up there? I've never seen it up there before." I see their enthusiasm in it. I really like that.

Jane Sibley

My early memories of McDonald Observatory are those of awe and curiosity. I must have been fourteen or fifteen when I rode with my mother and father from Ft. Stockton the 100 miles or so to Ft. Davis. I was amused today when coming to the Board of Visitors meeting to see a sign on the mountain road that said, "25-miles-per-hour." That was almost our speed on the highway. There was an enormous crowd of cars that day, each one trying to get to the mountaintop. It seemed to me we were in line for hours; no one had thought of parking arrangements. This must have been the day of the dedication in 1939. The delay did not matter because my mother had brought a picnic lunch. **I am Jane Sibley and a voice of McDonald Observatory.**

Pride and McDonald Observatory

I remember going into the 82-inch telescope building, looking inside the dome, being absolutely overcome and wondering, "What in the world will take place here?" My mother, father and I had never seen an observatory. We thought it was the grandest thing in the world and so special for West Texas. These were still the depression years and to think that somebody would even look at the stars was so grand, when everybody else was just trying to pay the grocery bill. It was a rather fantastic idea, but now we know what a benefit it has been to science.

I feel the same pride today when I have an early morning cup of coffee at our Glass Mountain Ranch, let my eyes move along the horizon to the right, and then suddenly the two domes flash in the sunlight. The night is over and McDonald Observatory is there—fifty miles away, just as magnificent as ever.

Preston Edward Lindsey, Jr.

My name is Preston Edward Lindsey, Jr. and that being such a mouthful, I am generally known as Ed Lindsey, and I am a voice of McDonald Observatory. My life's work has involved being a musician, a photographer, and currently, a banker. Growing up in rural East Texas—Jasper, Texas, kindled a general interest in the outdoors. I was given a small reflecting telescope as a child and developed an interest in the night sky and photography.

A long-time supporter and Board member named Josiah Wheat from Woodville, Texas, initially invited me to a BoV meeting. He failed to mention he had nominated me for membership on the board at the time, but I'm glad he did. I was immediately impressed with the research being conducted and helping support their efforts is definitely worthwhile.

Learning about our place in creation
The foundations of our knowledge of astronomy had their beginnings many years before the establishment of McDonald Observatory, and one visit to the top of Mt. Locke at night to view the expansive West Texas sky should be enough to convince anyone of how little we really know and how much there is to still be learned about our place in creation. I would advise anyone with an interest in the answers to the many questions we all have about our origins and our future, to take the time to visit McDonald Observatory to get a sense of the effort involved and the importance of the research this facility provides to increase our knowledge of our small part of the universe.

I hope that the importance of the work and the instruments this facility affords is realized and properly funded so that knowledge of our world, and other worlds, will continue for the benefit of us all. I also hope that continuing to expose new generations to the Observatory will keep the science of astronomy supplied with fresh approaches and bright young minds.

Jake Pickle
The next voice comes to you from the office of a Congressman. He is not a member of the Board of Visitors, but he shares their mission. When you come in here, it is impossible to keep your eyes off the walls. They are ALL here; everyone's photograph is on the walls of this Congressman's office. It is obvious the Congressman is important to the University of Texas; an aerial shot of Memorial Stadium shows The Longhorn Band is in formation and they have spelled out, "Thanks Jake." You can hear the "Eyes of Texas," and eighty thousand voices.

I have been here so long that I knew IH-35 when it was called East Avenue. It was a pretty little drive and there was a knoll right around where Brackenridge Hospital is now. You could go on top of that knoll and see the city of Austin. The world has changed. **I am Jake Pickle and I am a voice of McDonald Observatory.**

Helping my University of Texas and McDonald Observatory

When I was elected to the Congress, I obtained membership on the Interstate and Foreign Commerce Committee, a very key committee in Congress and one of the most powerful. It was not an exclusive committee, which means I could serve on other committees. There occurred a vacancy on the Science and Technology Committee and I decided I would like to be a member of that committee. I only had five or six years in Congress at that time, but I made application and I obtained it. Some people said to me, "Why do you want to be on that committee?" Well, I am not educated about technology or scientific findings of the universe, but I knew the Science and Technology Committee was involved in all kinds of science research and I wanted on it because it was valuable to *my University of Texas.*

Another reason I wanted on that committee was McDonald Observatory. It was very much a part of the University and it was growing in its importance. I got on the committee and I enjoyed it very much and I found it *fascinating.* I became enamored with McDonald Observatory because I would go out there and visit and realize the importance of science and technology and what we were going to find there. It was an exciting thing to visit McDonald Observatory and look through the big lens and see what the world beyond looks like.

Serving on the Science and Technology Committee, I could help McDonald Observatory by helping direct or endorse grants and monies appropriated from Congress for their programs. Therefore, a little unknown assignment to a committee might be unimportant, but in particular, it could be very important to McDonald Observatory and *my* University of Texas.

A lot of people in those days and in now times, question the wisdom or the viability of astronomy. It is a slow and very expensive process and a lot of people ask, Why do we spend millions and millions of dollars trying to look at the universe? It *is* hard sometimes to realize how much good you are doing, but I have become convinced in my term, in my life, particularly in my relation to Congress, *mankind always is going to reach out.* Mankind is always going to look beyond where they are, and who they are, and where they came from, and what is the universe, and where is it. Mankind is going to continue to try to understand the universe, and we can learn about it best through the findings and interpretations of observatories. So each day and month we learn a little bit more. *I don't think we'll ever stop.*

Although I was not a scientist, I found that I could make a contribution by being on the Science and Technology Committee. I found myself as an advocate of the McDonald Observatory, not because I was an astronomer, but I recognized the importance to the University of Texas.

On the honor of public service

My greatest honor in life has just been the privilege of being a public servant; I've always considered public service an honorable profession and it has meant more in my life than any one thing I have done. Now some people like to poke fun at politicians and that will always be the case because it is easy to criticize your elected officials, whether it is your Governor or the President, it is your right to criticize your public officials—and make fun of us, terribly at times. At the same time, that elected official is ultimately in a position to be of service to you. I have always had a staff around me, young people who are dedicated and work long hours with very little pay to get things done. I think we have helped as much as any other member; at least we have tried.

I haven't been out to McDonald now in three or four years. I just can't get out there and it is just hard for me to get around. And I miss it because McDonald Observatory is recognized now as one of the prime observatories in the world. I trust my members of Congress on the Science and Technology Committee will help McDonald Observatory now—the same as I tried to help them in any way I could.

Lillian Murray

I am Lillian Murray, a member of the Board of Visitors and one of the many voices of McDonald Observatory. I was born under the Texas flag in Liberal, Kansas, in October of 1943. During World War II, my dad, the commanding officer of a U.S. Air Force Military Reservation in Kansas, was determined that his first-born was going to be a Texan from the first breath. Thus, immediately prior to my birth, he asked the crew of the plane that went to and from San Antonio to go to the Alamo and bring back a flag and a box of dirt. With the flag hanging over the delivery table and my footprints placed in the box of dirt, I was baptized a true-blue Texan.

My family lived in San Antonio until the late 1950s, at which time, we moved to Corpus Christi. My parents found South Texas to be the ideal environment in which to keep all five of their children busy – hunting, fishing, sailing, camping, and all kinds of outdoor sports. Having lived in Corpus Christi for most of the past thirty-three years, my roots are deep in the sands of the Gulf of Mexico and this will always be home.

I graduated from the University of Texas – Austin in 1965 with a degree in education and a teaching certificate, which, of course, is what young women were advised to do by their fathers in that day and time. My first teaching position, however, was something I was totally unprepared for. Having done most of my work with gifted students in the Austin School District, my first teaching job was in Philadelphia as a special education teacher in the ghetto. It was quite a shock to my system, but I grew to love Special Education and when my husband and I returned to Texas two years later, I became certified in Special Ed and taught for another eight years.

After my two children were born, I became a community volunteer and since then have worked in both the profit and the non-profit world. My free time has been spent traveling around the world to satisfy my love of adventure, nature and the out-of-doors. As I still love to camp, hike, fish and kayak, I find many opportunities to be in the wilderness at night. I'm sharing this as a preface to why I became an enthusiastic supporter of McDonald Observatory and its educational programs. I am not a scientist or astronomer, nor do I aspire to be. I can't sit on a mountaintop at night and point out all the constellations, planets, galaxies, connecting the dots between them. Instead, I am constantly in awe of those who can, but in truth my passion is for the beauty of it all and what it means to those of us who enjoy life on this beautiful planet.

The family I married into bought a ranch in the 1970s in Marathon, Texas, less than a hundred miles from the Observatory. We spent many months every year in West Texas and I grew to dearly love the Big Bend area. When we sold the ranch in the mid 1980s, I experienced a great sense of loss, as if a significant part of my life had been stolen away. I always yearned to go back but never felt I had a real reason to return, nor did I have access to the land the way I had in the past. And then a dear and trusted friend stepped back into my life, becoming a mentor to my two teenagers and me. He was, and still is, deeply involved with the McDonald Observatory – his name is Harry Bovay.

Harry had been a friend of my husband's and mine for many years and had visited us often during the West Texas hunting season. And because he understood how much I loved the land, Harry gave me a special gift. He simply called one day and said, "Lillian, I really want to do something for you, to put you back in touch with something that is very important to you." He invited me to be his guest at the summer meeting of the Board of Visitors at McDonald Observatory. It was the perfect gift, given by a generous and most gracious gentleman; in truth, a magnificent gesture and one I will never, ever forget.

The best part was the people I met and with whom I've been blessed to serve with on the BoV—people who love the land and sky as much as

I do and who appreciate the need to protect the beauty of the region. As a group, we eagerly look forward to those clear dark nights when we sit together on the side of a mountain and simply enjoy the night sky. Some bring telescopes and sky maps and some don't. All know a lot more about astronomy than I do, but we all share the same sincere appreciation for the mission of the Observatory and the research of the astronomers. We continue to share the excitement and exhilaration of discovery the astronomers offer us and do appreciate being a part of the process. That's my story – how I became involved with the stars and the people who call them by name.

Seeing the big picture, special friends, and community
One of my most memorable trips to the Observatory included an evening of stargazing when we were a small enough group to still be able to use the telescopes along the ring road for night viewing. I had some friends from Corpus Christi with me that included the president of a bank as well as the CEO of Central Power and Light Company. After taking several turns looking through the telescope, my banking friend sauntered off into the night and disappeared. After a while I started looking for him and finally found him lying on his back in the middle of the ring road. I asked if he was OK and what had happened. His reply said it all: "You see so much more from this perspective than you do looking through the little eyepiece. I'd rather see the big picture!" So I joined him on the road and in a very short time we had two dozen people lying in the road at midnight, talking amongst ourselves, not really sure what we were looking at but loving every minute of it. Eventually some of the University graduate students joined us and continued with our astronomy lesson. That is a night I'll always carry in my heart; a beautiful evening shared with special friends.

Visitors to the Observatory always comment on the friendly welcome extended by the people that live on the mountain. Our staff lets it be known that you don't have to be a scientist, an astronomer, a Ph.D., or a college graduate to enjoy what McDonald Observatory has to offer. At any time of the year, you will find the inquiring minds of an elder hostel group, a Boy Scout troop, gray-haired ladies (and men) in tennis shoes, as well as families and students of all ages. Often you'll also find a frustrated mom and dad with a car full of kids who simply want to take a break, spot the Observatory's road sign, and realize that there will be a bathroom available and enough open space for the kids to stretch their legs! They generally end up staying longer (much longer) than planned because they have never had the opportunity to look through a telescope, much less know or understand what they are seeing. All go home richer for the experience and that's what makes it worthwhile… and why I continue my membership on the board.

Harry Bovay

I was born in Big Rapids, Michigan, and raised in Stuttgart, Arkansas, and Memphis, Tennessee. I graduated from Cornell University with a degree as "Civil Engineer" and worked for the U. S. Corps of Engineers at the time of the 1937 Mississippi River flood. Afterwards I was with Humble Oil Company at Baytown for nearly ten years, including one year with Petroleum Administration for World War II. I founded and was chairman of Bovay Engineers, headquartered in Houston for forty years and then guided it through merger with Armco Steel. After retiring, I founded Mid-South Telecommunications and I am still reporting for work at eighty-eight years of age. **This is Harry Bovay and I am a voice of the McDonald Observatory.** During my life, I am pleased to have been honored by my profession and the Boy Scouts of America while enjoying engineering as my life's work.

Scientific advance through worldwide partnering

I became interested in astronomy at Cornell through courses I took, then by books I read after graduation, and then even more when I was asked to be on the Board of Visitors at the Department of Astronomy of the University of Texas. I was asked to join the Board of Visitors by the chairman at the time, Otto Wetzel, and was very happy at the opportunity. Harlan Smith was director at the time I joined the Board of Visitors, and he requested me to be chairman of the fund raising for a 300-inch telescope. This effort barely got started when the business world slowed in the middle 1980s. Through the initiative and creativeness of the Astronomy Department, this effort, originally $60 million in eight years, was changed to a new design of ninety-one, 1-meter diameter mirrors for $15 million—the Hobby-Eberly Telescope. It not only succeeded but also gained valuable partners in Stanford University, Pennsylvania State University, and two German universities—Ludwig Maximilians Universität and Georg August Universität. It also created great new opportunities for the University due to the creative initiative of Frank Bash and his staff. My current particular interest in astronomy is helping the science advance by the partnering of universities worldwide.

Being on the Board of Visitors has added to my knowledge and interest of astronomy as well as my friendships and feeling of contributing to a great university and my fellow man. I have been on the board for so many years they've gotten all my ideas. I think I do have an effect by helping with the fundraisers for the new telescope and probably an even stronger effect in talking Frank into partnering, which I think is one of the great steps that they've made. With the Hobby-Eberly Telescope partnership, they now have five scientific bodies looking at the same picture instead of one. I'm a great believer in things like that.

McDonald Observatory and the Davis Mountains—everybody loves that climate out there. I guess the whole world would live out there if it weren't so far away!

I would suggest to the visitor today, and years from now, that they look at the entire Observatory thoroughly, its organization, why and where it is located, its outstanding growth and success, including service to the University and our nation through NASA, as well as other national interests and its unique and successful leadership over the years which has led to its outstanding success.

On the subject of light pollution, they have done a great job out there getting the citizens, ranch owners, and State Representatives to protect it. Even the cities and small towns shield their lights now. Outside of these efforts, the only thing left to do is maybe...raise the mountain higher.

I hope the visitors, when they come, will be sure they see and learn all they can, enjoy the wonderful area and admire all the work that all the wonderful astronomers are doing and the devotion they give to it. Just soak it up!

Jim Kruger

Sanctuary

"Secure yourself to heaven"...that is where I do that, McDonald Observatory. **Dear Visitor, I am Jim Kruger and I am McDonald Observatory.** I am speaking to you from my office in Kruger Jewelers. We are hometown folks; we have been here a long time. My wife and I have a mission...it is sanctuary—a place where people can come and be peaceful, calm, and happy. Everyone that comes into the environment of my store, I want them to leave with something that either makes them happy or peaceful, or makes someone they love happy or peaceful. I try to go out to the Observatory once a year. It is the place where I plug myself back into the universe and get recharged so that I can do what I do every day.

I have been out to the Observatory many times, but never enough. My first trip out to the Observatory was in Al Barrier's airplane—Al is another BoV member. He drove, I navigated, and it beats that stretch of Interstate 10. Anyway, we were supposed to have some scope time on the 36-inch and just as we were getting set up, this cold front came through and we had rain for the next two days. But what we did do was sit up for almost two days and two nights *talking* about everything I had been teaching myself about astronomy. And I found out I had a good understanding of what I was reading. If there is such a thing as a religious experience, I had one that weekend because I knew my life was going to change in major ways, and it did.

On a personal level, my life changed a whole lot within the next ten years. It affected my faith in the fact that, I'm Jewish by religion, but I believe there is one Great Spirit guiding the universe. The universe is not one of the things we studied in statistics as a *random* event. Well, there is very, very *little* randomness in the way the universe operates. It's an incredibly ordered place.

I don't know what my favorite experience has been at the Observatory, but you know, every time I go out there I learn something and I experience something different. To me, that is the holiest place I have ever been, because it puts you in such immediate and wonderful touch with the universe. Even if you are just *standing* out there, it's holy.

The first time my wife Julia and I drove out there, we stopped on a stretch of highway where there were no lights. I said to Julia, "You need to see what a really dark sky looks like, because you've never seen this before." There were so *many* stars I *could not* find Orion for a minute. I couldn't find *any* constellations the sky was so filled with stars.

McDonald Observatory is an awe-full place, in the true sense of that word. I think I would say to you, Dear Visitor, when you go out to the Observatory, try to put out of your mind everything except the immediate moment. Try to experience everything you can out there, because going to the McDonald Observatory will change your life. Let the experience into you and go with an inquisitive and open mind. I wonder…will we ever be able to build anything to see to the edge of the universe? God, that would be really cool if we could!

The involuntary " Wow!"

I have to tell you my *wow* story. The last time I went out to the Observatory, they were having a star party at the Visitors Center. There were probably two or three hundred people and Mark Wetzel was going a little crazy because he had ten telescopes operating at once. I was standing by the 16-inch scope and I said, "Look, Mark, go ahead and take care of what you need to do and I'll run this scope for you." Then this little kid, about nine years old climbs up the ladder to the scope. He looks through the eyepiece and says, *"Wow!"* That *wow* is so important. When he got through looking, I tapped him on the shoulder and I said, "I have to tell you; every time I look through a telescope, I say exactly the same thing, *'Wow!'"* Exactly. Even to this day.

Winston Crowder

I am Winston Crowder and I am a voice of McDonald Observatory and a Board of Visitors member. I was born two blocks inside Texas on June 25, 1934 in Texarkana. I was raised there, went through the public schools in Texarkana, and then went to the Rice Institute in 1952. Thought I wanted to be a physicist—I was always interested in science. My first two roommates were a playboy and the campus bookie. This wasn't a good crowd for me and I asked the folks in registration if they could change me and they put me in with a fifth year physics major. He was graduating and looking for jobs and when he came back from all of his interviews, we would talk. After hearing the kind of job openings he was looking at, I decided physics wasn't what I wanted to do. I was in NROTC; the Korean War was cranking down but they were still drafting everybody. We didn't have counselors in those days so I talked to my mother. She graduated in 1928 at The University of Texas and knew the Dean of Men and the Dean of Students, and one of them was married to one of her sorority sisters. So we went down and I transferred to UT. I stayed with the NROTC, took two years in the business school, then to law school, then active duty and back to law school. I took the Bar in February of 1960 and graduated in May. My legal job was with the State Attorney General in 1961, where I took over the files of a lawyer who was just leaving. He was John Wildenthal, later one of the founding members of the McDonald Observatory Board of Visitors.

The king of science

I've always looked to the heavens. Love seeing the stars. And, of course, my parents talked to us children about the constellations and what's there and these sorts of things. My wife, Julia, was raised very much that same way. In about 1985 she and I took a course on building a telescope. We built it; and it is good for seeing the planets, the Moon, and things like that. Shortly after this I had dinner with John Wildenthal and it came up that we'd built a telescope. At that point he says, "Oh, would you be interested in going to McDonald?" I said, "Oh, golly, would I ever." The next year, 1987, I came out with John and Carolyn Wildenthal.

I won't forget that trip. We were looking in the 82-inch telescope and we got locked in. I don't know how we got locked in but we did. But it was fun. It was eleven o'clock before we got out. We used the telephone and got somebody with a key to come get us. He took us back down then in a bus. It was a real experience and cold. It was a cold day in July.

For the future of McDonald, I would like to see us expand and have a big telescope in some place like Chile at a much higher altitude than we have here at McDonald. I would like that, as long as it can stay with the University of Texas.

I would like to say two things to the visitor. First, in my opinion, astronomy is the king of science, because it includes everything else. It includes physics, mathematics, chemistry, and biology. Astronomy is the one science that puts it all together and to me, astronomy is the one that ought to be taught first. Then, the kids can pick the part that they like.

Second, look at the ladybugs. Sometimes they are all over the domes.

Ki Allen
My name is Ki Allen and I am one of the many voices of McDonald Observatory. The nights of central Texas are filled with city lights, including baseball, soccer and football fields and you really can't see the dark skies. On my first trip to McDonald Observatory and the Davis Mountains, I was with my mother, Raye Virginia Allen, and I was just enamored with the clarity and number of stars I could see. That trip, I remember, was one of the years it had rained a lot. I looked down from the mountaintop and it looked like Christmas. There was the contrast between the red stone of the mountain and the very green, freshly watered vegetation.

Exploring creation and Harlan's legacy

There are so many discoveries going on right now, anywhere from the tiny atom to the stars that are billions of light years away. None of the discoveries has disturbed my faith in Christ; Christ is still my fulfillment. Science is the exploration of what and how God has put it all together. This is not true just for me, but for my entire family as our guiding light. God created heaven and Earth, and He created mankind. They can and do coexist together.

I always tell people, "You need to go out to McDonald Observatory. Your kids need to see this. You need to be out there with them, not only from the astronomy standpoint but also from the overall introduction into science."

I have very fond memories of Harlan Smith and his wisdom and encouragement to build the Board of Visitors, to help people learn about the Observatory and to be a resource to draw on if need be. I also have great respect for Frank Bash for taking on this legacy and moving it to the next level. We are very fortunate to have these men, their colleagues and visions at McDonald Observatory. I can sum it up by saying, whenever those astronomers speak, I can guarantee you "it's going to be out of this world."

Joan Baskin

I have been a housewife, mother of four children, and professional volunteer for these many fifty years. I became interested in astronomy because I grew up in Galveston, Texas, where I could sit on a pier, look up at the sky, and get things in perspective. By doing that I realized by the age of nine, by golly I am pretty small, things are pretty big, and I need to develop some understanding of all sorts of things. **I am Joan Baskin and I am a voice of McDonald Observatory.**

An interesting person who can make things happen

Much later, Harlan Smith asked me to come on the Board of Visitors. I said, "Harlan, I don't have any scientific knowledge, I don't have any money, and I don't know very many people who have money." Harlan said to me, "Oh, but Joan, come on and serve; these people need someone interesting to talk to." Well, anybody that good at being a snow artist, I want to be around. So we came up here between Christmas and New Year's, when that wonderful last bit of highway up to the dome was frozen solid. We made our way up and stayed at the director's residence with Harlan and Joan Smith. Harlan took all sorts of scientific ideas and made them accessible to our children and me. We all thought we were very smart because he was so wonderful at making it understandable.

Harry Bovay wants to give me credit for the first big donation to the HET from Abell-Hangar Foundation in Midland, Texas. It was really not my doing at all; I just helped get them back with the Abell-Hanger Foundation who made the lead donation for the telescope Harlan Smith started planning in the late seventies. When everything went south financially for Texas in the mid seventies, the plans for Harlan's telescope were revised to the innovative idea of the HET—to build a big telescope without the big price tag. We went back to Abell-Hanger Foundation and said, "Every cent you gave us for the planning of the first telescope fits the planning for this one. This was a wonderful investment you made, but now we need more." And they came back with a huge gift that helped start everything. The visitors' viewing room in the HET now carries the name of George T. Abell and that's what is fun about this; it has his name on it. In the past, their donations were always made anonymously.

The HET rising above the George T. Abell visitors gallery.

Photo by David Reaves.

To the visitors of McDonald Observatory, I always like to point out the scientific breakthrough of the Hobby-Eberly Telescope, how it is such a risk-taking, exciting idea and help them appreciate the difference, not only in the breakthrough science, but also in its low cost. I also like to explain that while most observatories tend to think of visitors as ants that have invaded the picnic, McDonald Observatory is the one major Observatory that lets people come in and look through their big telescopes from time to time. My hope for McDonald Observatory is that we can bring in more students and train the teachers through the new Visitors Center so that we can interest more people in science and math. We must be ready, as Texans, to have the kind of people who can enjoy good jobs and progress for themselves in this State.

John Cotton
I'm John Cotton, member of the Board of Visitors since the mid-1980s, a supporter of McDonald Observatory since the 1950s, and a voice of McDonald Observatory. I am presently teaching astronomy at SMU and I am on the staff at the planetarium at The Science Place in Fairpark, Dallas, Texas.

A lifelong love of astronomy and McDonald Observatory

My connection to McDonald Observatory goes back a long time—1956 to be exact. At that time, I was a member of the Junior Texas Astronomical Society of Dallas—a bunch of kids who were interested in astronomy—and there was a load of us. In the summer of 1956 we decided to make the pilgrimage to McDonald Observatory—take the trip down and see the place. At that time, of course, the only domes on the mountain were the 82- and the 36-inch. We got all our kids together in a couple of cars and two of the parents drove us down. We stayed at the Indian Lodge and had a wonderful time climbing the rocks.

At that time, the practice was to go up on the mountain in the afternoon, one or two o'clock, and get a tour of the dome in daylight when you could see the telescope and talk to the people there at the time. Then you would come back at night after dinner and look at something with the telescope. That is exactly what we did. We went up in the daytime, this bunch of bushy-tailed kids from Dallas, asking all kinds of questions, and just poking around everything trying to learn all we could. We went back that night for the nighttime viewing session, and Dr. Gerard Kuiper was using the telescope. It was 1956, the summer of an extremely favorable opposition of Mars, and Dr. Kuiper was going to be visually studying Mars with the 82-inch telescope. But it was too early for Mars, so all the public went in, us included, and looked through the telescope. You have to remember that in 1956, all the control room structure and enclosures now in the 82-inch dome, didn't exist—it was open to the walls. We looked at something with the 82-inch, Saturn most likely. (Reasonable—Saturn was in opposition in 1956)

We were having a great time, but there were a number of other people there, too, so we could not monopolize it. But I will never forget what happened as we were going down the stairs and out the door. Marlyn Krebs, the superintendent, said, "Hey, you guys, don't leave!" Now that was an invitation we could not turn down so we sort of hung around outside, waiting to see what was going to happen. After a while, Krebs came out the door and waved us back in. You don't think we were going to turn that down?! So back up the stairs we went, up to the observing floor, and found that Dr. Kuiper had turned the 82-inch around and aimed it at Mars, which had risen over in the east. There were some thunderstorms in the east and the turbulence was pretty bad, so he couldn't work. He invited this bunch of Junior astronomers from Dallas to come back up in the dome, and we spent the best part of an hour looking at Mars with the 82-inch telescope and talking to Dr. Gerard Kuiper. Absolutely fabulous experience. Kuiper didn't have to do that; he just saw this bunch of kids and did it.

156

That experience illustrates just how important something like that can be, because I know I never forgot it and I bet all the other Junior astronomers with me never forgot it. Dr. Kuiper just took a little time to spend with kids and it made a lasting impression. I mean *really* lasting. It is something I guess we could all learn from. We went back to McDonald the next summer in 1957, but it just wasn't quite the same—nothing ever beat that visit with Kuiper. That was my first really great experience with McDonald Observatory.

Intriguingly, just to add on to that, in 1986 we were back on the mountain for a Board of Visitors summer meeting. We were up in the 82-inch dome late at night with Karl Henize and, I think, Art Whipple, peering at Mars. I never thought in 1956 that I'd be back over thirty years later looking at Mars with the very same telescope.

In the following years, my connection with McDonald was through seeing Harlan Smith, partly as a result of my getting involved in planetariums in 1964, as well as staying active with the Astronomical Society here in Dallas. Harlan came to speak at some meetings up here, both the club and the planetarium society. He was sort of a pioneer in my book in outreach by observatories. He was out on the front lines talking to groups and, as you might say, doing the politicking long before it seemed to be fashionable in the field.

One story about Harlan relates to the dedication of the Austin Astronomical Society's telescope; Harlan made the dedication speech. The one thing I remember about the speech was when he coined a term. He said, "Really the basic difference between professional astronomers and amateur astronomers is that professional astronomers get paid for it." Then he coined the term, "Philastrophers," which means people who love the stars. That seemed to apply to everybody and it was particularly memorable.

Another memorable weekend up at the Observatory was back in 1986 when Halley's comet came around. For the BoV, Harlan organized a Halley's comet party up on the mountain. We planned to stay on the mountain both nights (any excuse to spend some time up on the mountain), and the first night was cloudy; we didn't see a thing. Harlan had planned to give little certificates that said, "John Cotton came to McDonald Observatory and saw Halley's Comet on this night." He did the best he could and made up certificates that said; "John Cotton did *not* see Halley's Comet from McDonald Observatory on this night."

The next night we tried again and it was clear. The only problem was the winds were peaking at about seventy miles an hour coming up over the hill and Ed Barker couldn't open the 107-inch. I had brought my 10-inch reflector and planned to set that up on the ring road by the 36-inch, but we couldn't do that because it would have been blown over.

All we could do was set up my big binoculars on a tripod in that little niche between the 36-inch's control room and the rocks where you could get a little shielding from the wind, because the wind would almost blow you off the mountain. We actually got a very good view of Halley with those binoculars; Harlan said so.

I have another fond memory of Harlan. I had taken my 10-inch telescope to a summer BoV meeting, and one night had it set up on the ring road in the usual spot near the 36-inch dome. Harlan and I were looking at M51 with the 10-inch. I remember our discussion about whether or not we could see the spiral structure of M51 with the 10-inch. I thought we couldn't and he thought we could. I know he had eagle eyes but thought that if we did "see" the structure, it was because we already knew it was there. He was truly a great astronomer who enjoyed such things.

Back about 1989, I spent several days out at the McDonald Observatory with Bob Shepler, pitching-in with the Visitors Center crew doing programs and tours, a practice I have continued off and on whenever my schedule allows. The tours with the crew have been very helpful to me personally and it is hard work. You can't really appreciate what kind of a job the Visitors Center crew does until you put on their shoes and staff shirt, go out, and do what they *do*. Then you *see* what kind of energy and dedication it takes to do the job. That has been an education for me and it has helped me support the Visitors Center.

I remember going up on the mountain one night with Bob; actually we had some visitors with us because it was a public viewing night. The weather was awful—cloudy, foggy, really miserable. Nobody was going to see anything but a few people showed up, so we said, "Well, we might as well take them up and see the 107-inch telescope; there is nobody going to be working tonight." So we all piled in the station wagon and went up the mountain. We parked, got out of the car, and decided to give the visitors a little demonstration. We turned off all the lights. If you haven't been up on the mountain on a cloudy night with no lights, you don't know what dark is.

Another feature of the summer BoV meetings I remember very fondly was Harlan being the first one to use the Laser Ranging Telescope as a sky pointer. He pointed the green beam of the laser at the stars, and since it converged with the sky, you could see what Harlan was pointing out. You could enjoy Harlan's star show from anywhere on the mountain!

I could go on and on. Sitting in the TQ lounge watching lighting fireworks out the window. Playing pool in that same lounge. Hiking down the hill to the firehouse with Bob Tull. Swapping teaching stories with everyone. Helping out at the 50th Anniversary party, when the tent contractor fouled up the reservation for the dinner tent (first time I ever saw Harlan give up on something). Looking at the Messier Objects with the 30-inch. Attending the Lunar Laser Ranging Symposium and watching Wendy Williams fire the laser at the Moon for the last time. Barbecues in the grove over at the Prudes'. Standing out on the catwalk looking at the sky. Frank Bash giving a talk to the Texas Astronomical Society and getting a standing ovation (likely the first for the TAS).

I guess you can get the idea that McDonald Observatory has been a pretty important factor of my life, and that certainly is true. The Observatory has had a major influence on me so I have always tried to contribute what I can. Not being one of the wealthiest members of the board, I have contributed time and some sweat equity by working with the Visitors Center crew. I also wrote a couple of versions of "One Night on the Mountain," a planetarium show about McDonald, which we ran at the Planetarium here in Dallas. I wouldn't trade anything for all the experiences I have had with and around McDonald Observatory.

Dick Evans

My name is Dick Evans, Richard C., if you wish, and I am a voice of McDonald Observatory. I was born in Chicago on January 17, 1929. I am thirty-four years and a few days old, of course, it is something over thirteen thousand days now.

My early astronomy story goes back to the first Tuesday of November 1936. I was seven years old and my parents were having an elections return party at our house in Tinsdale, Illinois. This was the first "adult party" I was allowed to stay up and attend. The guests were cigar and pipe smoking Republicans and they were all gathered around our little dome-top radio, listening to the returns come in. The later the evening got, the bluer the air got, and the longer their faces got because Mr. Roosevelt was winning by a landslide. This was in the middle of the Depression, and of course, I didn't know anything about the Depression. I listened to their discussions of how terrible the economic circumstances in the country were and how much worse they were going to be under Mr. Roosevelt's second term. I had just learned that stars wcre suns. I got to thinking, if stars are suns, maybe they have planets. If they have planets, maybe they have people. Let's go up and see if they have solved some of the problems we are having so much troublc with.

The darkest skies

The dark skies at McDonald Observatory are all important. I remember on one trip thinking, if I had a newspaper I could read it using only the light from the Milky Way. When you look up at the night sky in the cities, there is enough sky glow that you wonder who's got the lights turned on. You don't see that at McDonald and Ft. Davis, not ever. The dark skies are just fabulous.

Because I am a Board of Visitors member, I get to spend more time in Texas and I like that. One of the ways I help the Observatory as a board member is I contributed to the DIMM, the Differential Image Motion Monitor, which helps determine whether the turbulence is in the atmosphere or in the dome. As long as I am able, I plan to help support the Observatory. I don't think we will ever see a time when surface astronomy isn't important and since McDonald Observatory has the best skies on the continent, they are going to have to stay in the center of things for a very long time to come.

Saralee Tiede

I am Saralee Tiede, Board of Visitors member and Greater Austin Chamber of Austin Vice President for Communications, and I am a voice of McDonald Observatory. The first time I went out to McDonald Observatory was when I was working with Lieutenant Governor Bill Hobby in the 1980s. Harlan Smith wanted to build a new telescope and we went out for some preliminary fundraising meetings. This telescope, as you know, was revised and is now the Hobby-Eberly Telescope. We were guests of Harlan Smith and stayed in the director's house on the mountaintop. I can remember Harlan using the Lunar Laser to point out the stars, which was just wonderful and a terrific lesson. Harlan was so gifted at making people excited about his dreams. His enthusiasm, and just being out there in the cold clear wintertime, made Bill Hobby and Diana very excited about the project. I think this helped put the fundraising together because at that point, the University had not considered it on their priority list.

Look, listen, and learn at McDonald Observatory

The best part of being a Board of Visitors member is knowing that the Observatory makes it possible for many people to learn about the stars and the solar system. I hope we never get to the point that we think we don't need to learn any more. We need to keep looking up. McDonald Observatory is a great opportunity and a totally unique place. While you are here, you should look around and enjoy this beautiful part of Texas in the Davis Mountains. You should definitely, even if you are not there for a star party, just get out at night and look at the stars. Listen to StarDate to know what to look for. Maybe get a star chart, get some books and get interested. It's a lifetime pleasure and it's a lifetime learning experience.

Bill Guest
I am Bill Guest and I am a voice of McDonald Observatory. I practiced law in Houston for about twenty-five years after Yale and Harvard Law School. About twenty years ago, I crossed the line—that is a phrase I have used to say I left law practice and now head a life insurance company involved in acquisitions. I have done a number of things in my life in the way of athletics, but horses have been my main interest. I am interested in philosophical matters and science in particular. I have read a lot in science—astronomy, physics, and particle physics, as a layperson, and generally on the topic of where did it all come from, how is it made, and what is it?

Lt. Governor Bill Hobby

I became a Board of Visitors member through Bill Hobby. I would not like to compare Bill to an "iceberg," because he is a very warm, friendly, and giving person, but I think to evaluate what Bill has done for McDonald Observatory, it's like seeing only the tip of an iceberg. He is very interested in the Observatory and has done so much behind the scene that it is not apparent what he is doing or what he has done. With the HET it is somewhat obvious but the *amount* of effort he put in is not obvious.

Harlan Smith

One weekend—I guess it was about twenty years ago—Bill took several of us down to McDonald Observatory. He often takes people to the Observatory, not just for Board of Visitors meetings, but just for the weekend, on his own cuff, and his own initiative to introduce them to the Observatory and promote it. On that particular weekend, Harlan Smith was there, and one of the things we did was go up to Mt. Livermore. There were eight of us and everyone had started the descent except Harlan and me. Harlan stopped me and pointed in the direction of Mt. Locke. Way over in the distance we could clearly see the two observatories on the mountaintop. Harlan said, "You know, the Mexicans call that 'Dos Huevos.'" And it was very clear why they did because it looked like two eggs sitting on the distant horizon. It was at that time, standing there with Harlan on top of Mt. Livermore and looking at McDonald Observatory, Dos Huevos, that Harlan invited me to join the McDonald Observatory Board of Visitors. That was quite a nice thing, and a very special moment with Harlan.

Frank Bash

Like with Harlan, I have had a number of good conversations with Frank Bash. He is a wonderful person whose ability to communicate is absolutely extraordinary. He can address a lay audience and make things clear. You can easily follow him he is so good at it. I have had many good experiences with Frank. I admire him and what he has done at McDonald, and I have enjoyed very much my relationship with him.

McDonald Observatory is one of the few places on the face of the Earth where visitors can have access to technology, astronomical facilities, and information regarding the cosmos and the work that goes on at McDonald Observatory. I think that it is one of the most important things McDonald Observatory does. So visitor, my message is, "Go and enjoy!"

Allen C. King

I am Allen Carlisle King, Life Board of Visitors member, and a voice of McDonald Observatory. My son, David, and I have been coming to the McDonald Observatory since he was sixteen years old. He is thirty-six now and we have been out every year together for the Board of Visitors meetings. I joined the board not knowing much about astronomy but just having an interest in it, as I think most human beings do. David has developed a great interest in astronomy and he is a Board member now as well. You will hear from him next.

The quick mind of Harlan Smith

I have several Harlan Smith stories but one I would like to tell you demonstrates just a little bit of how he thinks. Once at a Board of Visitors meeting at Indian Lodge, Harlan gave a lecture on his trip to South America to find a site for the twin to the HET. Harlan was going through his slide show about his climb up a huge mountain when his picture of an alpaca came up and it was upside down in the projector. Just as quick as lightning Harlan said, "That's really how it looks in South America." He was a wonderful man and a genius with people.

David King

I am David King and I am a voice of McDonald Observatory. My father first brought me to the Observatory one summer almost thirty years ago—I was about ten years old. Much later, Chris Sneden, a professor at the University of Texas in the Astronomy Department, invited me out on an astronomy run. It was definitely not like going to a party; it was not high-level excitement, but I *really* enjoyed it. On the surface, all we did was gather data—little strips of spectra on the computer screen. But, being out here in the stillness of the night, all night with the 107-inch telescope, I could hear a little wind swirling around in the dome and in the observing area I could hear the cooling fans. It was not all glamour, but it was just one of the most peaceful experiences I have ever had.

Get away from it all and explore your childhood curiosity

I would like to say to the contemporary visitor to take advantage of being away from your everyday life in the darkest sky in the continental United States. Stop, listen, look, and reflect on things that your childhood curiosity just gets too busy to enjoy because there is no other place like McDonald Observatory.

To the visitor a hundred years from now—I hope you can still look up and see the Milky Way. I hope with our ongoing efforts, the skies will still be dark and we will still have a vibrant community.

Donna C. Pierce

I am Donna C. Pierce, a Board of Visitors member, and a voice of McDonald Observatory. I'm interested in the younger generation learning to "look up" and be aware of the astronomy in their past, present, and future. I teach Kindergarten to 12th graders and adult community courses and have been a planetarium director/astronomy teacher for thirty-six years. I became involved in astronomy as a docent for The Junior League of Dallas' docent museum program at the Dallas Health and Science Museum's Planetarium—The Science Place today— in the 1960s. I am also the American Field Service Student Exchange school sponsor and coach for the Highland Park High School Girls Golf Teams.

Harlan Smith, as my mentor, must have placed my name in nomination for a BoV member. I have felt privileged being on the cutting edge of astronomy, not only for my own knowledge but also in teaching to a wide spectrum of ages. Being a member of the Board of Visitors has given me the foundation for learning with the best of the best...the research astronomers at The University of Texas Astronomy Department have literally been my teachers and friends. Harlan was always on call and Craig Wheeler tutored me on SN87A before my talk at the International Planetarium Society's conference in Atlanta. What special information, not only for me but also for the community in which I teach!

Get up, look up, and stay in the dark

I would urge every person to *be an active member of your world*! Participate in the activities of astronomy, from viewing on a clear night, visiting museums such as McDonald Observatory, visiting local planetariums, and of course, taking classes in astronomy.

My biggest concern is light pollution. McDonald Observatory has done an excellent job in keeping "dark nights" but they must keep the fight each and every second. We must never, ever lose the advantage we have "Deep in the Heart of Texas."

John Poindexter

I am John Poindexter, a member of the Board of Visitors, and I am a voice of the McDonald Observatory. I am chairman, executive officer and owner of J. B. Poindexter & Co. Earlier in my career, I was a partner at various investment firms associated with the acquisition of industrial companies. Before that, I was a military officer and served in Europe, the United States, and Vietnam.

McDonald Observatory in the Big Bend community

My interest in astronomy, while strong, is probably not so keen as that of some of the other members of the Board of Visitors. I became interested in McDonald Observatory as a result of my ownership of the Cibolo Creek Ranch in Presidio County, located about fifty-five miles south of the astronomy site. As a strong supporter of the community in the Big Bend and its economic prospects, I, of course, became interested in the McDonald Observatory inasmuch as it is an important part of our life in the Big Bend.

Today, we house guests who visit the McDonald Observatory and have established a relationship with the administration, which I believe to be mutually beneficial. From time to time, we invite and compensate members of the staff to come to the Cibolo Creek Ranch and hold miniature star parties for our guests. McDonald Observatory has had a fairly large effect on our activities at the Cibolo Creek Ranch and I enjoy greatly my interactions with the administration and with my fellow Board of Visitors members.

I hope that in the future, the McDonald Observatory continues to grow in international stature and make significant scientific contributions that are worthy of the State of Texas, our region, and the institution.

As I accumulate more experience on the Board of Visitors, I hope to be able to revisit this project in order to share more of my thoughts.

Lloyd Bentsen, III

I was born in South Texas, McAllen, a couple of miles away from where my father was born in Mission. My great grandparents, who were Danish immigrants, settled in the 1880s and 1890s in the Dakotas. My great grandfather was a stowaway on a steamer that came to New York and went to the Dakotas because that is where the free land was. In

1920, he sent a couple of his sons, one was my namesake, to the Texas valley to check on an investment he had made in a citrus grove. My grandfather and his brother, Elmer, decided it was the land of milk and honey and they stayed there. In the thirties, they moved most of the Bentsen clan to South Texas. They prospered in real estate, banking, and insurance. My father, also my namesake, had the good fortune of being able to serve his country both in the service and politically, first in the Congress and then later in the U. S. Senate and then as Secretary/Treasurer. We moved to Houston in the 1950s where my father established an insurance company. Then, he moved on to Washington in 1970, which turned out to be a very wonderful thing for my own maturing because in 1970, at the age of twenty-six, I was on my own in Texas. **Today is March 16, 2001, my name is Lloyd Bentsen, and I am a voice of McDonald Observatory**.

With family backing, I started an investment banking firm and in the 1980s I moved our business into venture capital. Over the last fifteen years, I have managed or co-managed the founding of three venture funds; the most recent is a fifty-fifty partnership with the Texas A & M University System. I think it's the first partnership between a university, a public institution, and a private entity—our venture capital partnership. It has been very, very successful and our focus has been on technology. It's been a great twenty-two years. Most recently something has become a passion for me.

It goes back to one night about three years ago. We were guests at Board of Visitors member John Poindexter's ranch, Cibolo Creek, there in West Texas. We were spending the weekend with John and he asked one of the astronomers to come down from McDonald Observatory. Years ago, I had gone to McDonald Observatory during the day but I picked a particularly bad day to go because the public part of the Observatory was closed. It might have been a holiday and should have been closed. Anyway, John said, "We're going to have a star party and an astronomer is going to come here from McDonald Observatory." It was very cold but we agreed to go.

It was cold and dark, a perfect night—although I didn't know it at the time, and I complained bitterly that I couldn't see my hand in front of my face, I couldn't see my wife, I couldn't see the astronomer, I couldn't see anybody. In a human chain, one person holding onto the next person, we followed the astronomer up to the top of the hill where he had a telescope. I'll never ever forget that night. The temperature was in the 30s and we were freezing. We were typical people from Houston, out in West Texas, and hadn't brought enough warm clothing and we were just bitterly cold.

I was out there strictly to be a good guest. I had already checked with my wife, and I knew in the dark we could just sneak off and no one could see us as long as we didn't fall over anything. We could gracefully exit and no one would know. So we were all ready to go and Mark, the astronomer, said, "Would anyone like to take a look in the telescope?" Still the good guest, I said sure. I looked in the eyepiece, there were two galaxies right next to each other, and you could see them both in one eyepiece! I think it was M81 and M82. I was just floored. I mean I just could not believe it. I said, "Mark, I really appreciate this, but it's cold, and if you'll excuse me, we're going to sneak away." And he said, "Before you see a globular star cluster?" I said, "Well, whatever that is, Ok." So a few minutes went by and he moved the telescope around. I looked in it—I mean you could have... I just... my jaw dropped. I just could not believe what I was seeing. I had never even seen a *picture* of a globular star cluster and here was this huge snowball filled with stars. It was beyond anything I could comprehend, much less see. So I said, "That's really incredible and I really appreciate it Mark, but it's freezing and we're gonna sneak off." He said, "Before you see the great nebula of Orion?" And I said, "Nebula?" And he swung that thing around and, holy Toledo! there it was. But we were still cold and I said, "Mark, I'm really going to go." And he said, "Before you see the remnants of a supernova?" So then we saw the Crab Nebula. Anyway, the long, short of it, I was out there for about forty minutes. I leaned over to him and I said, "Tell me what this telescope is." And he said, it is a such and such, 12 and a half-inch.

I went home and after that weekend I said to my wife, "I want to buy one of those telescopes." She said, "Well now, Lloyd aren't you a little impulsive?" I said. "I am really sincere about this. I'm going to prove to you I'm sincere. I'm going to buy a pair of binoculars and I'm going to spend one year, going out every month, using those binoculars to learn the constellations. If at the end of that year I've stuck to that commitment to you, can I buy a telescope?" And I really was speaking more to myself than to her; we really don't negotiate like that.

At the end of that year I bought a telescope. It was an 8-inch telescope. I told her after a couple of days, "This is incredible. We're seeing things the likes of which you've never seen." I said to her, "I'll tell you what, if I stick with this for one year, if I go out every month and set this 8-inch telescope up and show you how I am really genuinely interested in this, can I buy a bigger one?" At the end of one year, she said, "You really are interested in this; you can buy a bigger telescope." I bought a 12-inch telescope.

After that, and this coincided with our 25th anniversary, she said, "Tell you what, why don't we exchange gifts for our 25th wedding anniversary." So I bought her some stars that she could wear on her fingers and ears and she gave me an observatory. We built the observatory and I moved the 12-inch telescope in to it.

So that guy Mark, he really set the hook in me. All of a sudden I realized there is this immense body of not only knowledge and information, but there's this immense body of potential discovery directly overhead *every night.* It's phenomenal how it just pulled me in to it. That's how I got hooked on astronomy.

On my second visit to McDonald Observatory, it was open. It was for an orientation for the new Board of Visitors members. When John Poindexter saw how enthusiastic I was, he put me up for the board and when that orientation finished, I was really on board. Not only was I hooked by looking through the eyepiece, I was interested in everyone who gets into the sport and really appreciates instrumentation and how much technology is increasing the capacity in astronomy and for astronomers to see and understand.

Basic research and the health of our nation

One time, I was on a plane coming from South Texas with a very well known individual. I will not identify him, but a person of great integrity, a delightful person to be with and talk to, and we happened to sit next to each other. It was a chance meeting; I didn't know who he was and he didn't know who I was, but we learned that both of our families had known each other for generations. This gentleman pulls out and reads the New York Times. He is looking at a picture of the Hubble Space Telescope and he says to me, "Isn't this a waste of money?" Well, he certainly asked the right person. I said, "It depends on your perspective." He said, "It's not serving any useful purpose is it?" And I said, "It depends on your timeframe." And he said, "But, yours and my life today aren't better for the billions of dollars they are spending on this telescope—now be honest!" We still had not introduced ourselves but I went into this little discussion with him about research and development and how important it was, but how slow it sometimes seems, and how one discovery becomes a tool to unveil another discovery. He kind of looked at me, and at the end of this fairly long discussion he said, "Well, I guess I'll share that with my wife, because she's on the Board of Regents of such and such University. They are confronted every day with how much they are going to spend on research and development." And I said, "When you share this with her, I hope you will encourage her to be a little more favorably disposed the next time someone comes up and asks for a research grant, because it is all so critical to the long-term well-being and strength of this country of ours." He smiled. Then we changed the conversation and moved on to talk about cattle.

Anyway, it's important to do a better job of explaining why we need, not only pure research and development dollars, but why we need to invest in the people who can use those dollars to create the discoveries and science upon which the ultimate well-being of our economy, our competitive edge, and the uniqueness of our country and the contributions it makes to the well-being of the rest of the world. We need to make a bigger point of that, not just lip service, I think that's short-sightedness.

With respect to McDonald Observatory, I would hope that individuals like myself can encourage people, foster thinking beyond the constraints of that mountain, those telescopes, and the State budget. I think that is one of the great gifts a Board of Visitors member can make. A Board of Visitors member is like a visitor going to a home, complementing it, being a good guest, and leaving a house-warming present or something behind with the thought of making the host or the home a better place for the next visitor. I think that's the ultimate challenge for us as Board of Visitors.

A lot of times people think that if you are interested in astronomy or you are an astrophysicist, or scientist, then you don't believe in God. I've found that is not really true. I've had people say, "Lloyd, you know you have a passion about this astronomy; how does that impact your faith in God?" I say, "I don't know how you can look at the universe and not appreciate it and not have your faith strengthened, because, it all seems so perfect. It is so challenging, so vast and so beyond our ability to comprehend, but on the other hand, it seems perfect. And it's in that perfection, the balance of it, the infiniteness of it, that it allows me to believe in the infiniteness of God."

To me the Big Bang is the best argument for God because you have to ask, What came before the Big Bang?

Wayne Alexander

Today is the July Board of Visitors Bar-B-Q. We are just below the Observatory at the firehouse and everyone is sitting around large tables eating, or wandering around outside under large tents. From the cool breeze, darkening sky, and occasional lightning flash, I know a typical West Texas thunderstorm is arriving.

I am going to start out a little differently. I have done a lot in my career over the last thirty years with Southwestern Bell Telephone Company, but what I am most honored to have achieved is the success of two fine young men, our sons. I give most of the credit to Barbara, my wife; she is incredible. She is definitely smarter than I am, more organized than I am, a lot more patient than I am, and could have done a lot better in business than I have done...and I have done OK. She elected to retire from teaching when she gave birth to our first son twenty-five years ago and stay at home to raise our boys. Both these guys, through mostly Barbara's efforts, but some of mine, have turned into great human beings. I am so proud of that. Everything else truly pales in comparison. **I am Wayne Alexander and I am a voice of the McDonald Observatory.**

I've always been fascinated with the unknown and I don't think there is anything we know less about than the universe, how it all came to be, and what's out there. I guess my first real series of questions I started to ask about the universe were with my grandfather. Both my grandfathers were very special guys to me, but one grandfather, who worked for fifty-seven years for the railroad, really loved this planet; he loved the Earth and he loved the universe. He didn't have but an 8th grade education but had a fabulous knowledge of things, because he was self-taught and did a lot of reading over the years. He would answer questions from the standpoint of science for what's out there as well as from a religious perspective. He blended his very strong Christian faith with his strong understanding of science in a very interesting way.

I do believe there is definitely a God; I am a Christian and I believe all this did not happen by chance. I believe that, clearly, we don't understand how it happened. I don't have any preconceived beliefs as to whether there is other life out there. I know my faith doesn't preclude me from thinking that there is other life and personally, I don't believe we are alone in the universe. Yes, I have been able to fit my Christian faith with my strong thirst for understanding of how the universe really happened. I don't take a literal interpretation of seven days, and then [flash of lightning...deafening clap of thunder] well, may... maybe I should. Maybe...*I*...should, oh my goodness, yes that was good.

All right, but anyway, my faith and my interest in science blend very nicely, no conflict there. So I guess my grandfather was the launching pad for me to become interested in astronomy. I finally got my own telescope about two years ago when we were living in California in some fairly dark skies. I started to get interested and I found out my two boys had a real, but latent, interest in astronomy. When they saw old Dad had a telescope, they started showing up a little bit more often.

I came to McDonald Observatory the first time with both my boys and Barbara and we stayed at the director's home. It was a fabulous weekend. We came in on Saturday. It was very rainy and overcast, so we were very crestfallen that we had just missed our opportunity for a star party. We still loved it out here for all the other natural assets this part of the country has, but really, my prime focus was getting to look through that 16-inch scope down at the Visitors Center. Through the graciousness of Frank Cianciolo, our guide that weekend, he opened up

169

the Visitors Center for a private viewing Sunday night. We had great viewing and it was a memorable weekend. One I will never forget. This was before I knew I could become a Board of Visitors person and it's all come together very nicely. Through the graciousness of board member, Curtis Vaughn, and our friendship, this developed into an invitation to join the board.

McDonald Observatory as a leader in public outreach

I don't know that I personally have an effect or ever will have an effect on the Observatory, but by virtue of my employer's generosity, I think *we* are having some effect. The SBC foundation had given a $150,000 grant to the Spanish Language version of StarDate, Universo, to keep it going through at least 2002—and who knows what the future will hold. Our corporate foundation is very interested in education and economic development. By helping the University of Texas McDonald Observatory's educational outreach efforts, we are helping both of our interests at the same time.

I think McDonald Observatory is a big economic generator for this part of Texas and clearly, to get kids interested in math and science, what better hook can there be than astronomy? Get kids interested at an early age, something Frank Bash speaks about so passionately and articulately. So why do we at SBC want to find ways in the astronomy program at McDonald to get kids interested in science at an early age? Because, we are finding it harder and harder to find employees with technology backgrounds for our company, as are other employers, because we are not producing as many young scientists. Industry needs people with technology backgrounds to go forward. We are a knowledge-based economy and we need to get kids interested in that.

Visitor, when you come out here I hope you have a clear night, but even if you don't, you are going to have a lot of fun. Get a lot of sleep the night before, come very alert, try to clear your mind of all the stress and distractions of everyday life, and prepare to learn and be exposed to some fabulous mind-expanding stuff. To those who are coming, you are going to have a great time!

To the visitor who is coming here in a hundred years, what do you think of the decisions we made back at the turn of the century, in the new millennium? Did we make the right decisions to move us on a trajectory of preserving this planet? It worries me that we are doing things to this planet that, over time, will create a poorer quality of life for our descendants. I am hoping that those who might be reading this a hundred years from now, will say, "Those men and women back in the year 2001 began to get their act together and make decisions over the next fifteen to twenty years that stopped an irreversible trend to destruction of this planet. We appreciate that!" If we don't start now, I am real worried we will pass the point of no return. So to the visitor one hundred years from now, I hope we did good by you—those of you who are hopefully around to hear this and read this.

Otto K. Wetzel

I am Otto K. Wetzel, Board of Visitors life member, and a voice of McDonald Observatory. The first time I saw the dark skies in the McDonald Observatory area was in the 1950s when we had been camping down on the Rio Grande. Of course, it was dark down in the Big Bend and we loved it; the dark skies were just fabulous.

Forever dark

I think all the work being done at the Observatory in keeping the skies dark, in spite of all the development, has been monumental and we'll keep them dark. To understand the problem, all you have to do is look at the photos from space and see how light polluted the planet is.

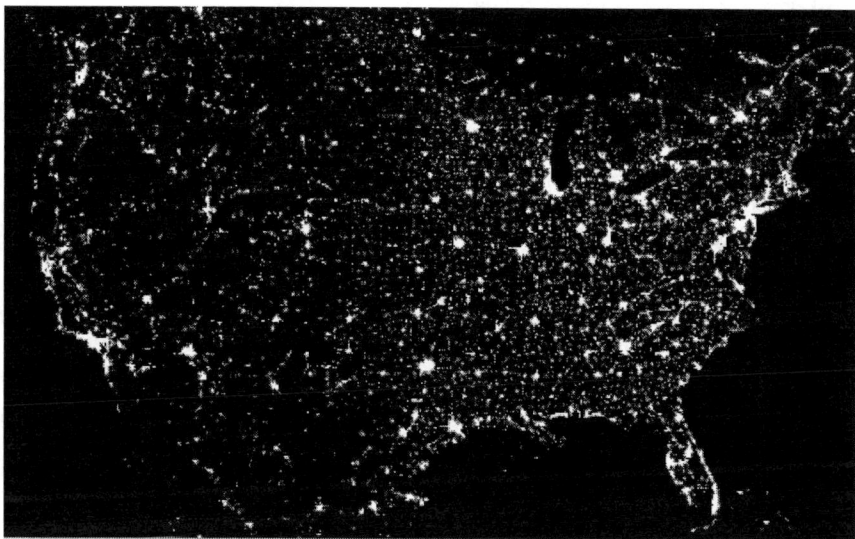

The United States at night. The place you can't see in West Texas is where you'll find McDonald Observatory. Reproduced from U.S. Air Force Defense Meteorological Satellite Program (DMSP).

I'd like to see more and bigger telescopes at the Observatory... the only problem is, we are going to run out of mountain one of these days. We really can't put too much more out there, I think our relationship

171

with South Africa, and building the Hobby-Eberly twin is a tremendous achievement and a great reflection on the Observatory.

We now have the technology that will enable us to find other solar systems and *that's* fascinating. We are finding there are other places out there, we are not unique, and this changes our perception of our place in the universe just like when we discovered the Earth was not the center of the universe. It is exciting times now and the new discoveries will change the future again. We need to be prepared for that.

Tom Wright

I became a Board of Visitors member a little bit differently than most of the members. My family and I were just visiting the West Texas area on our way elsewhere when I came across some of the people attending the July Board of Visitors meeting. We got to talking and came to a mutual interest in me joining the board. I had an underlying interest in cosmology—probably most people do, about our origin; and I had an astronomy course in college, which ended up being one of the most interesting courses I took in college. **I am Tom Wright, investor, and a voice of McDonald Observatory.**

My daughter was with me at the time of our meeting the McDonald Observatory BoV, and now has an interest in astronomy and ladybugs. Ladybugs are quite prevalent here at the Observatory. She was maybe three-years old when we were out here the first time, and the 82-inch telescope dome was covered with ladybugs. It looked like a blanket of flowers almost.

The nation's supply of future scientists

One key aspect of McDonald Observatory is drawing more people into it. We need to keep feeding the supply chain for future scientists, and I think in this country we are lacking in that area. It is awe inspiring when the conditions are right, the skies are right, and we go into the Observatory and witness the graduate students conducting their activities. It is impressive.

John Wildenthal

I was born in La Salle County's jailhouse, that is, on the second floor of the jailer's residence, in Cotulla, Texas, November 10, 1922. Dad was Chief Deputy Sheriff and Mother was a schoolteacher. **I am John Wildenthal and I am a voice of McDonald Observatory.**

Having applied for the Naval ROTC at the University of Texas, I was examined on Saturday, December 6, 1941, the day before Pearl Harbor. I was commissioned in the Navy and served on destroyers during World War II. My second destroyer was designed for radar picket duty for invasion of the home islands of Japan. Thanks to the atomic bomb, we did not have to enter that slaughterhouse. Thanks to the GI bill, I went to law school after the War.

After law school I went to Washington in 1950 to work for then Senator Lyndon Johnson, both on his staff and later on the staff of the Senate Armed Services Committee. From there I joined the office of General Counsel of the Renegotiation Board. My home judicial district, having had the good fortune to get a judge that I respected, I returned to Cotulla in November 1953 to practice Law. In 1959 I won election as County Attorney. Six months later Texas Attorney General Will Wilson invited me to join his staff in Austin. There, I met and married Carolyn Harris. We have a son and a daughter, both married. Each of them has a daughter and a son.

Having determined not to get stuck in any kind of government job, Carolyn and I moved to Houston in 1961. Mayor Louie Welch was elected in 1963. As his first City Attorney, I had the privilege of recruiting the first African Americans employed in City Hall above custodial rank. They were an assistant city attorney and a secretary. I quit in 1966 to run for Congress in Houston's new seventh district. The campaign was great fun, but I was plowed under politically by George H. W. Bush's army of voters. Engaged in law practice, mostly real estate, I had no intention of returning to public employment until 1976 when I was appointed a municipal judge in Houston. I retired in 2001.

My interest in astronomy became serious after hearing a Harlan Smith lecture in Austin during the fall of 1976. Harlan explained the resources available in the solar system, pointing out that the human race has all the energy and material resources it needs to prosper available to it in the solar system, without depending on Earth's resources. He supported development of resources of the Moon and asteroids to relieve pressure on Earth's biosphere that results from processing raw materials. He advocated using methods later developed for converting solar energy on the Moon's surface and beaming it to Earth to supply Earth's needs for electric power. I introduced Harlan to Ray Miller of Houston's TV Channel Two. Ray produced three television specials in 1977 featuring Harlan's presentation of these ideas.

By the time of Harlan's untimely death, Harlan was promoting the construction of astronomical observatories on the far side of the Moon where the potential to receive faint signals at all wavelengths far outstrips the potential ability of Earth-based telescopes or of orbiting observatories constructed on Earth.

Back to 1977, Harlan put my name on the list proposed for appointment to the McDonald Observatory Advisory Council (now, Board of Visitors) by the Board of Regents at their May meeting. I attended the July 1977 meeting of the Council. Then and later I was able to meet most of the original members of the Advisory Council. The Council's first meeting was held in June 1970 in the library of the Struve telescope (the 82-inch). The original members included S. T. (Buddy) Harris of Dallas, senior vice president of Texas Instruments, the first chairman. Other members were State Representative George Baker, publisher of the Ft. Stockton *Pioneer*; Dr. H. F. Connally, a physician from Waco and former UT System regent; Joe J. King, vice chairman of the board of Tenneco Chemicals of Houston—who attended many meetings after I came on the Council; R. N. Lane, president of Tracor Inc., from Austin; E. R. Lockhart, chairman and board president of El Paso Electric Company; Eugene McDermott, a founder of Texas Instruments; Don McIvor, a rancher from Jeff Davis County from whose family Mt. Locke was acquired; and W. E. (Pete) Snelson, then State Senator from Midland, who now lives in Austin and who is the only original member still active on the Board of Visitors, thirty-three years later!

Astronomy and civilization

I am fascinated with astronomy because of the role astronomy has played in the advance of civilization. This role leads me to believe there are revolutionary discoveries yet to be made in astronomy. Accurate observation of the *lights in the firmament of the heavens* (Genesis 1:14) was required for humanity to progress from the hunter-gatherer stage to an agricultural civilization. Agricultural civilization permits much larger numbers of humans to live much more prosperously than would have been possible by perpetual dependence on wild game. The calendar made agriculture possible. Without a reliable calendar, farmers would be liable to plant the seed corn during a false spring when a warm spell follows a long cold spell of winter. In a false spring, the seed would sprout, freezing would then destroy the sprouts when winter weather returned, and the people would come to grief. The earliest calendars, our first scientific instruments, consisted of stones such as circles and pyramids, aligned according to astronomical observations.

In the Copernican Revolution, astronomy fostered the development of other sciences. The major contribution was to shift scientific thinking from reliance on logic to reliance on measurable observations. Even after philosophers had to accept that Earth revolves around the Sun rather than vice-versa, the armchair pundits said that the orbits were perfect circles because this is a perfect universe. However, actual measurements showed the orbits of the Earth and other planets are elliptical. Newton's concept of gravity arose from his realizing the correspondence between the elliptical orbits of planets and the elliptical trajectories of projectiles on Earth. Astronomy aided chemistry by giving currency to the concept of small objects revolving around a heavy central object. This prepared the mind to accept the concept that atoms consist of electrons orbiting a heavy nucleus. Astronomy still provides a laboratory both for physics and chemistry. The most famous recent example being the verification of Einstein's physics, made by an astronomer during World War I. I believe the best is yet to come.

Darrell Windham

I am Darrell Windham, corporate finance and securities lawyer, and I am a voice of McDonald Observatory. I was born in Port Arthur, Texas, in the so-called "Golden Triangle" of southeast Texas and raised in my hometown of Nederland, Texas. I left Nederland in 1972 and came to Austin to attend the University of Texas. I knew I wanted to go to law school - don't ask me why but I always liked the law. I started out as a political science major, "government" it is called at UT. Then my cousin persuaded me to transfer into the business school, because even though he was a trial lawyer, he wished he had more of a business background. So I tried business, didn't like it at first, and then in my third class I had a really good accounting professor who was a pioneer in financial accounting. I liked it and that's why I went from thinking I was going to be a trial lawyer into gravitating to business law, which is what I do now.

I have always been interested in astronomy, and I took an astronomy class as one of my science requirements. Actually, believe it or not, while I was single in El Paso, I took dates to McDonald Observatory and the solar observatory in New Mexico. My dates probably thought I was a big dweeb, but anyway, it was something different and cool, and I have always been proud of the University of Texas' commitment to, and excellence in, astronomy and physics.

There is a combination of things that inspire me to be a Board of Visitors member of McDonald Observatory: my love of the University of Texas, my lifelong interest in astronomy, and my love of the Davis Mountains. I like tramping through the Davis Mountains; I think there are some little jewels in there.

I am not sure what I would say to a visitor of the Observatory; that's too profound a question for a corporate lawyer, but I will say, "Enjoy, appreciate!" My interrogator here has asked me to respond to this question, "Suppose in a hundred years, someone goes to the center for American History at the University of Texas, goes to the archives of the McDonald Observatory, and pulls out your file. What would you like to ask that person?" Well, one item I would ask is, "Don't you have anything better to do than read *my* file?" Well, speaking from the capacity of a Board of Visitors standpoint, "What advances have we made in our knowledge and what contributions have we made at McDonald Observatory and the UT Astronomy Department?"

Research shapes the future of technology
As far as space-based astronomy is concerned, like the Space Telescope, …whatever we can do to advance the learning curve is terrific. We have to be somewhat mindful of budgets and cost effectiveness. I'm not one that says just throw everything up there, but I do believe when you advance knowledge, in general, there are lots of tangible and intangible benefits. Think about the space program and how many products are now being used and the advances in other technology that came through that!

Tom Williams
I am Tom Williams, Board of Visitors member, and I am a voice of McDonald Observatory. I became a member of the Board of Visitors before I retired from Shell. I worked for Shell for about thirty-six and a half years and decided in November 1992 that was long enough. In about 1982 or 1983, I gave a paper at the first Texas Star Party about how amateur astronomers can contribute to astronomy in a scientific sense. There is a lot of useful work going on by amateurs in astronomy, much of which is available to, and some of which actually gets used by, the professional astronomers, and I was interested in involving more amateurs in that effort.

How can an amateur get involved?
Anyone who is interested in becoming involved in amateur astronomy at the level of making useful observations and/or collecting data for possible professional use can become a member of associations which facilitate that work. The associations, which you can join for this purpose, include The American Association of Variable Star Observers (AAVSO), the International Occultation Timing Association (IOTA), the Association of Lunar and Planetary Observers (ALPO), and the American Meteor Society (AMS). These associations have Websites and I would urge anyone interested to learn more about them that way. All have the capacity to embrace fledgling amateurs and help them get started in astronomy, even to the point of advising about the right equipment and books to get started with.

For someone who is more advanced in their background in astronomy and their equipment, there are two other organizations that conduct more sophisticated observing programs and support publication in professional journals, namely the Center for Backyard Astrophysics

(CBA) and the International Amateur Professional Photoelectric Photometry (IAPPP). These organizations also maintain Web pages.

Finally, I would urge that interested amateurs not overlook the possibility of organizing their own campaigns to do special types of observing through their local clubs. I would cite, as a fine example of such an effort, the Fort Bend Astronomical Society, which has for a number of years conducted a campaign to discover new or rediscover lost asteroids and have an amazingly successful record in that regard. Members of this group were also among the first ground-based observers to see the fading light of a gamma-ray burster. FBAS maintains a good Website that describes some of their programs.

If a local club doesn't exist, the Astronomical League has very useful information available that will help individuals get clubs organized. You can also join the Astronomical League as an individual member and enjoy their considerable benefits in terms of organized observing programs useful to train yourself as an observer, interesting meetings, and a regular magazine that discusses league activities. The AL website will guide you to these resources.

The best way to get started, then, is to get started. The opportunities have never been more numerous or productive at all levels of amateur astronomy.

Francis Wright
Transplant Surgeon at Texas Transplant Institute, in San Antonio, Texas.

We are at the Observatory Transient Quarters and a pool game is going on in background. It is great to sit down and have a chance to think about the Observatory and talk about it. It looks like it may rain this afternoon—and rain or shine, the summer Board of Visitors meetings are in July, which is monsoon season. We always said BoV also stands for "Bad Overhead Visibility" whenever we come out.

There are things that have happened out here during the BoV meetings, besides rain. I remember one BoV meeting we were all having cocktails on the back porch of the director's house, House A. This was when the group was still small enough to fit on the back porch. One of the members looked over the edge of the porch and there was a six-foot rattlesnake sitting down in the brush. Since there were a lot of people walking around up there at night, we thought maybe having a six-foot rattlesnake in close proximity wasn't such a great idea, so George Grubb grabbed a shovel and set out to dispatch the snake…which he did with cheerful readiness and no difficulty.

Some of the other Board of Visitors meetings have coincided with various events like the Comet Shoemaker/Levy impact with Jupiter. I can remember the excitement of seeing those initial images coming in over the Internet and everyone's enthusiasm about this unique event. It was certainly a privilege you don't get every day to sit around in the telescope control room during that time.

Harlan, Frank, public outreach and the Observatory people
We were out here with Harlan Smith during the Halley comet event. My kids got a nice certificate signed by Harlan and certifying them as "Official Observers of Halley's Comet." They still have that framed at home. I guess the biggest tragedy here was Harlan Smith's untimely death from cancer. It is one of my biggest regrets that I was unable to attend his retirement party out here...we did get videotape from that event. Frank Bash has done a wonderful job as the McDonald Observatory Director with his vision to reach out to the public with things like the new Visitors Center, StarDate, and the many PR activities the UT Astronomy Department has developed over the years.

The Hobby-Eberly Telescope was a wonderful project to watch go from concept, to a hole in the ground, to some foundation and telescope structures, a dome, a few mirrors, and then the whole thing together and working and being debugged. The HET is probably one of the greatest scientific bargains of the last 20 years.

It's also been fun to watch the people at the Observatory through the years as they have moved from position to position or even into retirement in some instances. I have enjoyed seeing Don Winget go from post doc, to faculty and professor. It's just great to see that kind of personal scientific growth, as well as the physical growth in projects, instruments and telescopes.

Brad Moody
It is July 21, 2001. We are in the TQ, transient quarters, waiting to go to the Board of Visitors Bar-B-Q, which is usually a wonderful meat fest. We are downstairs under the dining room where the pool table and TV are located. Pool balls are cracking in the background. As we look out the windows, which make up an entire wall overlooking the mountains and on over to the HET, an assortment of wilted lettuce, tomatoes and other vegetables fall through our view onto the ground below. This is part of the Observatory's effort to recycle, and feed the local animals at the same time. You are with Brad Moody, a Board of Visitors member who is a graduate of the University of Texas Law School, and has practiced law in Washington, D.C., and Texas, where he started his own practice in January 2001.

I am Brad Moody and I am a voice of McDonald Observatory. My interest in astronomy is probably a combination of being intensely interested in the space program and a meteor shower I experienced as a young person. Watching the Mercury, Gemini, and Apollo rockets was something of intense interest to me in elementary school. The idea of being able to explore the Moon and the planets was something that was always fascinating to me. I remember also being fascinated by a meteor storm I saw in 1968 or 1969. My parents woke us up and took us in the back yard where we saw more meteors than you could shake a stick at for about two hours. It was like a fireworks show.

I became a Board of Visitors member primarily through the good graces of Joan Baskin from Midland, who knew me as a two-year old. Her family, her kids, my brothers and sisters and I, and my wife, grew up together in Midland and our parents were good friends as well. I had attended Rice University and early on in my membership on the board, I was very involved with Frank Bash, trying to put Rice into the partnership that built the HET. Our efforts to get Rice in the partnership were unsuccessful, but we really had fun trying.

I have always been involved with trying to get the necessary political funding support for McDonald Observatory at the Texas Legislature. A critical point I would like to tell you, the visitor of McDonald Observatory, is that it *is* possible *and* necessary for you, the public, to affect the Texas Legislature through your local State Representatives.

I would say that anybody who has taken the trouble to come out here is a friend of McDonald Observatory forever. You will walk away with a very positive feeling about what you saw and a very good education about what McDonald Observatory does. You will be able to express yourself to your State Representatives, and I *strongly* encourage you to do so. The trouble is, only 125,000 people out of a statewide population of ten million people visit the Observatory every year.

What you can do to help McDonald Observatory

The *general* population's interest in astronomy obviously is not as strong as it was during the days of the Apollo program, so anything anyone does now helps. But, you are not going to get somebody to pick up the phone or write that letter unless they have made a connection to McDonald. If you talk to someone on the street about McDonald Observatory, the chances are overwhelming that they will say, "Well, I don't even know what you are talking about." But if you found someone who has been out here, they would say, "Oh, what a great thing." Then if you said, "Do you understand that McDonald Observatory is dependent upon the support of the legislature for it's existence?" They might say, "No, I didn't know that." You could say, "McDonald needs people like you to phone in or write letters and do your part to support the Observatory. Please call your State Representative or write a letter and say, 'I know about McDonald Observatory and I think the work they are doing is important. I want *you*, my State Representative, to support it because *I* support it.'"

If your legislature understands that there is a broad base of support for McDonald Observatory, it's going to do very well in the coming years as the funding requests come up. McDonald Observatory has a constituency just like any other interest group that is in front of the legislature asking for money. This is one of the reasons I think the McDonald Observatory outreach is important. Some of the kids who come out here and experience the Observatory and the new Visitors Center will grow up to be somebody who *really* has impact—one in ten thousand, but that one will make a huge difference.

Trail of car lights snaking their way to the Visitors Center for a star party. Time exposure taken from the ring road by Karen S. Winget.

Chapter 8 Current Scientists and a Bicycle Mechanic

Bob Tull

Late one night when I was about four or five years old, I was with my family in the old Willy's Knight. A Willy's Knight is a car—we called it the Wiggly's Knight, because as it aged it didn't run very well. We were driving from a visit with relatives in Brooklyn, Michigan, to my home in Jackson, Michigan, and I was, I think, sitting on the lap of one of my older sisters in the back seat of Wiggly's Knight. I looked out the left window and they were coming down like rain; this was a true meteor storm. At my young age I figured this was something that happens all the time. Anyway, that's one of my earliest memories, and particularly my earliest astronomical memory. I do recall one evening in Jackson when I was, oh, eight or nine years old, seeing a fireball go across the sky from horizon to horizon. I remember thinking to myself that when I grow up, I certainly want to be an amateur astronomer.

I am Bob Tull, Senior Research Scientist "retired" and I am a voice of McDonald Observatory. While I knew I wanted to be an astronomer from a very young age, it was just before I went to high school that I became aware of astronomical instrumentation, which is my field. After my family moved to Provo, Utah, I went to the local optician, a guy that makes eyeglasses, and said, "How big a lens blank have you got?" They had one that was 2 inches in diameter—pretty big for eyeglasses. I asked him, "Could you make a single lens with a six foot focal length from which I could make a telescope?" He said, "Sure." So he made it and charged me three dollars for it. I stuck that lens in the end of a cardboard tube, the kind used for rolling up carpets, stuck a magnifying glass in the other end which became the eyepiece, and I built myself a wooden equatorial mount. I was, fourteen, maybe.

I went to a boarding high school operated by the Presbyterian Board of National Missions, in Mount Pleasant, Utah. A school called Wasatch Academy, which is named for the Wasatch mountain range that runs down through the center of Utah. This school is now 125 years old and is where I was at the time of the Giacobinid, 1946 meteor shower. This, I think, is the same storm I saw in the Wiggly's Knight thirteen years earlier. We had been alerted of the storm prediction, so after dinner that night we all just went out onto the football field and waited for it. And it started. The Moon was bright and high, nearly full, and they started up. It lasted about half an hour and at any given instant at the peak, there were probably several hundred meteors visible. It was exciting. Some of them, many of them, in fact, exploded several times along their trek. It was like the Fourth of July.

About in my second year in high school, I decided to bring the telescope I had made to school with me. My advisor, who was our science teacher, heard about it, and knowing I had some interest in astronomy she told me about a book in the library, Amateur Telescope Making by Albert Ingalls; a good many amateur astronomers around the world have made use of it. I got that book out of the library and sat up all night reading it. It was so fascinating. My teacher then supplied me with some 8.5-inch diameter glass blanks, grinding materials, pitch, and space in the basement of the school building, so that I could make my first telescope mirror. It probably was the beginning of my instrumentation period. I was absolutely fascinated with the simplicity of it and the fact that a person could have the ability to make such a mirror without any machine tools or anything. This just fascinated me. I got started right in with it and kept on going.

South to Texas

As you know, in about 1959, The University of Texas decided to form an astronomy department. Frank Edmonds was here in the math department teaching astronomy and math. He became associate director of the McDonald Observatory, under W.W. Morgan, and acting chairman of the Department of Astronomy at UT. At some stage, he invited Gerard de Vaucouleurs to come and join him and Harold Johnson, who invented the UBV photometry system. Anyway, in 1961, I was at the University of Michigan working on my Ph.D. when I got a telephone call from Frank Edmonds. He said he was interested in having me come down to The University of Texas in Austin to help them build some instrumentation for the 82-inch telescope. I was still working on my dissertation at the University of Michigan and Cathie, my wife, and our two children, by now were visiting my mother in Florida. So I called her and said, "How would you like to go to Texas for a while?" She did jump at the opportunity and said, "Sure, let's do it." So in the late summer of 1961 we drove down to Texas for four months, during which time I worked with engineer Johnnie Floyd to design what became known as the big scanner for the 82-inch telescope. I had proposed an upgraded version of the scanner I designed for my dissertation.

During my stay here, Frank and Gerard invited me to return the following year and join the faculty. But first, I had to go back and finish the school year in Michigan. So at the end of the four-month period of our visit in Texas in 1961, my wife and two kids and I packed up our car and on the first of January. We left Austin at 70 something degrees and drove into Michigan at 0 degrees.

We came back to McDonald in the fall of 1962 to join the faculty without yet completing my dissertation and, in fact, it turned out I was able to do some of my dissertation observations on the new scanner and the 82-inch telescope at McDonald. I finished the dissertation while we were in Texas, or I should say, Cathie finished the dissertation for me with a typewriter and many sheets of onionskin paper, separated by carbon paper. It was a task for her. Anyway, we finished the dissertation and mailed it in to my advisor, Dean B. McLaughlin. In the fall of 1963 we were ready to go back, do the oral examination for the Ph.D., and have the required party, of which I do not remember…sorry about that. It was just sort of a punctuation mark between our completing our dissertation and heading back to McDonald Observatory. I observed for a week at the Observatory and then we headed back to Austin. One memory I have of that trip back to Austin was President Kennedy and his killer were shot during our trip from Texas to Michigan and now on our trip from the Observatory to Austin, we observed the many, many telephone linemen working along the highway between Johnson City and eastward, stringing up lines for the new presidential headquarters away from Washington.

Spectrographs, large telescopes, and Harlan's vision

I became an assistant professor at the University of Texas and that lasted until 1970. Also in 1963, Harlan Smith became the director of the McDonald Observatory and chairman of the Department of Astronomy at UT, a position that lasted twenty-seven years. There were five faculty members at the time and a handful of graduate students. There is a large photograph of the original five hanging in the Edmonds lounge in the Department of Astronomy—Harlan J. Smith, Gerard de Vaucouleurs, myself, Terence Deeming, and Frank Edmonds. Harlan came with dreams of expanding the department to perhaps 20 faculty members and 40 or 50 graduate students. All of which sounded pretty crazy to me *but he did it*. He really *did it*. He also had dreams of building larger telescopes at McDonald Observatory – *and he did that, too*.

I can remember a particular instance when Harlan, David Evans, I, and Johnnie Floyd were seated around a table thinking about how to build a large telescope and incidentally, a high-resolution spectrograph. I suggested some ideas on the spectrograph based on what I had learned from the 82-inch coudé spectrograph. David Evans turned to me and said, "You're a clever bastard, aren't you?!" I thought that was a very high compliment. Well, this was just a preamble of the next phase of my life at the University of Texas.

It was about that time that Harlan had taken on the task of building a new telescope, which might be 84 inches in diameter, it might be 100 inches, or it might be bigger. And he asked me to help build the telescope and the spectrograph. This was, I believe, the summer of 1964. I had obtained a University Research Institute grant to cover my summer salary while I did some data reduction of some spectra that I had obtained and I asked Harlan, "Are you asking me to give up this grant?" He said, "Yes." So I wrote to the administration and asked them to discontinue the grant and I went to work for Harlan, full-time salary and I think probably from that point on I have been salaried throughout all of the summers, even when I was on faculty, initially so that I could help build this telescope.

There had been several phases of upgrading the size of Harlan's telescope. The first idea was to borrow the blueprints of the 84-inch telescope from Kitt Peak and duplicate that telescope. It was about that time that Harlan heard about an available 100-inch mirror blank; I think it was in England. Therefore, he asked NASA to upgrade the grant to that size. After NASA agreed to this, we learned that that 100-inch blank was unsuitable for some reason, but by that time, the plan was at the 100-inch level.

Harlan went to Corning to get bids on a blank. The material chosen was fused silica. This was to become the first very large fused-silica primary mirror. We specified the size at something like a 105-inch diameter. By the time the blank was completed, it was 107 inches in diameter and, of course, Harlan would not allow them to cut this down to the size that we actually needed, so the telescope itself became a 107-inch.

The mirror was being figured at Davidson Optronics in California, and at some point we decided that things were not going fast enough to suit us so we went out there to inspect the Corning mirror. Jean Texereau, a French optician, became our consultant. To make sure things went well, I stayed out there for six months while the mirror was being figured. I moved into a hotel where I stayed all week and then on the weekends, came home. This was not an easy time for my family.

The mirror was finished in July, 1968, and shipped to the McDonald Observatory in the fall of that year.[16] The mirror was put in a steel jacket on a large truck and brought up to the mountain. The idea of the steel jacket with sloping sides was that Don Davidson didn't want any West Texas cowboys firing their rifles at this mirror as it went through the West Texas land. [This happened to the 200-inch that was sent to Hale Observatory so it is not an unfounded worry.] The irony of that, of

---

[16] The description of the overall project is in an article by Harlan J. Smith in the December 1968, Sky and Telescope Magazine, and the description of the Spectrograph in the September 1969, Sky and Telescope Magazine, by R. G. Tull.

course, is that we took the mirror out of its crate, mounted it in the telescope and it was shot up by one of our own employees the following year.

The damage from the shooting of the 107-inch

I remember I was in my office in Austin and Cathie telephoned me and told me that she had heard the news of the shooting. I had not heard a thing, nothing. I immediately went to Harlan's office and, of course, he already knew about it. Harlan and I immediately flew out to the Observatory to inspect the damage. Harlan called a meeting of the staff at the Observatory and talked to them about the man who had done the shooting, the fact that he had been captured and was now in jail down in Ft. Davis. Harlan tried, in the best way he could, to lend some support to this man who had shot the mirror, in spite of what he had done. He voiced that support in his talk to the staff who, as you can imagine, had some mixed feelings about Harlan's reaction to the shooting. In any case, this is Harlan's character; he cares about everyone, and he was supportive of this man who evidently had some mental instability. Eventually, we learned that the man's wife also supported him quite strongly and the man eventually graduated from the mental hospital and went into a different field.

As I said, Harlan and I went to the Observatory almost immediately and inspected the damage. We got the telescope pointed at the sky that night and did some Foucault tests which showed that the areas immediately surrounding the bullet impacts were the only areas that showed any damage to the figure of the mirror. Harlan got in touch with Don Davidson and asked him if he would come and make his recommendations about repairs to the mirror. He came and eventually he and I and Johnnie Floyd, and perhaps one or two others, got involved in actually grinding out the impact areas, in order to relieve the stress, and smoothing it out so that there would be no accumulation of grit or water during mirror-washing operations.

There were seven bullet impacts and a large area of damage done by a sledgehammer. He had used a sledgehammer to damage the telescope as well. Somehow, he managed to put all of that sledgehammer damage in the shadow of the secondary mirror. We ground that out also, smoothed it, and put the telescope back into operation. I personally after that, never felt like I could state that this is the world's best mirror. I stated that before.

The Hartman test of the mirror, prior to the shooting showed maximum deviations of the reflected wave front of only about 1/14 of a wavelength of light and an RMS [Root Mean Square] of about 1/33 of a wavelength of light. And that, in anybody's book, is an excellent

185

primary mirror. We did photographic Foucault tests in the telescope on starlight before and after the repair work was done. It showed there was no permanent damage done to the mirror but there is about two percent less light gathered by the mirror due to the areas that we had to simply remove from the mirror surface—the bullet impacts. So it remains a very excellent mirror.

McDonald Observatory 107-inch Harlan J. Smith Telescope.

Photo by David Reaves

The coudé for the 107-inch
During the time that the primary mirror was being made at Davidson Optronics, we were also building the coudé spectrograph. Davidson was doing the mirrors for that spectrograph, I designed the optical system, Johnnie helped with the mechanical specifications and we turned the mechanical design over to Boller and Chivens in Pasadena, California, to make what I think was an excellent spectrograph. We installed it in 1969. In fact, the 107-inch telescope, the spectrograph, and two other instruments—an interferometric spectrometer built by JPL and the Observatory's computer—all came into full operation on the same

day—March 8th of 1969—in the 30th anniversary year of the Observatory.

That evening at supper, Reinhard Beer from JPL, who built the interferometric spectrometer, said to me, "Well, you take the first observation and I will take the second one." I agreed to that and took the first observation: a photographic spectrogram of Arcturus at very high dispersion with the coudé spectrograph. Then Reinhard did his observation with his interferometric spectrograph.

Computer-controlled instruments in astronomy

In late April of that same year graduate student Don Wells and I were traveling to the Observatory on the leased plane for a two-week observing run. As we were flying, I outlined to Don my concept for a computer-controlled scanner for the 107-inch coudé spectrograph. This was something that, as far as I am aware, had never been done before, *anyplace.* Don had worked with Ed Nather in setting up the IBM 1800 computer for the Observatory. The computer was not intended as an instrument-control computer; it was intended primarily as an aid for the observer to take away the drudgery of having to calculate corrections to star positions. Since Don had been one of the guys that brought this computer into operation, he told me, "Well, I know how to take a soldering iron to the back plane of the computer; we can do it." I had a bunch of equipment left over from a previous experiment and between the two of us, Don and I, over the following two weeks built the first version of the scanner and had it fully operating on the 1800 computer.

One of my favorite memories was on the last night of our two-week observing run. We had it running successfully and suddenly realized that we had real spectra coming in from a nova! We were literally running up and down from the coudé room to the computer room, tripping on the steps, we were so excited about it. This project was not funded—too cheap; it was not an official project, *and* nobody knew we were doing it. That was how we did instrumentation in those days. I don't think this technique would be acceptable in developing instrumentation for McDonald Observatory today.

For that summer of 1969, I was invited for a position at the Jet Propulsion Laboratory in Pasadena, California. By the time I got back, the coudé scanner had become so popular that the photographic use of the instrument was basically at an end. Unfortunately, the coudé scanner was still using the IBM 1800 for control, and during the times that the scanner was in operation the 1800 computer was not available for its original purpose, which was as an aid to the observers on all the telescopes. So associate director Charlie Jenkins saw fit to get me a NOVA computer just as quickly as possible. This was probably the second computer the department had purchased. Ed Nather got the first one, Serial No. 1—I think it is in the Data General museum now. Ed taught us all how to use them, how to build circuit boards to interface with astronomical instruments. He is amazing. So from 1969 to about 1972 the primary observational mode was with the scanner.

Strange phones and a fire

At the time the 107-inch telescope first came into operation in 1969, it was time to update our out-moded telephone system at the Observatory. By out-moded I mean when I first arrived in 1961 and 1962, if you wanted to telephone somebody next door, it was a lot easier to just go next door and talk to them personally. Otherwise you'd find yourself shouting into the telephone. These phones were rather strange and, in particular, if you ever wanted to talk long distance to Austin, that was virtually a lost cause. These telephones were powered by batteries in the basements of the houses. Eventually that improved and at the time we finished the 107-inch telescope, it was time for yet another improvement. The telephone linemen came out to install the new lines from Ft. Davis to the Observatory. The telephone guys needed to take down some old lines and accidentally dropped some power lines onto a fence line along the state highway. This power line then created sparks along about a one-mile front, which caught the fields on fire. We had a grass fire that swept three-quarters of the way around the mountain and up towards the top. It passed, in fact, between the 36-inch dome and the dome a bit farther down the mountain, burning a communications cable in between the two.

The significant thing that I wanted to bring up was the fact that all the astronomers on the mountain, including myself, got involved in fighting this fire. There were also students from Sul Ross up there fighting it. I think it was Don McIvor, a local rancher, who brought up wet tote sacks by the truck load and requested help because his fields were in as much danger as ours and so anything we can do to put out the fire is a help to him and anything he can do to put out the fire is a help to us. He brought them up wet by the truckload and when they dried out, we brought them back to his truck and he got them wet again. There was no fire department there at that time and by the time we had been fighting this fire through a day and a night, fire crews from around the area finally arrived. But by the time they got there, we didn't need them.

There was not much observing the astronomers could do under those conditions and it was important to fight the fire so we were all down there doing it. None of us felt like we were in any particular danger. The brush in those mountains is fairly low so there was never a huge tall tree burning or a lot of them together—it is mostly brush. The flames were generally along a single line and it was easy enough to jump across this fire line to get into the burned out-area where it is safe. We fought that fire all day and then at night when it was dark and you could look down the mountain side and see all these glow spots where the trees were still burning. That was eerie. I am not aware that any of the scopes suffered any damage.

When Harlan Smith retired from the directorship, a committee was formed by the University to select a new director. By some fluke, I was made a member of that committee as was Frank Bash, Chris Sneden and a couple of others that I cannot recall at the moment. Our aim was to try to pull somebody in from outside the University, both to bring in new blood and to increase the strength of the department by the addition of another person. The university administration allowed us to proceed that way for some time, and each time we selected somebody they were summarily rejected. Eventually the committee was dissolved and the University president proclaimed that Frank Bash would be the director. It was a good decision; Frank has been an excellent director. His personality and mode of operations are quite different from those of Harlan Smith, and that is always as it should be. A new director should take us in new directions.

The High-Resolution Spectrograph for the HET

The next defining moment was when I was asked by Frank Bash to direct the project of building the High-Resolution Spectrograph for the Hobby-Eberly Telescope, the HET. The first thing to do was assemble a team of experts in all aspects of spectroscopy and, in particular, high-resolution spectroscopy, instrument design, and engineering. This would be a team to work out the details of the spectrograph in order to meet the scientific needs for that particular instrument. In this manner, one begins to build up a list of properties of the spectrograph, which are first, scientifically needed; second, possible; and third, affordable. Now the Hobby-Eberly Telescope was planned from the very beginning to be a very low-cost telescope. The spectrograph itself probably should not be comparable in cost to the telescope or the balance is not correct. Therefore, it is necessary to push for design aspects of the spectrograph that can save cost.

One of the first email conferences

So basically, a team is put together, a plan is put forth, funding is sought, and then the spectrograph construction can go forward. A technique that I used for putting together the plan or for gleaning ideas was an email conference. This was back in the relatively early days of the Internet and may well have been one of the first email conferences. I contacted everybody I could think of in the world that might be interested in discussing high-resolution spectrograph design.

Many of them came back and said, "Sure, count me in." This gave us the opportunity to have a conference, each of us being seated in the privacy of our own offices and allowed us all to brainstorm all kinds of ideas, circulate them without rejecting any until the true nature of the instrument began to crystallize. We didn't have to travel to a particular place so it was a very low-cost conference. The email conference ran from October 16, 1992, to December 18th of 1992, with a few random interchanges after that. I think everybody involved in it rather enjoyed the format and the leisure atmosphere of the auditorium.

The next stage was to organize a committee of half a dozen or so astronomers to advise on the aspects of the spectrograph and who, for the most part, would not have any responsibilities toward actually building the spectrograph, but were all potential users of the instrument. This always seems very important. I can't work in a vacuum; I have to have somebody to talk to. So I held semi-periodic meetings with my team over the lifetime of the project.

HET groundbreaking

Bob Eberly and Bill Hobby were present for groundbreaking in 1994 along with presidents of the various HET partners and many others. In full regalia, they were all standing in a row with gold-plated shovels. I was standing there with my camera, as everybody else was, of course, and I distinctly heard one of these gentlemen say, "Over the shoulder." They spaded away a little bit of the soil and that was the groundbreaking ceremony for the Hobby-Eberly Telescope.

The HRS camera

Probably one of the most difficult aspects of building a complex instrument is working out the schedule, any kind of realistic schedule of getting it completed. The single most important long-term item is the camera for the spectrograph and it was *the* item that took the most time. It is a complex optical instrument involving eight lenses, some of which were as large as 11 inches in diameter and of very exotic glasses. Two of the lenses are of pure crystalline calcium fluoride. All of the others, except the very last one, were made at a glass plant in Japan. One particular lens, the company had to make three times before they were able to succeed in getting a glass blank made. Then they had to be shipped to the United States. Once we received all of the glass blanks, the optical designer had to re-optimize the design based on the measured refractive indices of all of these lenses. Once this was completed, we shipped the blanks to a company in Florida and they very quickly turned

190

these into lenses. That was at about half the original budget and was the really shining part of the whole process.

The next aspect of getting this camera done was coating all the lenses to reduce reflections from their surfaces and to increase the amount of light that passes through them. The coatings on the lenses were completed successfully last Friday. Now we are preparing to do a test assembly. We have a tentative schedule set up for installing them at the HET during mid-April, so we have about two weeks to check them out, test the assembly and the alignment of the individual lenses in the assembly. We have a preliminary schedule that places the engineering installation run on the Hobby-Eberly Telescope for May 15 to May 22, 2000. During that run we hope to be able to put in the CCD camera, attach it to the optical camera that we have just been talking about, and install the fiber optic cable. With those in place, then we could conceivably have some first light, starlight flowing through the telescope, the fiber optic cable, to the spectrograph and detected by the CCD, possibly by May 22, 2000. But this is not necessarily the end of all the de-bugging. [17]

The spectrograph for the HET is located inside the pier of the telescope in the basement of the building. The pier is the circular wall that supports the telescope on its air-bearing pads. That pier is large enough in diameter to house all of the spectrographs. Hopefully, you got to see the HET on your visit. John Booth can tell you some interesting things about the telescope itself.

Rewards and sacrifices of a career in astronomy

I always feel like one of the greatest rewards of the observational astronomer is the experience of walking out onto the dome catwalk just before sunrise and seeing that beautiful sky as the Sun comes up. After a long, hard night's work, *now* you can go down to the TQ and go to sleep. One of the differences between an engineering astronomer and an optical astronomer is if it is cloudy, an observational astronomer cannot work. But, if you are an engineering astronomer, you can work in the clouds and even in the day.

What's bad about being either one is it takes me away from my family quite a bit. Not so much now that I am retired, but it still will to some extent until the HRS for the HET project is completed. I guess it took me away more during the critical growing years of my children than any other time and that has always been a bother to both my wife and

---

[17] The Hobby-Eberly Telescope was dedicated on October 8, 1997, thus establishing the 29-year cycle of large telescope dedications from which Bob predicts the next one in – maybe – 2026.

me. They do, however, like to come up to the Observatory to visit, so there is a trade off. And now, my grandchildren have come!

John Booth

I have always had an interest in engineering and science and the way things work. I went to SMU for undergraduate school, the first time around, and eventually got a degree in philosophy. Along the way…well…I actually dropped out of SMU for a while and went hitchhiking. I wound up in Afghanistan. I was just burned out on school so I flew to Europe on a prop plane for $180, landed in Luxembourg, and wound up in Yugoslavia. I was hitchhiking in Yugoslavia one day and an eastern looking guy came up and said, "What's going on?" I said, "Well, I'm hitchhiking." We talked for a while and he finally let on that he and his brother were driving an old, *old* Mercedes bus back to Kabul, Afghanistan, from Hamburg. I was on my way to Athens, they were going through Istanbul, and I thought, heck, why not. So, I helped them drive the bus. We went to Istanbul and spent a week there picking up a bunch of hippies along the way. We were backpacking and sleeping outside so this cost almost nothing, maybe fifty bucks a month. In fact, I made money buying a bunch of turquoise in Iran. I brought it back, sold it in Europe, and ended up ahead. Anyway, did that, that was a great thing and I am still in contact with those guys. They are still in Afghanistan. We hooked up again later on in Austria.

That was 1974. I came back and graduated from SMU in philosophy. You can't do a whole lot with that unless you go on to get a doctorate, but by then I had met this family in Austria, so I left Dallas and went to a little town outside of Graz, Austria. I spent a year and a half there living on a farm with a family, learning German. I just kind of worked for them and helped run their farm and really, I just wanted to learn another language and learn about another culture. So I did that.

Finally, I decided to come back to the States in 1977. I kicked around Dallas and places and was working as a bicycle mechanic. I finally decided I should be an engineer; I kind of had an epiphany. I checked into UT and it looked like a good program so I applied. I came here, and through a concentrated course got an engineering degree in about two and a half years.

I got out in 1980 and had met my future wife, Susan. We got married and moved to Kansas City, where I grew up. It was coincidental; she is an engineer and we just both found engineering jobs up in Kansas, City. We moved up there for three and a half years or so but she didn't like it much—didn't like the cold weather, and she got transferred back down here in the spring of 1985. I was looking for a job and a buddy pointed out a little blurb in a mechanical engineering magazine that was for some kind of an instrumentation engineer for McDonald Observatory. The applicant just needed to know about optics, integrating mechanics and electronics and ideally, things about astronomical instrumentation. None of which I knew anything about, but I applied anyway.

I got an interview with Tom Barnes, along with Harlan Smith and Al Mitchell. I had a great interview. It looked like real interesting work and stuff I could learn and do. I remember Harlan came into Tom's office for a while during the interview and the thing he was most interested in was the fact that I had been a bicycle mechanic. Harlan was looking for a hands-on engineer who could actually build stuff, was very practical, and not just somebody who was real good in their field. He wanted somebody who could actually go in and run machines and build stuff with his own hands. So that was it. They picked me for this job and that was the beginning; July of 1985 I started at McDonald Observatory. **My name is John Booth and I am a voice of McDonald Observatory.**

I had some interest in astronomy and I remember listening to Debra Byrd and StarDate back when I came to school here. I remember going out with binoculars to the Hancock Golf Course, lying on the greens at night, and looking up at the stars…just doing binocular stargazing. Nothing beyond that, never owned a telescope, just binoculars.

I was a mechanical design engineer and there had been a problem with instrumentation at McDonald for a long time. They were working on too many instruments at one time and not enough progress was made on any one instrument. Harlan and Tom had this notion to take an engineer and have him work on one project at a time. My first project was to create an instrument for the 82-inch that would both shrink the field down to a size so that more of the field could fit onto a CCD chip, and to speed up the focal ratio so it would take less time to make an exposure. This went along for a while until the inevitable happened and the reason they were working on so many different projects at one time; another instrument needed working on. The new Cassegrain camera was in trouble. There were all kinds of different problems with the thing, so I was asked to come and figure out what the problems were. I did that, and it ended up being a successful project. The instrument was used for tracking and getting orbits for asteroids. It had an (x,y)-guiding stage, driven by a photomultiplier tube, and was really new technology at the time.

The HET cranks up

In the spring of 1987 I was asked to take over the mechanical engineering group and become supervisor. It's funny, there are a couple of people from that group who are still in it: David Boyd and Jimmy Welborn, and we hired George Barczak not too long after that. Now the HET was just starting to crank up. You know all about the beginnings of this idea because Frank Bash has talked about it earlier. It began as an extremely simple idea at Penn State; just put mirrors in a truss, focus it, and have a little corrector at the top, light weight, very simple fiber feed from the corrector down to the ground. No instruments at the top, just a corrector, and the fiber feed. If you look at what we have now, I am fond of saying that it was a good idea that got completely out of control. It really did, but in a lot of good ways. Texas joined up with Penn State and as usually happens when you join up with other interest groups, you start adding features. The tracker went from a few hundred pounds to twelve thousand pounds; the tilt went from the zenith—straight up—to 35 degrees to give us even wider coverage; the mirrors aren't round and made of Pyrex; they are hexagonal, which improved the light collection area, and are made of Zerodur, which is a glassy ceramic that is not sensitive to temperature changes that would affect the telescope image.

In August of 1989, Harlan stepped down and Frank Bash took over. Frank realized he had a tiger by the tail. He very much realized the Observatory had never done a project of this scale before and he began getting things out of an *ongoing survival effort* to more of a *project going somewhere*.

Tom Sebring, project manager
The big change happened in August of 1992 when Tom Sebring was hired as project manager. Before Tom, we had everybody with a hand in everything. Tom divided the project up into discrete parts, like the telescope structure, the tracker, the payload, the control and service building, and the dome. He did what a good project manager would do. He chunked it up into pieces and then he assigned an individual to each one of those pieces. It wasn't always pretty; it was bloody in some cases because this wasn't the way we had thought about the project before. But it got things going and the project became much, much simpler and straightforward.

Tom basically raked through the whole telescope project and found things that looked extremely complicated or extremely difficult to engineer and build, and he had us look for new technical approaches. One of his things was part count; he wanted a low part count. If it has ninety thousand parts, it's not a design we want to use. The case of the azimuth drive is the most obvious one. That went from hundreds of parts to virtually no moving parts—just the eight air bearings.

194

The air bearings

The air bearings are like gigantic, 3-foot diameter rubber inner tubes that are sort of flattened out. They are the bearings of the telescope structure and they are sitting on top of the circular cement wall that is the pier of the telescope. There are neat things about these air bearings. Imagine taking an inner tube from a great big truck and squash it with a flat plate. This plate has a very heavy weight on it that you want to lift. Now picture inflating the inner tube with compressed air. Now think about the donut hole part of the inner tube. Suppose that you have drilled four holes on the inside of the donut hole so the air leaks out of the inner tube, but it only leaks into the inside of the donut hole, the center. So now this inner tube is filled up, you have lifted your heavy weight (the telescope), since the pier provides the seal around the bottom and has formed a sealed chamber in the donut hole center. If you keep pumping air into the inner tube, the air is going to keep leaking to the inside hole and eventually the inside hole will pressurize and start to leak air out under the tube. As soon as it starts doing that, you have two things. One, you've lifted up your heavy weight; and two, you are leaking out air evenly under the bottom of the inner tube and you are on a frictionless platform because there is a little film of air between the pier of the telescope and your inner tube. Now you can move the weight. It is as simple as that.

It is neat. You can really see the light turn on with elementary and middle school age kids when I turn off the air, pull one of the air bearings out, stand it up, and show them how it works. That is really fun.

Mick Jagger and Jerry Hall

Bill Gresler, who was our optical guy, told me Mick Jagger and Jerry Hall came by for a special tour one night. They stayed at Cibolo Creek, a dude ranch, and it was a big hush-hush thing. Bill gave them a tour of the HET and like most people, they sort of looked up at the tracker and said, yeah, yeah. They looked at the mirror and said, "Yeah that looks like a lot of mirrors, isn't it pretty?" Then, he showed them the air bearings and they said, "That's *really* neat!" Mick Jagger went back out to the car, got his video camera, came back in and videoed the air bearings going up and down. That was a fun thing.

Big presentations

By March of 1993 we had to have a preliminary design done, cost it to pretty good accuracy, and represent our reviews to the Board of Regents and our administration. This was critical because our goal was to convince them we were ready to release funding, start the final design of the telescope, and start building the thing. We had a big two-day presentation planned in March.

The first day of that review I remember well because my now ten-year-old son was born that morning. The night before the review, we were having dinner at the Four Seasons Hotel with some of the consulting engineers who were also part of the review. Susan, who was quite pregnant, kicked me under the table, gave me a meaningful look and we made our excuses. We took off and Michael was born about four o'clock the next morning. This was quite a day for me because this was the biggest presentation I have ever given in my career and the importance of the future of the project, and it was obviously one of the biggest presentations Susan had ever given, our third child. So, Michael was born that morning, I think at 4:19 a.m. I just stayed with them as long as I could—till about 7:00 a.m., then I went home, took a shower, put on a suit, went to the presentation and gave my talk on the structure and the tracker—slipping in as my first slide, Michael Booth. All that went real well and I think of that day as Michael's birthday and as the birthday of the modern version of the HET, so it's easy for me to keep track of.

The unique design of the HET

The unique part about this design for the HET is the way it works. A telescope is attached to Earth, which is turning and makes the stars appear to move across the sky. With a normal telescope, like the 107-inch, you want the telescope to move and track the star while the star goes across the sky. With the HET, we rotate the telescope structure around on its air bearings, set it down on its four feet and wait for the star to cross the mirror. Then we don't move the telescope structure; we just move the tracking part, which is up above the mirrors, and track the star as it moves across the mirrors.

The stars move along a shallow spherical surface that is about thirteen feet across, a shape that Frank Bash appropriately likens to "a contact lens for the Jolly Green Giant."

Milestones

OK, so what else? That was 1993. We had various people working on the HET. John Good was doing the dome, the control building, the dirt work, and the civil works. Victor Krabbendam was responsible for the primary mirror. Joan Sage was doing the software. Larry Long was hired and did the electrical engineering. Mary Lou Akin was our administrative assistant.

Milestones...looking back now from 2003 it's amazing how quickly the telescope was built. We went from that original meeting in March of 1993 through the summer, and ground breaking was just a year later in March of 1994. The parts of it that I am most familiar with were the telescope structure, the tracker, and the payload. The structure, which was delivered in April 1995, and in June the contractor was essentially done. They did have problems with the air bearings at first. The company hired to make the bearings tried a new experimental air bearing which did not work. They asked if it would be a tragedy if they came back in six to eight weeks with a new design. Well, the telescope structure was just about ready to go but the mirrors were behind schedule, the payload—corrector and so forth—were behind schedule so we said that would be fine.

Baby powder and tacky stuff

Oh, their first design was interesting; they suggested all sorts of things. The air bearings sort of rubbed on the concrete pier and one thing they suggested was baby powder—it actually worked. Victor and Stephanie Krabbendam had just had a baby and we ran down and got Kelsey Krabbendam's baby powder. We smeared it all over the pier and sure enough, it provided just enough lubrication between the rubber bag of the air bearing and the concrete top of the pier. The problem was we could not have a job designation of "baby powderer" or "baby powder spreader" every night, and we couldn't always make sure we had enough baby powder on the pier. It was a temporary solution but it wasn't going to work long term. Then they suggested sealing the top of the concrete pier, which we did with some sort of a coating that would prevent the air from seeping down into the concrete. But we had to strip it off because it was too tacky. But that stripped off coating turned out to work pretty well keeping the air out of the concrete, and the new air bearings, when they came in, worked like champs. We really bought off the telescope structure in its entirety in mid-October, 1995.

That all went pretty well, considering it was two and a half years after that original meeting. Still, there was no tracker—that was in the works—and still no mirror segments on the telescope.

Allie's telescope

I should tell you the story of my daughter Allison, Allie, in the construction of the telescope. In April of 1995 the construction of the telescope structure began. Remember the telescope sits on a great-big, flattop, concrete circular wall. The very first part of the telescope is a great-big square, 10.5-meters on the sides. And the square sits on four feet, which sit on the pier. They built this square, with a bunch of structure in the middle, and then they built the superstructure on top of that. Underneath this square is a huge metal cone about seven feet tall that holds the bearing that the telescope rotates around and keeps it from sliding off the pier. The huge cone arrived with the bearing in it and was set into place with a crane using cables strung from the *inside* of the cone. It was the first thing off the truck and in their haste to unload the truck, they just unhooked the cables from the crane and threw them down inside the cone—they are called choker cables. Now these cables are shackled to steel eyes or rings that are welded to the inside of this cone about half way down, and now the choker cables are just hanging there inside the cone. Nobody thought too much about them because you could, at that point, easily reach in, undo the shackles, undo the cable loops, and drag the cables out. But, they were in a hurry, the truck was full of steel, the next truck was waiting, so they just threw these short coiled cables down inside this great big steel cone and started unloading the rest of the trucks.

Well, within days they start to build the square part over the cone. What no one realized was once that square was completed, you could not reach down through the center part of the square and get the cables out. Cables are no big deal, unless they are where the fibers go from the tracker to the instruments below and they need a clear path with no obstructions to drop down through the cone.

All of this came to light the week before my family and I were to come out to the Observatory for the Harlan J. Smith dedication of the 107-inch. They had tried to get the cables undone, but nobody had long enough arms to do it. They used broomsticks and stuff duct taped to poles and things and they just couldn't undo the shackles.

We had a meeting on the spot with the contractor and tried to decide what to do. But nobody could come up with a good solution. It finally dawned on me that I did know somebody who was small enough to get in the 12-inch hole, strong enough, I thought, to undo the shackles, and just smart enough to do it. That is Allie, who was seven years old at the time. I told the contractor I thought I had a solution and would be back next weekend with the family for the dedication. So I got a shackle, a paper bag, and went back home to Austin.

Within the next day or two I cut an 11-inch hole in the paper bag and told Allie to hold her hands up over her head. Then I slipped the bag over her and sure enough, it just passed right over her without touching, all the way down. I didn't want to get her stuck down there so now I knew I had a little bit of margin. Then I gave Allie the shackle and I told her if she could undo the shackle, she could help me out at the telescope. I tightened up the shackle pin really tightly because I thought the one at the telescope would be pretty tight and I wanted to make sure she could do it. So she took it and tried, and tried, and tried to undo the shackle pin and couldn't undo it. But then, she went into our little workshop at home—I kind of brought them up with tools—and she got a big pair of vice grips. She chunked the vice grips onto the shackle pin and just undid it very easily. She was all set; she could do it.

We went out the next weekend for the dedication and Allie's sister, Emily (our back up), who was six years old, was very interested in doing this in case Allie chickened out. We went out and I explained to the foreman and the steel workers what I was proposing. They thought about it and they thought, Yeah, could be a kid could get down there and undo that.

Now to fully understand our worries, there is a two-foot passageway to the cone, the cone itself is about six and a half feet tall, and then it is five feet or so down to the shackles. But below the cone is another 12-inch hole in the concrete floor and below that it is a 16-foot drop to the spectrometer room floor. We were not interested in that.

We tied a French bowline, which has a double loop, so Allie could stand in one of the loops and have the other loop around her waist so that we wouldn't lose her through the bottom of the cone. We got Allie rigged up; she had a little hard hat, tool belt, her vice grips, all the little tools, gloves, and everything. The riggers and ironworkers were just petrified by all this because the sight of this little girl being lowered looked like the little girl in the news at the time, Jessica, who was rescued from a well in Midland, only Allie was going down instead of coming out. I tried to explain this to my wife, but when I got a little ways into the explanation, she thought she would much rather be over in the TQ not watching—good idea.

We lowered Allie down in this hole and she disappeared. Down in the hole, she had a flashlight and found the shackle. She unscrewed the pin, screwed it in the other side like a rigger would, so she did not have to hold it, and passed up the shackle—the riggers are amazed—then she passed up the choker cable. Then she went over to the other one—all this time she is suspended in this loop with both feet standing in one loop and one loop around her waist so she could have both hands free—she broke the other shackle loose, reversed the pin, passed it up, and passed the choker up. By then, we had a big crowd and when she came out, there was this huge roar of applause and cheering. Ever since then, Allie has just felt like she's owned part of the telescope because she was a crucial little player at the time.

Dad, John Booth, lowers Allie down the 12-inch hole. Photo courtesy of John Booth

Allie is fixed in position down the shaft. She's not worried but you should see Mom! Photo courtesy of John Booth.

Just so you will know, holding Allie up on the other end of the rope were about twelve people, including four iron workers, and of course, me. The rope also wrapped over a bar in the mirror truss, which took most of the strain. I did tell Allie before she went down, "If this doesn't work out, can I have all your stuff?" She said, "Dad, if you drop me, you'll never hear the end of it from Mom." I said, "You're right about that!" But, she did it, never missed a beat, and really did a great job. It was obvious nobody else could get those cables out, none of these great big men, try though they had, including me. None of us could do it. It was a great day for Allie.

The dome

Oh, the dome was a great thing. The dome was built on site by, as George Grubb put it, "Three hippies in a van with a rivet gun." You know George. George Grubb, as the former physical plant superintendent, actually worked as a young man on the 107-inch dome. The difference between the two constructions just struck him. The 107-inch required two huge arch girders that supported the dome crane: tens and tens of steel workers; riggers, trucks, cranes, and all kinds of people. For the HET geodesic dome, there were literally three guys in a van with rivet guns and a flat bed truck with aluminum prefab parts—any member of which would fit inside a 9- by 14-foot office. There were no huge pieces; the HET dome is just a geodesic frame with a skin of aluminum triangles pop riveted all over it. The dome lift was July 10th of 1995. We had a huge 400-ton crane from El Paso come out and it just picked the whole geodesic dome up and set it on top of the ring wall. We did need a crane to build the crane that lifted the dome.

The tracker

In September of 1996, the company hired to build the tracker, Orbital Sciences Corporation, was finished and we had a successful acceptance test run. The tracker passed with flying colors; it is quite an impressive machine. At the end of September, they completely disassembled the tracker, packed it up onto a flat bed truck and shipped it to us. I was out there to meet it. It showed up in a whole bunch of packing crates and, of course, the tracker beam was on the back of the truck. The bazillion packing crates contained all the different components of the tracker, which we had to put all back together. We took the tracker off with the old McDonald crane, loaded it into the tracker beam and put it into the spectrometer room. The spectrometer room had been completely bare, a gigantic fifty-foot concrete hollow cylinder, and now it was full of the beam and all those crates. We spent the next seven weeks assembling all the different parts of the tracker.

When you are in the HET building, look for the tracker; it looks sort of like an upside down railroad bridge kind of flying on the top. It's the great big black thing that is up on top of the telescope.

I spent pretty much the whole seven weeks at the Observatory; I think I came back to Austin twice. There was Frank Ray, Fred Harvey, George Barczak, just probably no more than about five people, and some folks down at the mountain. It was a very small team. We were pretty much working constantly for seven weeks. I remember we were all staying at House 14. We would get up at five o'clock in the morning; work for a couple of hours, then go get breakfast at the TQ. We would come back and often work until ten o'clock at night. Then we would go back down to House 14, and typically we would have about a half-inch of Jack Daniels, start a conversation and all fall asleep. We'd get up at five o'clock the next morning and do it again.

Engineer's perspective

So that was a lot of hard work. We finally got it put together in November. We had a crane put the tracker in through the slit of the dome, then lower it down onto its support points. This was one of the unique things about this project. On most other projects if you are the engineer, you'd design the instrument, you would maybe oversee the construction of it, but the actual installation of the equipment... you probably wouldn't participate in it. In this project, I was the guy at the top end of the tracker as it was lowered down onto the telescope structure. Tom Sebring, the project manager, was the guy at the bottom end of the tracker. We were both on the telescope structure waiting for this thing to come down and we were the guys that actually bolted the bolts to attach it onto the telescope structure. Same thing for the mirror truss; it was Tom, Victor Krabbendam, and I at the three points when that turquoise mirror truss was lowered into the structure. We were physically attaching things at those critical junctures. It was a neat mix of people and it was a very involved role. It was sort of Harlan's thing, from the original bicycle mechanical design to the actual implementation of it. And with the eight inner tubes for bearings, it's kind of like a giant bicycle.

First light

Now we needed mirror segments in the mirror truss for "first light." I think the agreed upon definition of "first light" was seven segments in the mirror truss which made the reflecting area larger than the 107-inch. First light was an incredible night. It was astonishing that we got that close, that early. We picked a good star and we picked a good trajectory. I will never forget sitting up in the tracker with my little eyepiece looking at the images on the mirrors for the first part of the night. I couldn't translate what I could see of the image into what I wanted them to do in the control room with the telescope, so I finally came down and did the image analysis on the computer screens below. We started tracking on a star; the star image was perfectly round and it just sat there in the middle of the screen. If the thing is not tracking correctly the star image will change and drift when you update the image, so I asked Joan Sage to go ahead an update the image so that I could see the motion of the star. She said, "It *is* updating!"

It was a huge success, a really *defining* moment. I just thought the star image was sitting in the middle of the screen because it had not been updated, but the computer had been updating the image all along. Phillip McQueen was on the 30-inch that night and it was mostly cloudy, so he had come over to the HET to see the show. I remember going out in the dome with Philip at about three o'clock in the morning and he said, "Well, there is no doubt at all now that the telescope will work. You made a round image out of seven separate mirrors, you have stuck it to the monitor so you can track a moving star, and all the worries about jitter and inability to track and so forth are over." We still had to suffer many, many things, but at that point we had one good example of the thing working, and it was all over but the shouting. The night of December 10th, first light, really does stand out. Then we all went home and slept for two weeks. I know I did.

Then gradually more and more mirrors became available and began to populate more and more of the truss. First, we did a great big X of twenty-one mirrors, just laterally across the face of the truss, which was the best thing for running trajectories and testing the tracker. Spring of 1997, John Glaspey, the first facility manager for HET, helped play a big role in aligning the tracker. The alignment is such that the tracker payload, the spherical aberration corrector, always has to be pointing directly at whatever part of the primary mirror it is looking at.

Aligning the mirrors on the HET

Once the mirrors are aligned, we have to have a system to keep them aligned. The SAMS (Segment Alignment Maintenance System) is a system of electrical sensors, six on the back of each mirror, that keep all the different segments in alignment with each other. This project officially started in November of 1999. We asked ourselves, where are we going to rustle up people who can work intensely for a short period of time and do an unusual thing—it's not hard but it is an unusual activity climbing around up in this truss. So if you think about theatrical set design and stage production, the work is similar; you are working high up in catwalks with the lighting, you have sets that have to be built and some of them are tall and they have to be hoisted in and out. It ended up that the sub-contractor on the SAMS project knew some people in the theatrical business in Colorado Springs and could put a crew together. He trained them in Colorado Springs, loaded them up, and they came down and did a fantastic job. The theatrical company really did a professional job with the sensors. They were very safe and very organized. They told us what they were going to do, they got in and did it, and they got out. That was August of 2001.

The cost, louver doors, Chrome Dome, clean up

By the end of this calendar year, 2003, total, we will have spent $24 million. That is for the original telescope, the instruments, the commissioning time, the whole package. $24 million, compared to a Keck telescope, which is just another telescope, which costs $90 to $100 million. If we can be competitive by the end of this year, get down to just the site seeing issues, we will have a telescope that we can say, "That's a good value."

We have solved a couple of the dome seeing issues by installing louver doors and the "Chrome Dome." When we open a telescope dome in the evening to work, the air inside the dome is going to be warmer than the outside temperature—the ambient temperature—and we need to equalize the temperature inside the dome. One solution was we installed louver doors in the bottom of the dome structure to allow ventilation.

The most recent project to help equalize the dome temperature was what we call Chrome Dome, which was putting aluminum foil—it is actually sticky backed aluminum foil—on the dome. It is an industrial foil and meant for this kind of thing. There was a problem with the dome super-cooling. The white paint on the dome previously reflected sunlight pretty well, but it radiated the heat into the night sky *really* well. The problem is it radiated so well that it super-cooled the inside of the dome well below ambient temperature—the outside temperature. It created something like a refrigerator with cold air falling down from the inside of the dome panels. The foil, which does not radiate well, allows something like a half a degree difference in the inside and outside temperatures at the panels, where the white paint caused a nine-degree difference.

The parts kit for the guys putting on the Chrome Dome included sunglasses and sun block. The foil reflects a huge amount of solar energy and when you are up there putting this stuff on, you can be roasted. Physical plant came in and really did a super job working with the HET crew. They did a super job just like they did on the louvers. With the louver doors open at sunset and the Chrome Dome on, it is just amazing how much of the temperature problem we solved.

Right now there is a lot of stuff going on with what we call the "Completion Project." This is kind of a clean-up project to finish up all the systems that were either not done or not thought of in the original construction project.

My family

I think my family really likes being associated with the Observatory. They love to go out to the Observatory. I can go in my house and say, "Let's go to the mountain." And all the kids will jump in the car, ready to go. I know there was a long period of time when I had to spend a whole lot of time out at the mountain and that burden fell to Susan. I was gone a lot and it makes me appreciate Susan and my kids. When I am at home, I try to spend as much time as possible with my family because I am just not going to get that time back.

The Booth family. Susan and John Booth with daughters Allie and Emily, the tall guy in the middle with the hard hat is son Michael.
Photo courtesy of John Booth.

Reflections of the HET project

I am still involved in trying to fix things on the scope so I have to spend time away; it is sort of a two-edge sword. I think about image quality. I think about trying to make the star image quality better. That's been the goal for so long now. Maybe it is rose-colored glasses but I think about those air bearings just very quietly picking up the telescope and rotating it around. I think about the tens, and tens, and tens of nights, actually riding up in the tracker with an eyepiece and looking at star images and tracking star images and talking on a walkie-talkie with people down in the control room and telling them, "Go this way, go that way." It is what I love about engineering. Engineering is a wonderful merger of theory and the real world. You learn a physical principal, and then with your hands you get to apply it to the real world.

Thanks

McDonald Observatory, in my mind, just represents the best of the scientific part of humanity. We had W. J. McDonald, whose heirs used his dedication of his fortune to build an astronomical observatory as evidence that he was crazy. I just love that; it's just ironic because now we have visitors coming from all over to see the Observatory and have uniformly good comments about what they see and learn.

My message to the visitor: thank you for supporting this effort because it is your science; it is supported by your money and I never lose sight of the fact that we are trying to do the best we can do with your money. I just appreciate the fact that we all pay taxes and make contributions to the Observatory and believe in this endeavor. Also, I'd like to say, "Let us know what else we can do at the Observatory. Just what else can we do to make your experience better?"

Gunvor and Jan-Erik Solheim

This is Jan-Erik Solheim, Professor Institutt for fysikk, in Tromso, Norway, and my wife Gunvor, and we are voices of McDonald Observatory. I started as everybody else in natural science: physics and atomic physics was at that time the big thing. Everybody should go into atomic physics, but I realized there were so many students and so crowded auditoriums that I sneaked over to the Institute of Astrophysics one day and took an introductory course. During that time, I also read one book of Fred Hoyle. I think that was really the one thing that turned me on to astronomy, his book: "Frontiers of Astronomy." In this, Hoyle explained stellar evolution and I became very fascinated by the H-R diagram—that it was possible to follow a star in the H-R diagram and predict its life and so on. Professor Svein Rosseland, the most famous Norwegian astrophysicist, who later became my thesis advisor, gave the introductory course.

I had, during my stay in Texas, a fellowship from Norway and I took over a McDonald fellowship in 1967. At that time, there was no TQ so we stayed in the small houses at the mountain. We had a very good time because we had small children and my wife was with me many times. One of our children was born in Texas, and she was less than one-year old when we lived at the Observatory.

A snack under the table

The story I remember, which, for me it was not any problem with snakes and things like this because I am a very quiet person; I don't react vividly. My wife is more active in that respect. Sometimes I could hear a snake outside the 36-inch dome in the night but it did not bother me. When I came to the Observatory, there was another astronomer having the McDonald fellowship and he was from Italy. He had also family, a wife and two small children. The first time they went out there, they were shown one of these small houses to live in and when they went down to the house, there was a snake under the table.

He was Italian, very upset, of course, and ran up to the main building and shouted, "There is a *snack* under my table, a *snack* under my table!" They said, "Snack? Well, there was no problem, we can have a cleaning person come down and clean for you." He said, " No, no, no, *snack* under my table!" He was so excited you know. Finally, someone realized it could be a snake and went down with a gun and shot it.

We were at the mountain when they built the 107-inch telescope. For me it was interesting to watch. One thing very different from other constructions is when they came in with the lorries, big trucks, with the steel and all these materials. It was so well planned that they never stored anything—what came in the morning was more or less used during that day or the next day. Normally in a building place, you see big piles of this and that. But here, no; these trucks came and it was fascinating to watch because we were up there every month during that year. So that was really an impressive time for us.

Both the Italian guy, Cesare Barbieri, and myself became later engaged with large telescope projects—he with the Italian Gallilean Large Telescope project, and I with the Nordic Optical Telescope—both at La Palma, Canary Islands. This must be the inspiration from our McDonald time!

Observatory as community

In the first years, there were small houses we could live in as a family and we met other young people out there. We met George and Linda Grubb, and Fred and Karen Harvey. It was like a big family. At the BBQ where they invited us we saw these big Texans with the big hats. We went into their pickup trucks and saw their gun over the seats, of course, for the snakes. We got the impression that this was real western cowboy life that we have heard about and didn't know existed any more. We certainly learned from that period.

That was a very interesting time because Harlan Smith invited the young astronomers to his house, especially when there was some famous astronomer visiting. One time was Fritz Zwicky visiting. He is a very famous, outspoken German, strong words and so on. But he said something that I took to my heart, "A good astronomer, observer, should have a cloudy-night project to work on, not sitting there and just playing cards or whatever." I invented a couple of cloudy night projects, which my wife helped me with, and these resulted in papers in the prestigious journal, "Nature."

We had a good time. We think back and that's why we came this year to visit McDonald Observatory. It made such an impression on us as young parents. Our kids are older now and they wanted really to come back, too. Our daughter, Inger, was born in Texas in 1966, and her first steps were taken at McDonald.

Gunvor Solheim

Yes, she has an American passport. She is Texan as well as Norwegian. As soon as she could decide herself, being eighteen and after school, she went back with her American passport. She bought a car, she found a job, and worked for half a year. Then she spent the money traveling in South America. We were very relieved when she came back home.

Three real West Texas cowboys

Jan-Erik and some of his astronomer colleagues were down at Ft. Davis and there were tourists taking pictures. Of course, Jan-Erik wore a cowboy hat and cowboy boots and so did the other two; one was from Poland and one was from Sweden. But the tourist took his picture of "three real West Texas cowboys." Luckily, none of them opened their mouths.

When we traveled to the Observatory from Austin, we went by car. We did not know that in Texas you should take water when you drive. We never thought we could not always find running water. One time our radiator started to boil. The first car stopped, asked if they could help us, and they provided water. It also turned out they had a baby deer in their truck and we played with the baby deer. That was an enchanted moment. Why there was a baby deer, I didn't ask. They were very nice people and from then on, we followed their advice to always take some water for the car and for ourselves.

Life in astronomy is very interesting and is very enriching. It brought us to so many interesting places. I am a pharmacist, which is a more down-to-earth profession. I thought that when Jan-Erik went on sabbaticals to Texas, I would have to quit my job and find a new job when I returned. I thought, I will lose a year; I will lose income and everything. But in the long run it turned out that because I could not work in this country, I could be a student again and I could really plunge deeper into the subjects than when I was a young student. I took classes at the University in Clinical Pharmacy and it helped my professional role to have this aspect. So what I thought would be a disadvantage to my career, turned out to be an advantage.

I especially like visiting observatories because they are located in very interesting places. We have met many people from conferences and when we go, we meet friends from a lifetime. We have been very happy in marriage with astronomy as a profession. I think to our children, Texas has been sort of our second home country because one daughter was born here.

I would like to say one more thing about living up at McDonald. In Norway, we do hiking a lot. Actually, both Jan-Erik and I grew up thinking that every Sunday we had to go up in the nature; that's the Norwegian way of living. It's very important and that was the way to be healthy.

All Easter holidays we spent in the mountains skiing; also, a very Norwegian thing to do. We were sitting there at McDonald looking at all the slopes but there was no snow, no skiing, no nothing. But at least we wanted to go hiking so we asked where could we go—we wanted to climb Mt. Livermore. I think it was George Grubb who came back and said, "No, the man owning Mt. Livermore didn't want people up there." To us that was something. In our country we have a law that everybody can use the land and walk; you have the right to trespass and put up a tent for up to three nights if it is a certain distance from the houses.

George said he knew a man owning some land in a canyon and if we wanted to go there, he could give us directions. We said, "Oh yes, we will try for the canyon." We drove to the land, parked the car, and started walking off. After a while, a man came toward us and actually held us at gunpoint. I don't think he was high up in society because he was riding a donkey, not a horse. He looked like he was out of a cowboy movie. He didn't speak any English and he held us at gunpoint until some other people came. They said, "Oh, yes, we heard about it. It is all right; they are going down into the canyon." I thought this is really strange, but it was beautiful to go down to the canyon and we spent the day hiking.

Caught in the dark
We had a good day. Also, to us in the summer, the night is not really dark in Norway and we don't worry about being caught in the dark. But we experienced it in the canyon. It was rather scary to be caught in the dark; it became really dark, and there were no lights anywhere. I didn't know the meaning of that expression until I came to McDonald.

Anita Cochran

I was born in New York and grew up right outside of New York City. I went to Cornell University for my undergraduate work, and then came to The University of Texas in 1976 as a graduate student. I have never left. **I am Anita Cochran and I am a voice of the McDonald Observatory**.

I met my husband, Bill Cochran, when I came here to graduate school. When I arrived, I was to work for Larry Trafton as a Research Associate and he said, "Let me introduce you to my post-doc; he will teach you what to do." Bill started teaching me what to do and eventually we went on a date. Our first date was to the Armadillo World Headquarters—old-time Austin.

It's funny, because we don't observe together very often. I very often need dark time and he doesn't care because he is looking at bright stars. So we are rarely out at the Observatory at the same time. We sometimes do projects together—we get along quite well. Because of my comet schedule, we have shared a telescope on occasion. But then, I take the telescope from him. We've had runs where he's on the sunset to 3:00 a.m. in the morning shift and I'm on the 3:00 a.m. and onward shift, and that's very, very awkward. You can't go into the room because the other is sleeping and that doesn't generally work well. In December of 2001 we shared a telescope; I had the first half of the night and he did the second half and we just stayed up the whole night together. That's nice to have a companion.

Frozen remnants from the origin of the solar system
I spend most of my time studying comets and other primitive bodies in the solar system; the things left over from when the solar system formed. They are the building blocks of the major planets but they are also the left over debris. We care about comets because they have not

been altered since the time they were originally formed, four-and-a-half billion years ago. By studying them, we can learn about the origins of our solar system. Over the history of the solar system, comets have hit all of the planets, including Earth, and there is debate whether comets brought some of the volatile materials, like water, that are necessary for life. In general, comets played two roles. One, in helping life; and another, in frustrating life because they were some of the impactors that could have wiped out life on Earth early on. There are trillions of comets out there; basically there are more comets than anything else in the solar system—they are just tiny.

When Earth passes through the debris left behind after a comet has passed, then we've got a meteor storm. One of my favorite nights at McDonald Observatory was during 2001 when we had a significant Leonid meteor shower. I was going to feel guilty watching the storm while observing at McDonald except the humidity went up so high we had to close the dome. The fog stayed in the valley just below us and I stayed on the catwalk, freezing to death, to watch. Nairn Baliber, a graduate student, was on the ground below me. We saw hundreds and hundreds of meteors. People were various places, somebody would go, "Wow", and everybody else would go "W*ow*." People were seeing different ones; some of them were seeing the same ones. Sometimes you'd flip around to see what someone had seen and it was *still there*. One meteor trail lasted for a couple of minutes. None of us could believe it. It was a spectacular sight.

What we were seeing was comet debris burning up as it encountered Earth's atmosphere—and they look magnificent. The debris pieces are about the size of a grain of sand—none of them get much bigger than a few millimeters in size. These don't survive the atmosphere to land on Earth.

I study comets by using spectroscopy. Basically that is breaking up the light into its component colors and looking for different signatures of the molecules of gas in the atmosphere around the comet. I use every single telescope at McDonald, including the old Millimeter Wave telescope. Primarily now, I use the 107-inch. Studying comets is a bit different than studying stars. Stars are always there but comets are up at funny hours. Because they are closest to the Sun, they tend not to be up in the middle of the night, but you can observe them at either sunset or sunrise. I keep funny schedules getting out of bed at 2:30 in the morning and starting my day at 3:00 a.m. It gets a little bit weird.

We have an opportunity coming up in the fall of 2003 when there is a close passage of Comet Encke, the famous comet that has the shortest known period—it comes past the Sun every 3.3 years. What is so significant about this year is it is one of the best approaches in decades, and the next time we can predict any similar comet to be this good will be in 2020, so this is quite an opportunity. Comet Encke is just on the verge of a naked-eye object; a naked-eye object is one you can see without an instrument. With binoculars you'll see it and with small telescopes you'll see it. In your instrument, it will be recognizable as a comet in the sense that it's a big fuzzy patch but it will not have a tail.

Every comet that comes by looks different. One of the more amusing ones was IRAS-Araki-Alcock in 1983. IRAS is a satellite; the other two are peoples' names. Comet IRAS-Araki-Alcock has come closer to the Earth than any comet in the modern era and the second closest to the Earth of any comet we know of that hasn't hit the Earth. It was very, very close. The funny thing about it is, it was only a little fuzzy blob—it didn't have a tail—but you could look up at the comet and then turn around and talk to somebody and look up five minutes later and the comet had moved. You could watch its motion. One night it was in the evening sky and the next night it was in the morning sky. Three or four days later it was gone. It was so close to the Earth that it was just an amazing sight.

Observing stories
Harlan

Back when Harlan Smith was director and would be on the mountain, he would show up in the middle of the night just visiting each of the four domes. The next morning there would be four new Harlan Smith stories because he always said something interesting and outrageous. One of my funniest memories was a night we were on the 107-inch and it was just after sunset when he showed up. After sunset, we should have had things running, but the motor on the mirror cover had failed and we had the telescope in its service position. There were six of us standing inside the 107-inch tube, trying to open the mirror cover with a screwdriver, turning the motors by hand—a very slow process. You would think that the director of the Observatory would find this very upsetting because it is now getting dark and we still don't have the biggest telescope on the mountain open and working. But, no, Harlan had something that was amusing him and we had to come and see it. He had found a glowworm. He was going to the different domes to show everyone the glowworm. He was something. He was a great guy. Some days you just sort of shook your head, but it was always good.

Some observing procedures and critters at night

To stay awake sometimes while observing, I play games like spreading my night lunch over as long a time as possible. I say, forty-five minutes from now I can have a cookie, forty-five minutes from then,

I can have my banana. And actually it's better to eat small things all night because if you eat too much food at one time, you fall asleep. I spread it out as the incentive to keep going. Four o'clock in the morning is a difficult time; it's about the worst hour for me. I am playing solitaire on the computer, I sing to my music, whatever works to stay awake and ignore the mouse that just ran over my feet. If you want to wake up quickly, have a mouse come running over your feet. Sometimes I get other visitors like Dave Doss' cats and dogs—maybe they are after the mouse. But I am more likely to get something like a scorpion or a tarantula while working on the little telescopes. Or bats. These creatures in the middle of the night are a little unnerving at times. We had a rattlesnake outside of the 36-inch one night, which we chased away. It kept coming back wanting to be right next to our dome. This was not a safe situation so somebody went and got their car and ran over it.

We get lots of moths. A moth laying on your slit and looking at it with high magnification is a very large object. We had one blocking the slit one night and we had to dig it out of the instrument. The worst things are the centipedes. They are orangeish-red and 5 inches long.

In the winter you think the night will go on forever and all you have time to do on those observing runs is eat, sleep, and observe. Nights are incredibly long and you're always a little on the cold side.

Snow, sledding, and Christmas caroling at McDonald

One winter we had a lot of fun. It was November and we had the largest snowstorm I've seen out there—about ten inches. Needless to say, we weren't able to open the domes so we had to find something to do. As it turned out, the snowplows ran out of sand and salt way up the mountain. They were still plowing the road, but in essence, they were just packing it down and making it really slippery. So now we are bored astronomers who see all this nice white stuff out there so we're going to go play in the snow. We borrowed a sled from one of the families who lives at the bottom of the mountain, trays from the TQ kitchen, cardboard, and photographic development trays. We went sledding down the main road and, of course, it gradually got dark. So we just took some flashlights, imbedded them in the snow banks down each side of the road, and kept on sledding. Needless to say the next day none of us could move—we were sort of sore. In the snow, you can't tell how old you are.

Just a note…photographic development trays on snow are the fastest. They arc slick, fast, you have no control, and you spin around in circles. You could tell if someone was on a developing tray because you could see their flashlight going around and around and around really fast as they went down he road. It was really very funny.

That was fun. You need to have a little fun. We were very fortunate, too, because one of the cooks decided even though she could get off the mountain and go home, she wasn't sure somebody would be able to get back the next day. So she stayed to feed us and make us hot chocolate. We also went Christmas caroling. It was November, but it seemed the right thing to do. We woke up David Doss and his family Christmas caroling.

Most times, though, the snow is just a nuisance. It makes it hard to walk, and we have to rotate the domes to get them heated so the snow will melt off. Otherwise, if there is a lot of snow on the 107-inch and you open the 36-inch dome, the 107-inch will just snow in on you. One night, every time the wind would blow, the 107-inch would snow on us. Because there was no observer on the 30-inch, we took our instrument off the 36-inch, carried it down to the 30-inch, put it on that scope, and observed the rest of the night on the 30-inch.

Sometimes we have people just wander in the domes and this has been a problem on occasion. But, in general, most of the people we encounter are just curious about the place so I'll stop and talk to them. The best person at doing this is David Lambert. If he's there in the afternoon and he's not too busy, he'll go down to the visitors' gallery, find people hanging around and show them things.

One of the best things about McDonald is the dark skies. Sometimes I can see so many stars I cannot find the constellations. That's one of the advantages of McDonald; it is isolated. One of the disadvantages of McDonald is, it *is* isolated. But it is one of the most beautiful places I know. It definitely grows on you. My favorite night was one of the nights comet Hale-Bopp was in the morning sky and I watched it rise tail first. That was quite spectacular to watch.

Bill Cochran

How I got here is actually very simple. I was an undergraduate at Duke University with a physics major. I went from there to Princeton and got a Ph.D. in astrophysics. In 1976, I came to Texas as a post-doc and I am still here. **My name is Bill Cochran and I am a voice of McDonald Observatory.** Actually, Harlan Smith is the one who convinced me to come to Texas.

Harlan's crystal ball

When I was a graduate student, my advisor, Bob Danielson, took me to a meeting of the American Astronomical Society's Division for Planetary Sciences. This is about a year or so before I was finishing up and we were out there looking for jobs for me. I was sitting down just before one of the sessions started and this man plopped himself down next to me. He said, "I'm Harlan Smith, I'm director of McDonald Observatory." He goes on and says, "I'm probably the only astronomer who has a crystal ball on his desk." And this is true; he had a crystal ball on his desk. He said, "Before I left my office, I consulted my crystal ball and it told me that you were going to come and join our program at Texas and I want to talk to you about that." I just looked at him and figured, anybody with a line like that, I've got to talk to.

That's how I ended up here and I met Anita here. She arrived a couple of months after I did. As she told you, we are married and it actually works very well. We try to leave the office in the office. We have another life out there and we keep them separate, and that's great. We have an awful lot of friends who have nothing to do with astronomy, and that's what we do when we're not here.

I have always been interested in planetary work and I guess, in some sense, I was trying to do that at Princeton...I was a bit of a rebel because they don't do much of that there. Bob Danielson was doing planetary astronomy and I was working with him doing observations of outer planet atmospheres. At that time, we didn't know anything about extra-solar planets. It was the outer planets in our solar system—Jupiter, Saturn, Uranus and Neptune. When I came to Texas I started out as a post-doc working with Larry Trafton. We worked together for several years and then my interest started to diverge from his. I had been studying outer planet atmospheres for about ten years and I realized, hey, there are only four outer planets, there are a lot of people studying these four planets and the field is getting very crowded. So I began to get interested in the question of planets around other stars. Are there planets around other stars and what techniques can I try to discover them? This was in the early to mid-1980s. With the help and support from Harlan Smith, I started looking at ways to find planets around other stars and that's how we started our radial velocity program of searching for extra-solar planets.

Extra-solar planets and their detection

I do a lot of public lectures and people want to know: do other stars have planets around them? Do all the stars have planets like Earth? They want to know if there is life on those planets. The answer to the question, "Do other stars have planets around them?" Is, "Yes." But I always tell them right now we have one successful technique for finding planets around other stars and it is most sensitive to certain types of planets. The fact that we are not finding other types of planets simply means that we do not yet have techniques that are sensitive to finding those planets. It's the old thing that absence of evidence is not evidence of absence. The fact that we don't see them yet doesn't mean that they

215

are not there. It just means we haven't looked in the right way or we don't yet have the technology to look in the right way. That applies especially to Earth-like planets. Right now, we can't detect Earth-like planets around other stars. That's coming. It's coming in the very near future.

Right now from the ground, we can detect a transit of a Jupiter size planet around a star the size of the Sun. But to get down to an Earth size planet, we have to go into space. Earths have to be out there. I don't see how you can build Jupiters without also building Earths. I think we are going to be surprised by the diversity of the types of systems that we have found. When we started this game fifteen or twenty years ago we thought all the systems have to look exactly like ours. But, we have yet to find a Jupiter in a Jupiter-type orbit around another star. So I think it just shows that nature is a little cleverer than we think and it's going to be a really fascinating type of search when we find these things.

Life on extra-solar planets?

What about life on extra-solar planets? Well, life got started here somehow. The Sun is really just a garden-variety star. There is absolutely nothing special about the Sun to distinguish it from all the other millions of stars that are out there. So I find it very hard to believe that there is something about this Earth and this Sun that would cause it to be the only place where there is life of some kind. Just looking at the numbers I think that the universe *has* to be teeming with life; it's just difficult to find. Intelligent life is another matter. I think that, yes, there is bacteria out there, but is there intelligent life, who knows? I don't know. Are we alone in the universe? Either answer is fascinating.

What do you need to be an astronomer?

The drive to explore and to discover new worlds is something that has always been with mankind. We have explored Earth and people have visited every place possible on Earth. A hundred years ago you could still explore new areas on Earth. Astronomy is the only place where you can discover completely new worlds. You have to have talent in order to do astronomy and you have to want to do it. It takes an awful lot of persistence and drive. There are talented people who simply don't succeed because they expect somebody to say, "Go work on this." You have to be able to recognize important problems and then run like mad to be the first person doing it. It takes an awful lot of drive to succeed in this field. It is extremely competitive. You have to be clever. You have to bang your head against the wall trying to understand what is limiting you. You have to be able to come up with the angle that nobody else has thought of. That is why I like Don Winget's project. I don't know if he will succeed, but it's a great thing to try.

To make real progress, you have to be bold. You have to take steps and look at possibilities that five years ago you thought were crazy. That is the way progress gets made. A hundred meter telescope on the ground? Let's put it on the Moon! Let's be bold.

Science as a process

I would like to say to you, Visitor, astronomy in many ways is exploration, as is almost all science. You are trying to explore the frontiers. What I find when I talk to the public is they don't really understand what science is. Science is not a body of knowledge. Science is a process. It's a way of looking at our world and it is continually evolving. One of the fun things I have learned studying science is that a large number of things I learned in college and graduate school are wrong. The great part of science is being able to prove it wrong. Science, our ideas, and our theories are constantly changing. Just because you pick up the paper and read that this long-held theory has been overturned, doesn't mean that science is bad, evil, or wrong. That is just the way the process works. And that's something good.

Pete Shelus

Today is January 3, 2003. I actually formally left the McDonald Observatory about a year and a half ago. I am now, officially, a University of Texas Center for Space Research person. But, I am here to tell you about McDonald Observatory and the three things I spent most of my life with—Lunar Laser Ranging, Astrometry, and the Hubble Space Telescope. It's been a glorious time. **I am Pete Shelus and I am a voice of McDonald Observatory**.

I was born in Philadelphia, Pennsylvania, longer ago than I would care to admit—1942—I reached the big "six zero" last year. I spent the first twenty-five years of my life in Pennsylvania. I went to elementary school, high school, and got my undergraduate degree at Penn, i.e., the University of Pennsylvania, in astronomy. Then I went to the University of Virginia in Charlottesville and received my masters and a Ph.D. in astronomy in 1971, right at the time the Apollo program looked like it was going to go down the tubes. My post-doc was at the Manned Spacecraft Center in Houston, Texas. I spent most of my time there trying to find a real job, but it was a fantastic post-doc.

In the summer of 1971, the Department of Aerospace Engineering at the University of Texas at Austin was sponsoring a series of summer institutes in Dynamical Astronomy. Dynamical astronomy deals with what drives the solar system, satellites, how masses work under gravity. Since I was just down the road a little bit I thought it would be interesting to come here and "press the flesh"—try and meet as many people as I could and maybe find a job.

I was staying at the Castilian, which is just off the "drag" in Austin. I was there for a week, attended all the sessions, and spoke with as many people as I possibly could, but I absolutely came up empty. Now it's Friday afternoon and I'm going to go back to Houston. I'm on the 18th floor of the Castilian and I'm all packed. I had pushed the elevator button when a fellow by the name of Derral Mulholland came sidling up to me and says, "Hey, I hear you're looking for a job." It's kind of frightening to think that if it were five or ten seconds either way, I would have been completely unaware of Derral. So I sort "interviewed" with him for ten or fifteen minutes and he says, "Hey, okay, you want a job, it's yours." He made me the offer, I accepted, and I came to the University of Texas August 1, 1971.

Lunar laser ranging comes to McDonald Observatory

I came here specifically to work with Derral on the Lunar Laser Ranging experiment at McDonald Observatory. Apollo 11 put a reflector on the Moon in the summer of 1969, and there were other reflectors landed by the Apollo 14 and 15 missions. So there are three NASA built retro-reflector packages on the surface of the Moon and McDonald Observatory was one of the original sites selected to work with this experiment. That is a story unto itself—the way McDonald got into the lunar laser ranging business, even before Derral or I were here.

Spearheading the effort during the early Apollo program was the University of Hawaii. The multi-institutional LURE Team, LUnar Ranging Experiment team, was going to do the observing from Maui. At some point it became obvious that UH was not going to be ready. Of course at McDonald Observatory, director Dr. Harlan Smith is building the 107-inch telescope with NASA planetary money with the intention of building one of the biggest telescopes in the world at that time to do solar system type studies. Hey, is there some sort of a match here? And, of course, Dr. Smith, being the wonderful scientist, politician, entrepreneur, called it a "marriage made in heaven." This started a crash program in order to get the 107-inch up and able to do lunar laser ranging.

The science of lunar laser ranging

The lunar laser ranging program was a relativity-based experiment to help us understand the effects of gravity. You could also use the data to learn a great deal about the Earth's rotation and if you understood the Earth's rotation, you can find out what's going on inside the Earth. You then turn the experiment around and by seeing the way the Moon rotates, you can tell something about the inside of the Moon. With lunar laser ranging, you can do Earth physics, you can do Moon physics, you can do relativity, and you can also do solar system dynamics and orbital mechanics. There are many, many different things that you can do by using a single experiment. One of the drivers of this experiment was one could model the gravitational motion of the Earth-Moon system at unprecedented accuracy.

The travels of a lunar laser pulse

Essentially, the experiment is done like this: the laser pulse, which is between ten to the fourteenth and ten to the sixteenth photons in a single pulse—a huge number of photons—is fired through the 107-inch. The laser beam hits the reflector on the Moon and the beam comes back to the 107-inch. You have looked at your watch and noted when the beam left the 107 and when it returned to the 107. Then if you subtract when the laser fired from the time it returned, you've got the round-trip time, which is about two and one-half seconds. If you then divide by the speed of light, and divide by two, you've got the measurement of separation of the reflector on the Moon and the 107-inch on the Earth.

That's the very basic observation and gives you the two pieces of data: time and range. Well, that's all very simple, but you have many things going on during this experiment. You are using imperfect instrumentation; I mean, there is no such thing as a perfect machine and we need the time of day very, very accurately, like to a microsecond—a millionth of a second. Then the laser pulse is three nanoseconds in length, which is about 4 inches thick. When the laser pulse is fired, it goes through all the optics of the telescope and when it exits the telescope, it is a pancake of light 107 inches across and 4 inches thick. Now your pancake of light is going through Earth's atmosphere and is spreading out, just like your flashlight beam spreads out. When the beam lands on the Moon, it is about one kilometer across.

The reflector package

Now, your reflector package on the Moon left by the Apollo astronauts is about one foot square—one, the largest (Apollo 15), is about 12 inches by 18 inches. These reflector arrays are "corner cube reflectors." Your corner cube reflector is made so that no matter where an incoming beam of light comes from, these reflectors are going to send that beam right back along the same track it came in on. You can think of the corner reflector as a corner of a room and if you take a rubber ball, stand anywhere in the room and throw it into the corner, as long as the ball bounces off three of the walls, the ball is going to bounce right back to you. That's a corner reflector.

Your corner reflector has intercepted almost an infinitesimal part of this one kilometer-across laser beam and all the rest of the light is just scattered away. It is only that light from the reflector that is going to be sent back towards the Earth. The returning beam is now one foot square, about, and it will again expand to about a kilometer across. It will also be much, much fainter. Remember, the Earth and the Moon are moving all this time, so when you fire the beam it has to lead the Moon, like a duck hunter leads a duck before firing. You have also built your reflector in such a way it will lead the Earth and the 107-inch telescope will still be in the one-kilometer beam of light. Then your beam of light still has to get through all the optics of the telescope and get down to the photocell to say, "Hey, here I am."

You fire about one pulse every three seconds and it turns out, after the laser goes through all of the gymnastics of travel, one shot in ten will give a signal back to the photo cell (if you have been lucky). That is, one in ten under good conditions. Everything is affecting that original laser pulse. Have you lead the Moon the proper amount? Did we really illuminate the reflector? Coming back, did some atmospheric effect bend the beam outside of the field of view of the telescope? Was there a lot of atmospheric absorption? Were there clouds we didn't even see? If you put all of that under the best of circumstances, we should get about one in ten. But then you have to wonder, just because some photon hit the phototube, how do you know it came from the Moon? They don't have a sticker on their luggage saying, "Hey, I've been to the Moon."

The characteristics of a well- traveled lunar laser pulse

The next part of my job was now to say, okay, out of all the returns that we get, which are the real bona fide returns from the Moon. So we go through all kinds of machinations in order to filter out the interlopers, the volunteers. We've got to get rid of the volunteers. We've got to know which of the returns are really from the Moon. That's where I'm doing more than just programming grunge. I'm now starting to use a little bit of what I learned in school. The early days were probably my most rewarding because I was responsible for identifying the real photons. All of the data collected at McDonald Observatory on the lunar laser for the first fifteen years of the experiment, went through my software. I was the judge to say *yea* or *nay*.

Filters

We have several physical filters in the system to solve this problem. One is a spatial filter so that we look only at the part of the Moon where the reflector is. The second is a spectral filter, which only lets the right color photon come through. The third is a filter in time. We know approximately when the return should come back, so we don't open the gate to our phototube until we expect the return to come in.

We sent out a huge number of photons but we are looking for only one return. Even so, there are a lot of volunteers coming in the telescope and it could be anything. It might be a car headlight reflecting off a cloud. It may be stray starlight; it may be stray moonlight. Anything of the right color coming through the aperture at the right time, the system will say, "Hey, I got one." So our fourth filter is a statistical filter. We use the same mathematics that one uses to determine how many tollbooths there should be at a bridge or how many phone lines do we need for this organization. So it is that fourth mathematical filter which kind of narrows things down to say we have almost perfect confidence that these returns came from the Moon. We then use our mathematics again to form a "normal point" to eliminate the effect of any interloper which might be in there…meaning you take several returns over a measured interval of time, and in some sense take an average. That is essentially what lunar laser ranging is really all about.

Now, of course, it's a matter that things don't stay static. Now we have better lasers, we have better telescopes, we have better mathematics, we have better electronics, we have better timers, we have better photo-cells and over the course of the experiment, it is subject to changes. In the mid-eighties we actually came off of the 107-inch and we went to the MRS. The McDonald Laser Ranging System. That is the trailer out on Mount Fowlkes. We've been there since the mid-eighties. We are doing exactly the same thing in theory but using different equipment, and we have been doing it for over thirty years. Almost thirty-five years now.

Astrometry of satellites and asteroids

The next thing that I got involved with was observing the natural satellites of the other planets using the 82-inch telescope and photographic astrometry. This was something my schooling at UVA was really good for because the University of Virginia was world famous for doing astrometric observations—getting parallaxes of stars, proper motions, and things like that. Here we were doing exactly the same thing, only instead of observing stars, we are observing natural satellites. And, here again, Derral Mulholland had a hand in getting me into this game. The space program was sending out spacecraft to observe other planets and needed to get the orbits of the satellites improved so that when their spacecraft arrived in the vicinity, they know where to point in order to observe these things. That was expanded a little bit and we started observing asteroids as well. It was a matter that there are only a limited number of natural satellites and after you've made two or three observations of them in one night, you don't need any more, but you still have observing time. So we observed the asteroids.

I am now working with Ed Barker and Judit Reese and we are in the middle of a ten-year NASA project. We are doing only asteroids but we're looking at near-Earth approaching asteroids—looking for that asteroid with our number on it, in essence. There are three parts of this experiment. One part of the experiment is to find these objects, just discover them. Then we have to obtain enough information from them to understand and maintain their orbits so we know where they will be five years from now, ten years from now, and fifteen years from now. So you've got finders, you've got the maintainers, and the third part is to look at the physical characteristics of these objects. If the object is just a light snowball-type thing, even though it's a mile across it's just made of snow and it's just going to vaporize when it hits the Earth's atmosphere. It will do nothing to the Earth.

Hubble Space Telescope

So, I have told you about laser ranging to the Moon and astrometry of the natural satellites of other planets. Now, another big part of my stay at McDonald was with Hubble Space Telescope. One of our group said, Hey, there's this space telescope thing coming on, it's going to be a multi-instrument telescope and they're going to need to do astrometry— we know something about astrometry. We said, Let's see if we can become a part of this space telescope team. We got together, Paul Hemenway, Fritz Benedict, Bill Jefferys, Ray Duncombe and I, and we wrote up a proposal just to sort of get our foot in the door. We wrote up a proposal—it takes us two or three days—and we asked for something like a hundred thousand dollars. We took it to the Observatory director, Harlan Smith. Harlan reads the proposal and says, "I don't think this is going to fly...rewrite it and don't come back to me until it is at least a million and a half dollars."

So we looked at it and said, The space telescope is dependent on being very, very, very stable in the sky. It needs to be able to *point* very accurately and stay *fixed* in that direction. Hey, you know, they are going to need some sort of auto-guider. We say, What are they going to do for guide stars? Well, gee, I don't know. What's available? In the late eighties, the Smithsonian Astrophysical Catalog was the only thing available and it goes down to about 10th magnitude in brightness. Magnitude is a term astronomers use to describe the apparent brightness of a star: the larger the number, the less the apparent brightness. We weeded through the space telescope specs and they need 13th to 15th magnitude guide stars. These stars are, of course, in the sky but we don't know where they are. The faintest stars we've got good positions on, from catalogues, are just down to 10th magnitude.

We sat down and spent a week inventing something called the "Guide Star Selection System." We took the Palomar Sky Survey plates, glass plates of star fields—not a catalogue, go to 19th magnitude, and that is what we need. So we scan the plates with the microdensitometer (Fritz Benedict is our microdensitometer man) and catalog all the 13th to 15th magnitude stars. We wrote another proposal. This time it was a lot of money, over two million dollars. We handed it to Harlan; he got a big smile and said, "Now, you've done something!" We submitted the proposal, but there are many proposals and there are proposals from people, famous people, who have been in the business much, much longer than the five of us. So we wait.

About nine months later I was at McDonald Observatory for an observing run. I had just sat down to dinner and the TQ phone rings. The cook answers it, looks at me and says, "It's for you." It was Paul calling…we won the contract! Wow, man that was exciting! I'm telling you, that was maybe even better than Derral Mulholland coming up to me at the Castilian. There were other proposals but we were the only ones who attacked the guide-star problem. Not only did we attack it, but also we designed it on paper. We had noted the problem, we came up with the solution, and that's why we won. That job started us on a ride for fifteen years. We were the Space Telescope Astrometry Team, the STAT. We were involved in almost every part of the design and building of the space telescope in order to do astrometry. What a ride!

Those are the three things I spent most of my life with. Lunar laser ranging, astrometry, and then the Space Telescope. It's been a glorious time. I hope you have enjoyed learning a little bit about all three.

Craig Wheeler

I was born in Glendale, California, April 5, 1943—I just turned sixty last Saturday so I still have that on my mind. When I was younger, my father kept us moving. He had a bachelor degree in physics from Berkley, became an engineer in practice, and worked on all sorts of interesting things. He worked on inertial guidance systems for some of the early-guided missiles; he worked on a solar eclipse expedition; he worked on the first hydrogen bomb; he was in the south Pacific and came home to Boulder, Colorado, in the snow with a tan and wearing flip-flops. He worked on the nuclear airplane before President Kennedy canceled that; he worked on weather satellites and ended up working on the Apollo program. Moving around to these various technical undertakings was like being in the service, although we weren't in the service. All this happened while I was young, but it is still a distinct memory. The atmosphere I grew up in was not exactly scientific, but scientific and technical topics were part of the conversation. My parents would talk about ideas and specifically the task my dad was working on at the time, so this type of thing was in the air all the time.

Things definitely turned scientific in high school when my dad helped me with a series of ever more complex science projects and my mom helped with the "selling" of them in local science fairs. We built a monorail, a spectroscope that vaporized samples with an electrical arc, a nuclear magnetic resonance spectrometer, a plasma jet that required vats of water and 220-volt lines strung in my bedroom, and designed a (totally impractical) "point emitter, colliding-beam proton accelerator" in my senior year that earned me one of the top forty spots in the (then) Westinghouse Science Talent Search and a trip to Washington to meet President Kennedy.

I am Craig Wheeler and I am a voice of the McDonald Observatory. I went toward physics, not by a specific draw, but by process of elimination. I knew there were things I did not want to do and I guess I had some instinct that I wanted to do something basic. We were in Idaho when I applied to college. I went to MIT and was a physics major there. I got my Ph.D. from The University of Colorado, went to Cal Tech as a post-doc, Harvard as assistant professor. Then the University of Texas offered me a job and I moved down here in 1974.

Harlan J. Smith

When I moved to Austin, this was still a very young department in the sense that Harlan Smith had been hired and the University of Texas Astronomy Department was less than a decade old. My first interaction with the University was through the Astronomy Department, not the Observatory—I'm a theorist and I spent most of my time on campus. But this is all connected through Harlan Smith. The enterprise was very democratic. The particular thing that just shocked me was, as faculty, we all look at one another's salaries and vote whether we think they are appropriate. That level of democracy would be absolutely unheard of in a place like Harvard.

Harlan left his character stamped on the Department and the Observatory. Everybody from the graduate students and the staff, on up to the faculty and the Observatory people, are all part of this family. I'm thinking back to the yearly department picnics when Harlan would come out, lead the charge at the baseball diamond, then turn around, lead the charge on the volleyball court, and out-spike everybody. It wasn't that he was just active, he was *there* participating. It was just part of what he did. There is a family spirit here and looking back on it, I realize how important that was. It didn't sink into me until Harlan died and Joan, his wife, asked me to give one of the little talks at his funeral. I had to sit back and think of what he did to impose this spirit. In thinking retrospectively, it was the atmosphere he established here, which has been tremendously important to how great a place this is to work. I think it has just been one of the best things about being here. The fact that all the full professors were expected to teach and teach well; I don't think Harlan ever said that. He didn't stand up and give a lecture on it; you just understood this was something you were expected to do. I think we still owe him a great deal of credit for it.

Of course, now we have people that never met him and that memory will fade. That is one reason I want to say this here. Harlan thought of the department and the Observatory as family; mechanical or contrived, it was his family, he was the boss, and it was his enterprise. He was kind of a gentle guy, but he was a strong personality at the same time. He was just absolutely genuine.

Supernovae and gamma-ray bursts

For my Ph.D., I worked on exploding stars, supernovae. I fantasized when I graduated about giving it up, going down to Baja, California, hanging my sheepskin on the wall and never looking at another supernova again, but I had a wife and a young son and it just wasn't practical. So I went off to Cal Tech and continued to work on supernovae, and amazingly enough, they continued to be completely stimulating through my whole career. There was always something new happening.

We have answered some problems, but other things have come up like using the supernovae to discover the so-called dark energy that accelerates the universe. That is a dramatic new thing that just happened a few years ago and came completely out of left field. Now, gamma-ray bursts and their possible association with supernovae is another brand-new idea that came along about the same time. Both of them are just complete left turns that nobody anticipated coming at all. So it's not just been stimulating, it's been over-stimulating my whole career. Supernova 1987A happened the year I became chairman, so I was trying to be chairman with one hand and do the biggest thing in supernova science in 400 years with the other hand.

A gamma-ray burst is detected by a satellite that can detect x-rays and gamma rays. The first burst lasts about thirty seconds and they take that information and where they saw it and relay that to the ground and we start working with ground-based instruments.

The question that's been around is, "When a gamma-ray burst goes off, does it represent an exploding star—a supernova? Do gamma-ray bursts come out effectively instantaneously when the explosion happens?" The supernovae take a couple of weeks to rise to maximum light so when this recent gamma-ray burst went (March 29, 2003), it was relatively nearby in a cosmological sense, and it caused everybody to understand that this one would be a good one to look for a supernova. So we immediately got on the Hobby-Eberly Telescope and we got a spectrum or two every night to see if we could see some supernova-like features coming up. We think maybe we did but some guys at Harvard beat us to it. They got the first announcement out.

These bursts will happen in this Galaxy, the Milky Way. They certainly have happened in this Galaxy once every ten or a hundred million years. All the ones we are seeing now are in very, very distant galaxies.

I do not use the Observatory directly. Once rather early in my career, I went out to make an observation. It was cloudy, and I thought, well this stinks, so I never went back. I do use the Observatory indirectly by coordinating with other observers. Harlan and I had a running joke about the weather. The weather always cleared up when Harlan went to the Observatory, and I had the experience when I went out it tended to get cloudy. So when Harlan and I went out together, there was this great battle of the karma. Harlan would tend to win. It would tend to be clear when we were there at the same time.

I did get involved in the Observatory when I wrote a document called, "In case of Supernova: Break Glass." The point of the document was what we, or any observatory, should do if a supernova goes off. I wrote this after we scrambled when we had a very bright supernova in 1981 and I tried to mobilize people to observe it. I didn't actually go out to the Observatory myself so all I could do was beg people, in a mature and conscious way, to help out at the Observatory. Anita Cochran and Bev Wills used the same kind of instrumentation we would like to use, so I would call them. By and large, they were willing to help. Anita and I still have a running joke that I had to reward her with a chocolate sundae at one point. I always feel a little guilty about it because they're the ones who wrote their own proposals and they are out there to do their own science, but largely that worked pretty well and we got some good data.

Now that the Hobby-Eberly Telescope is up and running, we are starting to get regular data on the supernova. The HET is queue scheduled, which means your observations are scheduled individually, not by the night, so you are guaranteed first clear-weather opportunity. You must have a target-of-opportunity program approved in advance so you can just call the HET observer, who is living at the Observatory, and tell them where to look, and they get the data. So now, I don't have to go out there myself and make it cloudy; my colleagues and I can order up the data and get it nightly. Before the HET, we got data in snap shots that could be weeks apart. We knew what the supernova did in big steps, but we could not know how they got to the next step. So now, we have a wonderful database on a supernova that went off about six weeks ago (SN 2003du) that we haven't had time to look at because the gamma-ray burst we talked about earlier went off just after that and just completely flooded us. But we are able to do the same thing and we got nightly spectra of the gamma-ray bursts. The guys at Harvard using the MMT telescope in Arizona kind of snuck by us on this one but the principal is we have one of the few tools in the world that can do this: a big telescope on which you can get time quickly and night after night after night.

Board of Visitors members

One of the times I do go out to the Observatory is occasionally for the July Board of Visitors meeting. Whether the BoV meetings are here in Austin, or out in the Davis Mountains, they are really quite mind-boggling. The people on the Board of Visitors just appreciate what we do so much; it is almost embarrassing how much they like what we do. Of course, we're all happy to talk about our science and interact with them, so it's a real love fest.

Harlan set the Board of Visitors up and made it one of the best. I don't think there is a better, more viable, or more vital board at the University of Texas or associated with another astronomy program. It's really just incredible. The first one I attended I just quietly sat and listened. It became immediately clear that this room was full of very powerful, potent people, and they were all lined up behind Harlan. I think we still don't fully appreciate the amount of clout that sits down in those rooms. And on top of it, they are all enthusiastic about astronomy.

If there were no McDonald Observatory

As a theorist, I would still find other things to do, although McDonald Observatory has been a formative part of my scientific career. There is just no question that having our own observatory really shapes the place in so many ways, scientifically, socially, politically, all sorts of things. If there were no McDonald Observatory, it would radically change Texas astronomy.

If I could not be an astronomer...I had some vague idea earlier in life that I might like to go into architecture or I might like to be a geologist. But the real answer is, I do like to write, and I would like to do more writing when I get a chance to. I have two popular books out: "Cosmic Catastrophes" and a novel, "The Krone Experiment." I have a book on supernovae and another novel I'm working on now.

Vaporware—just an idea in my head

I've been using these words but really haven't brought it together coherently in my own mind yet. I think we should be collectively sitting back and thinking, not in just in terms of individual telescopes, but what could they do as an enterprise. Right now, you tend to see what's right in front of your nose. I just have this sense that we could use the telescopes in a coordinated way—the whole is greater than the sum of the parts. Having said that, I don't know exactly what to do. I've got to turn that over to brighter people than I am who could actually figure out what to do with it.

Fritz Benedict

The date is March 19, 2003. This voice comes to you from an office in the Astronomy Department on the University of Texas at Austin campus. This Senior Research Scientist's office is shaped like a shoebox with a door at one end and a window at the other. On the walls are pictures, but you could imagine they are windows into other places. Through the only actual window is the Texas sky, which could be a picture of a clear blue sky with particularly placed, puffy white clouds.

When I was eight years old, a friend of my dad's came over for dinner. He was an engineer and an amateur astronomer. After dinner, we went outside into our northern California winter night, and there was Orion riding high in the sky. He told me things about the stars and the constellation and just off-hand, he mentioned that there are people who make a living finding out things about stars. Something inside me snapped; I knew I wanted to be an astronomer. **I am Fritz Benedict and I am a voice of McDonald Observatory.**

I am occasionally touched by the odd coincidence that a distant relative of mine, H. Y. Benedict, was an astronomer and president of the University, who helped found McDonald Observatory. It just gives me a real sense of joy when I go out to the Observatory knowing that it's genetic. I feel a match with the place. We have genealogy books of all the Benedicts in America since 1636 and as far as I know, he is the only other Benedict that was an astronomer. Somebody was very kind to me one day and gave me a copy of his textbook, with his marginalia in it, from the course he taught in astronomy here at the University of Texas in the 1920s and 1930s. Evidentially, he had given it to someone else when he retired and it eventually got back to me.

Thirty years I've been here now and it has been wonderful. This has always been a temporary job, but I am lucky, I found the right people to work with. If you have the right people, you can do incredible things. I have no doubt that I'm not going to retire, ever.

I was born in Los Angeles and lived in Northern California for a while. When Dad moved to Saudi Arabia to work with an oil company, I lived there, too, and went to high school in Beirut, Lebanon. Then I was an undergraduate at Michigan and went to grad school at Northwestern.

My thesis advisor at Northwestern was Jim Wray. He worked with Karl Henize, who was in training to be an astronaut. He wanted his project to be closer to Johnson Space Flight Center, so he moved his project here to Austin. This was about the time I got my Ph.D., and in 1972 there weren't any jobs so I took whatever I could get. I came to Austin as a scientific programmer with the Skylab project.

Searching for hidden satellites

The critical point in my career came in about 1975. The Skylab project was winding down and I had to decide whether I was going to throw myself back into the job market or try to stay here. I really liked Austin and there was a project called the Digital Area Photometer that, to my knowledge, is the only Department of Defense project ever done at McDonald Observatory. Harlan Smith decided that even though he was a Pacifist and a Quaker, he could support the Air Force's interest in understanding if satellites could be hidden. It would be an interesting result either way but Harlan suspected, I think, that satellites couldn't be hidden. The Air Force painted the satellites different shades of black, launched them, and asked us to find them. We found every one of them; never had any trouble at all.

The Air Force gave us an ephemeris, a position, so it was cheating a little bit, but we knew where the satellite would be and when it was going to pass over. We were on the 2.7-meter, the 107-inch, and somebody would be in the control room and somebody else would be out on the dome floor with the telescope. This was twenty-five years ago and I was the low man on the totem pole so I was out in the dome. I could see a star near where the satellite would soon be through the finder scope and say, "Yes, we got it." Then the person in the control room would start taking the data—measuring how bright the satellite was. Quite often it would take a long time to acquire these things and I would lose track of the time. I'm working up at the Cassegrain focus [just behind the primary mirror] and over a period of about an hour, the telescope would be pointed lower, which made the rear end of it higher. In the meantime, this was back in the good old days when we had night assistants. The night assistant was very carefully raising the floor so that I wouldn't have to stretch or climb on a ladder to get to the focus. After I got done with what I needed to do, I tucked my calculator under my arm, walked right over to the edge of the floor, and stepped off. Now the floor, instead of being a foot from the ground, was about six feet up. I fell through in complete darkness, hit the ground, rolled, got up with the calculator still under my arm, and said, "I'm fine, I'm fine." Nothing was broken, not even the calculator.

The Air Force project got me started working with McDonald

Observatory directly rather than being a project from the outside. That was a very important transition for me because in 1977 we got Hubble Space Telescope, which has been the linchpin of my career and allows me to stay here at the University of Texas by supporting myself with grants. I've been very fortunate in my grants that I can pay for my observing runs. They are not rich, but they are flush enough that I can always take my current undergraduate student with me so they can get very useful and interesting experience. Most of them are either physics or astronomy undergraduates, and they've all had sufficiently interesting and enjoyable times that none of them has decided not to become an astronomer.

Astrometry and weighing the stars

What I am doing now is measuring the radial velocities of binary stars as an aid in determining their masses. It turns out that with radial velocities alone, all you can detect is that there are two things going around a common center of mass. You can figure out what the period is and what the orbit shape is, but you don't really know the masses until you do astrometry. With the Hubble Space Telescope, we have been doing astrometry of a particular kind of binary star—low-mass binary stars. You can determine the mass if you can measure a process in every possible way. With Hubble, we actually see the two stars going around a common center of mass in the sky, and with the radial velocities we can detect the velocity changes as they go towards us and go away from us. We combine all that into a model, and out pops the mass. We get very precise masses that way. What we are doing is weighing the stars with a giant scale.

I must admit, for many years I didn't get to go to McDonald very often at all, but for the last seven or eight years I've been out there two or three times a year. I really like going observing. In my very best "old man" voice I'll say, "It used…to be…better…in the old days." We had a little twin engine Aztec we could fly out to Marfa in. It was a five-minute drive from campus to the airport, a two and a half hour flight to Marfa, and an hour drive to the Observatory. You were there in half the time it takes now. Now it is an hour drive from my house to the Austin airport, because I have to go through the Ben White and I-35 intersection, which is the intersection from hell, then a two-hour wait at the airport because of increased security, a one-hour flight to Midland, then rent a car and drive three and a half hours to the Observatory. It's actually faster for me to drive from my house straight to the Observatory.

Flying with Jake

One of the early flights out to the Observatory in the small airplane, the ride was bouncing and it was cloudy. There were no thunderstorms, but there was a front coming in and it was going to snow. The ceiling was very, very, very low. My pilot, Jake—you heard about him earlier from Fritz Kahl—flew us into the airport at Marfa. If you have been to the Observatory, you know there are mountains and you are practically flying between the peaks, or at least right next to them. We couldn't see anything at all and I wondered, How the hell are we going to get there, we can't see, there is no radar—we're gonna die! I think Wayne Van Citters was in the co-pilot's seat on this flight and Jake said, "Wayne, all right, give me a count of five when I say 'mark.'" Then Jake says, "Mark," and Wayne says, "One Mississippi, two Mississippi, ..." up to five Mississippi. Then Jake turns the plane 20 degrees and puts the flaps on. Still, we can't see anything at all. We are going slower and lower and lower, and suddenly we see the runway and we have already landed. The ceiling was maybe eight feet, we just came out of it, and there's the runway. I think, this guy is good, I'm so happy he's flying me. He is a terrific pilot.

Weather and observing

I have never had an observing run that I didn't thoroughly enjoy, except for one. Even the ones when I didn't get any data because the weather was *bad*. I like weather. I think weather is fascinating. When there are thunderstorms...*especially* when there are thunderstorms, it's just wonderful to be out there and watch. For me, if the weather is "not suitable for observing," it's very suitable for looking at interesting weather. One trip that wasn't any good at all was in 1998 during the fires in Mexico and in the Davis Mountains. Standing on the catwalk at the 82-inch, I could not see *any* mountains *anywhere*. It was that hazy. I was five nights out there and never opened the dome once. It was a total waste of time. It wasn't any fun because there wasn't any weather to look at. All there was to do was worry about the Observatory burning down, which recently happened to an observatory in Australia.

In the wintertime, observing is usually a twelve-hour night which allows for a lot of data, but I also thoroughly enjoy summer observing. It's very gentlemanly. The nights are fairly short, about seven hours, but you get plenty of sleep and it's nice to observe in shorts. For today's modern astronomy, the long, cold winter nights are spent in the warm control room with few, if any, trips into the dome and the ambient temperature. When I first started, there was no control room so I was in ambient conditions most of the time. I had a meat-locker suit, which no longer fits me, to wear when I observed. On my most recent run, we had five different kinds of weather in four days. We had snow, we had ice, we had rain, we had high winds, and then we had to close the dome because of dust. This was the first time I couldn't get out on the catwalk because ice was all over everything, and if you slipped and grabbed the rail, it was ice, too, and you'd slip right down and fall forty feet.

Going to the Observatory is just wonderful. The surroundings out there are terrific and it's nice to be mollycoddled. It's the only place in the world that I can go and everybody, because I am an astronomer, is really nice to me, and they feed me well. I think you could plot the quality of food versus time—kind of a low, slow, rolling curve, like a sine wave. Right now, the food is pretty good out there, they don't wake me up in the middle of the day unless it's absolutely necessary, there are nice walks, and there is weather to look at. I love it out there.

McDonald Observatory bugs

My kids got to go when they were middle-school age. It was during a time when the apartment at the TQ was available and we stayed there. It was, in a sense, a mistake because I would observe all night and had to sleep during the day. It was very difficult for my wife, Ann, to keep the kids quiet during the day so I could sleep. They did not like that. Also, we were out there during moth season and Mike, my son, woke up with a moth in his mouth and now has a very bad memory of McDonald.

I have a wonderful memory about bugs and my kids out at McDonald. Sarah, my daughter, was about four years old and after we ate dinner, we would always go for a walk around the mountaintop. It was a beautiful evening, a great sunset, and we are around the 30-inch dome looking off to the south. We're toddling along and Sarah has my hand. All of a sudden she just stops. I tug on her hand, but no, she didn't want to come. She says, "Bug, Daddy, bug!" I said, "Oh, bugs, yes, there are bugs everywhere." She says, "No! Bug, Daddy Bug!" I'm still tugging on her when I look, and right in front of her is a tarantula about the size of her foot. "Oh, that *is* a bug." I just lifted her up and over it and kept on going.

Another bug story is when I was by myself walking around the mountaintop. I hear this "clitter clatter, clatter clitter, clatter," something is walking through the brush. I look, and it is a foot-long centipede! It's the only insect I've ever seen in my life that you can actually hear walking around. That night I was on the 30-inch, and I set up chairs so I could hop from chair to chair in the dome and not step on the floor. Ever since then I always shake my shoes, but if there were a foot-long centipede in your shoe, it would hang out the end of it so you wouldn't have to worry about shaking it.

My favorite telescope is the 82-inch, Otto Struve's telescope. I don't hear or see a wall-eyed ghost anywhere, but it's nice to hang around a telescope that's got history like that. My favorite place on the mountain is the back porch of House A. I have a draconian regime where I will allow myself *a* beer each night. I take it down to that porch, as long as there is nobody staying in House A, and I'll drink it just before dinner. It is soul satisfying.

Coffee and artificial intelligence

One of the tragedies of my life was about ten years ago; I had to stop drinking caffeinated coffee. They were not life threatening, but I developed very, very unsettling heart arrhythmias and it was just from overdosing on caffeine. After decaffeinating, I came to work and all my colleagues would be speaking rapidly and clearly, and moving with grace and style. I would come in and I could only…talk…like…this, and every thought was agony. Finally, though, I was able to get back on decaf and I can even get a buzz from decaf now. They say a mathematician is a machine for turning coffee into theorems, an astronomer is a machine for turning coffee into theories or observations, but I say, "Coffee is a machine to make artificial intelligence." Well, when I observe, I sin, slightly, because in one of those big Styrofoam cups, I will put about a quarter full of regular coffee and then fill it up with water. I'll drink that at midnight and it gets me through until seven in the morning without any problems at all.

I helped a great deal in putting the new Visitors Center together and I hope you enjoy it. I particularly am enamored with the solar spectrum and the little words of wisdom next to it—you get a taste of what it's like to be an astronomer. If it's cloudy you're not going to see the spectrum and that's a very important lesson about doing astronomy. There's a real element of having good fortune in being a successful astronomer, and that exhibit is a demonstration right there before you.

Music and the mountain

I especially like to drive out to the Observatory because I can take a hundred CDs with me. For me, music is an integral part of the observing process. I listen so much when I observe that I very rarely listen to my CD collection when I am at home. I listen to everything from Jimmy Dale Gilmore to Bach. I listen to a lot of jazz and classical. I have one particular CD that I don't listen to on the mountain, but when I get in the car outside the TQ to drive home, I listen to "Hot Rocks" by the Rolling Stones. I think of it as being like the lei you must get when you leave Hawaii or you don't get to come back. So I listen to the Rolling Stones off the mountain and it's worked so far—I've been able to go back each time.

Summing up

I've lived an uneventful life. I have nothing to say about McDonald Observatory other than I dearly love going there...now where did I put that coffee cup...oh yeah, here it is. It's got to be one of the best jobs in the world.

Scot Kleinman

I came to UT because it was the only school that accepted me, although, I probably would have picked it if I had another choice. But, Hawaii never responded—didn't even tell me no. I defended my Ph.D. at the University of Texas in 1995, stayed for a little while in the job search pattern, and now I am an Observer for the Sloan Digital Sky Survey (also called the Site Science Manager) at Apache Point Observatory in New Mexico, with my wife, Atsuko; I will tell you about her shortly. **I am Scot Kleinman and I am a voice of McDonald Observatory.**

As an undergraduate at Harvey Mudd College in California, I studied stars with star spots and flare stars. That is, large analogies of sunspots where they take up a large percentage of the physical hemisphere of the star. You see them when the star rotates and the light output changes. I came to UT to look at spotted and flare stars, but I ended up not doing that.

One group at UT, run by Ed Nather and Don Winget, was doing an around the world telescope run—the Whole Earth Telescope (WET) or XCov as we called it for "eXtended Coverage". They were doing observations of a, presumably, pulsating white dwarf star in the system called V471-Tau. This is a binary system, one of the objects being a white dwarf star and the other one being a chromospherically active star with spots and flares. They asked me to come up and join the lunch meetings to see if there was anything to do with the data on the flare star. They didn't care about the flare star and at the time, I didn't care about the white dwarf. But, as we discussed the possibilities, the white dwarf became much more exciting to me than the flare star, so I said, "Look, even if we don't do anything with this flare star data, I would like to hang around the group because I think this white dwarf stuff is kind of interesting." I ended up working on white dwarf stars and going on that observing run.

It was my first observing run at the University of Texas and it was with *the* Dr. Ed Nather, and with a brand new instrument finished just a couple of days before our run in Australia and not completely tested. Besides all of that, getting in a car accident in Sydney, and blowing up a laptop, the instrument performed fine. The machinists had done an excellent job with the instrument and we took some of the best data of the run with it. The end of this story is; by the end of the run, I had found my research project, was a member of the group, and it pretty much set my way for my career at UT.

Several of us ended up working in this group with Don and Ed in the Whole Earth Telescope lab. The lab is a very large room Ed Nather got for giving up his corner office. We had a fairly large contingent for lunch meetings that met at least three days a week and anything could happen during them. We might talk about the baseball game the night before or we might talk about your science project or where you are stuck, who knows, but it was a time to come together as a group and make progress on whatever you were working on. If I hadn't been going to these meetings but just talked to someone about what I knew, we would have exchanged some information and that would be the end of it. It was coming to these meetings, seeing what everybody was working on, and learning that everybody was doing a different part of the same puzzle, is what made it very exciting.

The process of observing

All throughout my career, we had to write proposals to the local McDonald TAC, Time Allocation Committee. Grad students usually got some preference in assigning telescope time but it was not guaranteed; you still had to write a good proposal.

Having access to the 36-inch telescope was extremely beneficial for me because it gave me the amount of telescope time I needed to complete my project. I was going up to the Observatory roughly every month for one to three weeks a month. Nowhere else can a graduate student get that much telescope time.

Most other students in my class were using instruments that lived at McDonald Observatory. They could just drive out or fly out and the instrument would be mounted on the telescope by the staff and ready to go to work when they arrived. Our instrument, a photometer, lived in the lab in Austin when we weren't using it. We brought it out ourselves, mounted it to the telescope with help from the day staff, observed, took the instrument off the telescope, brought it back to Austin, and set it up again in the lab to make sure it was still working. It remained in the lab until the next run.

I usually ended up driving out to the Observatory because I had to bring a hundred pounds of instrument and a car full of equipment. The instrument fit in a large suitcase type box, which did not fit in my car, a VW KarmannGhia, so I had to take it in halves. The box we used split in two, and I would leave it split in two. I used seatbelts or anything I could find to strap it in. Occasionally, if I didn't have the box, I would just wrap some towels and bubble wrap or something around the photometer and sit it in the back of the car with my suitcases and computers and drive on out.

While observing, I stayed at the TQ, on site at McDonald. When I started there, we were served night lunches that someone would cook for us. Shortly after I started, they changed the night lunch system, got rid of the night cook, and gave us TV dinners. Unfortunately, they made this switch at the start of a clear, three-week observing run I had in September. It was one of the best data sets I had on my star and better than some of the Whole Earth Telescope observations on this object. However, the TV dinners were *not* high quality and they had only three or four varieties. It was awful. So for three weeks I had macaroni and cheese TV dinners and I didn't want to see another one ever again. But, of course, I did, every night for the next several months afterwards. Otherwise, the food quality was variable. Now I hear it is much better.

I had a room I prefer in the TQ. It is downstairs, second from the end on the right hand side. I preferred downstairs because upstairs was where the kitchen was and it was sometimes noisy when the day staff came in for lunch. I was usually sleeping then, on the verge of sleep, or a few hours away from waking up, and if there was a lot of noise as people came in for lunch, I would often wake up. Downstairs however, you had the pool table and the TV room and I wanted to be far away from that, which put me towards the end of the hall. The last room was too close to the outside and there was a lot of outside noise from the machine shop, which is why I liked one room in from the last room. And I wanted the right hand side because it had the better view of the mountain.

Each room usually has two single beds, a dresser, a bathroom, and towels, which didn't get you very dry as water somewhat just beaded up on them. I actually brought my own towels and toilet paper because theirs were like sandpaper. They got new blankets sometime during my career and I think even new mattresses. That was a big improvement. There are laundry facilities and humidifiers because it is very dry up there. Also, there are good light-blocking shades on the windows so sunlight isn't a problem.

One particular run I remember was with Chris Clemens. We drove his car up because you could fit my car in the trunk of his car, and hence our instruments and computers were no problem at all for Chris. We had been a few days with terribly cloudy, socked-in nights and had done all of our ambitious late-night stuff already. We reduced all our data, did our class work, and whatever else we had to do, and we were getting a little stir crazy. So, we decided to go into town. Ft. Davis was the first suggestion but there is nothing in Ft. Davis to go to, so we went to

Alpine because there is a bar there called the Wooden Nickel. It was about an hour away. Of course, being careful observers, we were constantly going out to check the sky to make sure it was not clearing; we did not want to be away from the mountain when it cleared up. I don't know if we were officially allowed to leave the mountain, but we did.

We met some interesting people at the bar as I remember and everybody knew everybody there, so when we walked in they knew we weren't local. Some people took that as an invitation to come talk to us, and some people took that as an invitation to ignore us. But we had a good time, talked to a lot of people and every fifteen minutes somebody would get up and check the weather. At one point we could see some stars and we said, "Oh no! We gotta get up there." So we piled in Chris' car, which was a 1967 Pontiac Executive, a fairly rare model from what I understand (at least at the time of the early nineties). We left the parking lot, driving quickly because we were afraid it was clearing up, we weren't on the mountain, and this would be terrible, especially if Ed or Don found out that we were slacking off when we could have been observing. As we drove off, two people standing outside the Wooden Nickel said, "I think that *is* a Pontiac Executive." Anyway, Chris drove very fast to the Observatory, getting there in probably thirty minutes or less. We get to Ft. Davis, get up the mountain, and it was *exactly* the same weather conditions as when we left, completely cloudy and totally fogged in. The scare was for nothing.

Comparing other observatories

The Whole Earth Telescope involvement allowed me to meet astronomers from all over the world. They are some of the best in their field and I would not have met them otherwise. I had a goal: to travel to all seven continents, observe in all seven continents, and bare-foot water-ski in all seven continents. I have only bare-foot skied in one continent, traveled to six continents, and observed in six continents. Each one but Antarctica.

McDonald is a great observatory but it is only one longitude. When it is daytime at McDonald, it is nighttime somewhere else. We had to send people somewhere else to follow the star around the globe as the night progresses. So that's the Whole Earth Telescope, the WET, and all of my other continental observing was for the Whole Earth Telescope.

All of the observatories were *very* different. At Siding Springs, Australia where I first observed, it was similar to McDonald in that it is a University-run facility. They do have more telescopes, however. The day staff was very conscientious, but if you were working on something with them at ten, noon, or two, they would get up and leave because they had to have their tea. You could be right in the middle of fixing something and they will say, "Have to run now, it's teatime!" But fifteen minutes later, they came back and always did a good job.

At La Palma in the Canary Islands, their TQ was *very* fancy and *very* expensive. We had monogrammed plates for dinner, a choice of two entrées, and if you did not like those, you could make up something yourself like steak, for example, which was always available. The waiter came and served you soup at every meal, there was wine at every meal as well as juices, soft drinks, and almost anything you wanted. Very good food, very expensive, but when you are a thousand miles away from home it is nice to have a good meal you can depend on.

At ESO, the European Southern Observatory, in Chile, I observed on the 40-inch telescope. They deliver your night lunch to the dome, which is quite nice, and you could go down to the kitchen for a night lunch and get cooked-to-order dinners. They also had a TV/Video/Movie room and we went down on some cloudy nights with our European collaborator and his other friends to watch movies. They said, "Look, let's go watch a movie." And one of his friends said, "Well, let's not watch any American movies; they're all terrible!" I took only slight offense to this because when I looked at their movie collection, all they had were American B movies so, of course, they were all terrible.

I observed in China at the Xing Long Station near Beijing. The food there–well, they served us different food than they served the Chinese astronomers; we had our own table, our own set of drinks, and our own food. We felt very awkward because we didn't want to be singled out and given special treatment. We are observers, we eat good food, we eat bad food, but we shouldn't receive special treatment. But, they would have none of it. The food there was fine until I ate a pear without peeling the skin off. I thought I was being very good because I washed it in bottled water, which is more than I *ever* do when I travel. I don't worry about it and it never seems to get me. So I washed the pear in bottled water, ate the pear, and I was sick as a dog the next day. Even the Chinese said, "What? You didn't peel it?" I said, "No, it's a pear; why would I peel it?" "We always peel the fruit here," they said. So it was two or three days before I ate again but I did feel better after eating Ed's granola bars for a couple of days before I was able to get back to their Chinese food.

The staff there was very interesting. We needed a focus mechanism at the telescope. Focusing the CCD guider was performed in the control room at the computer screen. But, we needed to look through the eyepiece to focus and there was no way to do both at the same time. We talked to the engineer and said, "We need a way to do this." He said, "OK," and came back with a very nice switch. It had two buttons, and I can't remember if it was a soda can or a juice can, but basically they had taken a can, cut it in half, made a little cylinder out of it, and embedded two buttons in the bottom. It had very good tactile feedback and the buttons were not at all sloppy. We used it and saw how well it worked and made a point of thanking the engineer who built it the next day. The main engineer, as soon as Ed thanked him, got this huge smile on his face and they shook hands for, it must have been two or three minutes, because the engineer was so happy that we appreciated the work he had done for us. At least that is what it seemed from my point of point of view. There wasn't any English or Chinese spoken, except for the very heart-felt thank-you and the smile on the Chinese engineer's face.

In South Africa, I did not observe on a WET run but went there to work with a WET collaborator at the Sotherland Observatory on CCD data reduction processes because the Whole Earth Telescope was starting to think about switching to CCDs from a largely phototube-based network. The telescope worked very nicely, but I usually comment about the food first. They served very large meals, as I remember, and a night lunch of sandwiches and stuff, which was quite good. We didn't have any problems and we didn't meet much of the day staff because everything worked. Cape Town was a very nice place to visit and I enjoyed spending time there. Yes, they had teatime and also ping-pong during lunch.

Unique experiences at McDonald Observatory

I never took my guitar out to McDonald Observatory but now that I think about it, that would have been nice. I used to play drums on the 36-inch dome though. If you hit the dome in the right spot, you can get different resonances and actually different notes and sounds out of it. That is a cloudy-night activity or daytime when we were waiting for it to get dark. We would climb up on top of the roof of the 36-inch dome control room and get good access to the dome. We also climbed the 107-inch many times. We climbed from the inside of the dome on the ladders and then got out on top through a hatch. We went out there just mostly to *say* we went out there, although it was also a nice view from there.

I spilled hot chocolate on one of Ed Nather's laptops once. The display immediately fritzed and it started flashing at me. I turned it off and just figured I was dead. I did my best to clean it up and when I turned it back on, it worked, and I only lost about twenty minutes of data. Chuck Claver went out a month later with the same laptop and when he came back he said, "By the way, Scot, I cleaned up the hot chocolate on the laptop. Ed won't notice it."

My wife and I met in the lab. Atsuko Nitta was a student in the same lab and the day we met was probably the most angriest I had ever been. I was told I had to take the place of another student who could not, for some reason, go out to the Observatory to do her science. So it was decided, by someone, that I would go and take her place. I think I said, "I will go but I want to observe my stars." I was being told no, you must go and observe her stars. So I was discussing my displeasure with this decision when Atsuko walked in. She says she said, "Hi," to me and I just scowled at her. That was her first impression of me.

How things changed from that is a good question. I guess it is the usual story. I did train Atsuko a lot at observing and we did spend some time at McDonald together. I found that me on my knees was about the same height as her standing. So rather than moving the floor of the 36-inch up and down all the time to check the instrument, we just left the floor at her height and I got down on my knees to see through the telescope. Maybe that's what got me into kneeling down and asking her to marry me.

Atsuko Nitta at the Controls of the 36-inch telescope. Time exposure while dome is rotated.
Photo by Karen S. Winget.

When we were both looking for jobs, we wanted to be together but we were not limiting our choices. We figured, if we get any job offer we will see what we can do from there—maybe we can find something else and maybe not. So I applied for my current job at Apache Point Observatory as a Sloan Survey observer. At the same time, Atsuko had an interview for Subaru Telescope in Hawaii, which we thought was the perfect job for her because it was in a Japanese facility, in the United States. She came back from her interview with a very bad feeling. They had not asked if she was married, what she wanted to do, or what her spouse was doing... nothing like that came up at all. While conducting the interview in Japanese, they even asked her if she could read and write Japanese, despite knowing that she got her master's degree at a prestigious women's university in Tokyo.

Whereas, in my interview at Apache Point, we discussed yes, I have a spouse, and they said, "Oh, maybe we can find something for her here, too." They were willing to work at it and hired us both.

Advice on becoming an astronomer

Ten years ago was a time when jobs in astronomy were fairly hard to come by and a lot of astronomy departments were not admitting people, thinking it irresponsible to train people for a job they can't possibly get. But in my point of view, if I could do astronomy for however long I am in grad school and that's it, well then, I'll spend that many years doing astronomy. It is what I enjoy doing and that will be great. Besides, there are other skills I can learn as an astronomer that will parlay into other types of jobs. But, if I get one job after that, well then, it is two more years I can be an astronomer. So whenever it ends, it's over and I have had this much time being an astronomer. I am grateful that I was given a chance despite poor job prospects. If you really want to do astronomy and you enjoy it, don't be intimidated by the lack of jobs or anything else. You know you can do what you love as long as you can, and enjoy it for what it's worth.

McDonald Observatory provided me a chance to do a thesis that I could not have done anywhere else because I got large telescope time on equipment that worked, telescopes that worked, and staff that supported me. I couldn't have done it anywhere else and no one else could have done it elsewhere. I didn't have to worry about somebody *scooping* me because no one else could get the telescope time I got. McDonald Observatory made a very valuable contribution to my career and made one career possible that would not have been otherwise.

As you walk into the 36-inch telescope dome from the local road, on the cement platform that the 36-inch control room and telescope dome sit on, there is a little wall just three or four feet off the ground. On nice summer nights, between guiding the telescope every few minutes, and if things were going well, I would just lie down on that wall, look straight up at the sky, and ponder the universe while my data were being collected on my laptop. That was one of my favorite things to do on that telescope. To this day, when I think of McDonald Observatory, I think of the 36-inch telescope.

Michel Breger

Prof. Dr. Breger is at the Institut für Astronomie, Wien, Austria and an adjunct professor at the University of Texas at Austin. This interview takes place at an outdoor café in Vienna, Austria, near Dr. Breger's home.

I had no astronomy awareness when I was a child; none whatsoever. I had no astronomy awareness when I was an undergraduate; none whatsoever. I was a physicist, I was a mathematician, and I never even gave a thought to astronomy or astronomers. To me astronomers were strange old men with hats looking through telescopes, enjoying the beauty of the heavens to find something, some new star. This is a typical misconception.

When I was looking for a masters project, I investigated plasma physics and a few other branches of physics, and I was told I should investigate astronomy. So I thought, I'll just go and have a look at the Observatory. It was the Royal Observatory in Cape Town, South Africa. As soon as I knew there were actually physicists and scientists looking for laws of the universe, investigating what made the stars tick, I went from one extreme to the other. I became an astronomer within five minutes and I was hooked.

When I came to McDonald Observatory my impression was very positive. The entire Observatory, the atmosphere, the food, and the scientific flavor, were great - we discussed science at dinnertime around the table, intermixed with gossip, of course. It was a very positive experience to observe at McDonald, which is why I went back so much. I didn't *have* to observe as much as I did in the beginning, but I did.

Advice to young astronomers

My advice to a high school senior interested in astronomy and thinking about studying astronomy is this: in addition to astronomy, an astronomer has to be a very capable mathematician, a very capable astrophysicist, and a very capable chemist. Astronomy alone is not enough. The most highly motivated people are often the amateur astronomers and this is great. It is not enough, however. Today you also have to be a manager. Everybody has to manage grant proposals, get money to hire people, be able to handle bureaucracy, without it killing you and your science. Usually now, you are part of a bigger team, so you have to be a team player and you have to enjoy working on a team.

If you want to be an amateur astronomer, this is a great time to be one because you can now buy good astronomical equipment for little money. You can have a lot of fun, you can do many projects, and you can see a lot of objects. If you want to do research, it is not expensive to buy a CCD photometer. You can do real astronomy even as an amateur if you want to. You can stay a complete amateur, enjoy the heavens or do research. You can go as far as you want.

Don Winget

I am a professor at the University of Texas, with the Astronomy Department and McDonald Observatory. Dear Visitor, you are at my favorite spot on this Earth. It is a portal to the unimaginably vast, and endlessly fascinating, final frontier. **My name is Don Winget and I am a voice of McDonald Observatory.** I can't remember a time when I wasn't interested in astronomy and horses. I read articles on space in "Highlights" magazine when I was old enough to read; after I was married, we discovered my wife's grandmother had written the articles I read. I later read, "We Are Not Alone," by Walter Sullivan and this fueled a serious interest in extraterrestrial life. One of my most vivid early memories was watching a parade, after dark in Champaign, Illinois, where I grew up. I forgot all about the parade and lay on my back on the curb, wondering about those points of light in the sky.

When we were in junior high, one of my best friends, John Brinegar, and I used to borrow the high school's small refracting telescope for stargazing. We also used his folks' short-wave radio to time lunar occultations—when the Moon passes in front of a star, then we sent our timings along with our exact location to the U.S. Naval Observatory, to Lt. David Dunham, if I recall correctly, for use in accurately determining the position of the Moon; this gave us a sense of contributing in some small way to the Apollo program. We also were among the first, if not the first, to visually report observations of the disaster on Apollo 13. We were outside in John's backyard just looking to see if we could see it pass over when we saw a large, gray, sort-of cloud about the size of the Moon—and it was moving!

If you can, always work with the best

John and I went to the monthly open house usually put on by the University of Illinois. Professor Stan Wyatt usually did the public lecture and slide show; he would take the time to talk to us about a career in astronomy. He adviscd an undergrad degree in physics, so that is what we did. I got involved in some upper division astronomy classes, and a graduate physics class with Jim Truran and Don Lamb. They steered me to the University of Rochester to work with Hugh Van Horn on the theory of white dwarf stars for my Ph.D. They reasoned that if you want to do something, find out who is the best in the world at it, and go work with them. That is what I did. I recommend this philosophy to you; you have to flap just as hard to fly with the buzzards as with the eagles.

243

At Hugh's suggestion, I started working on pulsating white dwarf stars; it seemed like an interesting way to probe the interiors of these collapsed stars. That is how Carl Hansen, of the University of Colorado, became my co-advisor: Hugh was the leading expert in the theory of white dwarf stars, and Carl was the leading expert in the computation of nonradial pulsation properties of stars. By then we knew that white dwarf stars pulsated in nonradial g-modes, which were mostly sloshing back and forth horizontally, moving only slightly vertically against the strong gravity of the white dwarf. This sloshing causes periodic heating, which shows up as brightness variations with the period of the pulsations.

I finished up my Ph.D. explaining why the known pulsating white dwarf stars pulsated, and predicting the existence of another class of white dwarf pulsators. By this time Hugh and Carl had managed to turn me into a scientist; I'll never know *how* they did it, but they did it. Interestingly, I thought of Hugh as my professional father, and found out his other students, all close friends, thought of him the same way. I feel the same way about my students: they are my professional children and friends.

I was finishing up my Ph.D. and I found myself thinking about where to go for a postdoc—the typical next step in astronomy, and talking a lot with Hugh about it. Theory, observation, and instrumentation have to move forward hand-in-hand, if rapid progress is to be made. I knew I could do theoretical astrophysics, so I didn't need to go where there were a lot of other theorists. Following the same logic as when I went to work with Hugh and Carl, I wanted to go where the two best observers in the field were: Texas. Hugh agreed. Rob Robinson was, and still is, the best observer I have ever known. Ed Nather is the best instrumentalist in the field and a terrific observer in his own right. They were a team, they were the best, and I wanted to work with them. Somehow they managed to talk Harlan Smith into hiring me as a McDonald Observatory Postdoctoral Fellow—and me a theorist. I defended my thesis, packed my bags and came to Texas in October 1981.

I knew that the job prospects were rotten, and so were my chances for staying in the field and realizing my dream of being a professional astronomer—they sent a letter cautioning undergrads applying for graduate school in astronomy that there weren't any jobs. I figured when my two years as a postdoc ran out, I would have had the time of my life playing astronomer and when they discovered I was an idiot, and unsuitable for any future employment, I would fade away to the Ozark Mountains in Missouri—a place I particularly liked, and try to combine training horses and running a grocery store and somehow earn a living.

So I was prepared when I got the news from the National Science Foundation that they were going to turn down my application for a grant.

A bolt from the blue

I started searching for the kind of pulsating white dwarf star I had predicted in my thesis should exist. Rob was teaching me how to observe, and Ed had written some new software especially for the search project. They believed in me, but thought I should put my own efforts into testing my theory if *I* believed it. That is probably good advice for other theorists.

There were only twenty-six candidates possible, and only one that was really hot enough to fill the bill—at least according to our theory. It was a star called by the poetic name GD 358. But Rob had pointed out, in the beginning of the project, that we must determine not only if there were stars pulsating at the temperature we expected, but that the other stars we did not expect to pulsate did not. So we went out every two months or so, systematically observing each object for four hours to see if it pulsated.

It was the end of May; we were not scheduled to observe GD 358 until our July run. There was a big meeting scheduled in Boulder, Colorado, on stellar pulsations a few days after this run. Gilles Fontaine—my best friend, professional brother, and collaborator on all this science, and I were to give a joint review on the theory and observations of pulsating white dwarf stars, and some of the real pundits in the field were going to explain why our results were wrong—or so we had heard. I had just gotten the bad news from the NSF about my grant, and so knew that not just my observing run, but my run in astronomy was coming to an end. Even if GD 358 pulsated, finding it in July *after* the big Boulder meeting would not be soon enough to save my career; it would be only a minor footnote in astronomy. My thoughts turned to training horses and the Ozark Mountains...

So there we were, Rob and I, on the 36-inch telescope, observing a star that wasn't a good candidate to pulsate. Gilles was up in the library of the 82-inch, preparing our talk for the Boulder meeting—in all probability my swan song in astronomy. We were watching the data come in; Ed's software painted the light curve of the target star and a nearby comparison star on an CRT screen display, updating with a new point coming at the end of every integration, typically every five seconds or so. The brightness of the target star was on top, with the comparison star plotted below it. If the comparison star, presumed a constant star, goes up and down in the same way as the target star you know you've got cloud, or some sort of variable atmospheric extinction, or sky brightness, or something that is not in the target star—this was the genius of Ed's two-star photometer, which we were using in those days. If the star was not a pulsator, the two stars would "dance together" as we liked to say. If conditions were good, you got two parallel lines we called "railroad tracks." We had two hours of data by then, so we were pretty sure this target was a constant star—the data were nothing but railroad tracks.

All of the sudden a West Texas thunderstorm blows up. The clouds and rain were a good ways off, but we had been watching the lightning strikes in the distance between guiding on our quite uninteresting target. We were ready to close as soon as the rain got close enough—if it did. We saw a flash, heard a loud crack, and all the power went off in the dome.

Lightning strikes at McDonald. The 82-inch is in the foreground at left. Note the fires near the horizon at the right. Photo by Pamela Gay.

When the power returned, I fully expected Rob to say, let's go back and get our last two hours on that object. Surprisingly, at least to me, he said, "Let's set up on one of your July objects..." I think he knew GD 358 was on our July list. Every time he looked at my list he saw it sitting there with five asterisks beside it as my best candidate for pulsations. Well, I set up on that puppy quicker than you would believe.

I watched the first few points of the light curve come in to make sure I had set up the target and comparison star properly. Only a few points had come in and I was just beside myself with anticipation. I looked at Rob, and said, as casually as I could manage, "Watched pots never boil, and a watched star never pulsates…I'll go grab some night lunch at the TQ; let me know if it pulsates." I went slowly, or so it seemed, to the TQ and sat down with my night lunch. I had put about one bite in my mouth when the phone rang. I turned and said to the astronomer sitting next to me—I've forgotten who it was—and said very calmly, "That's Rob, calling to tell me that our star pulsates…" That was the last calm thing I said. I went back to the dome, and the target light curve was rising, but the comparison star was flat. Rob said, "There are a lot of things that can make a light curve to go down, but very few that will make it go up. This is a pulsator." We got Gilles from the 82-inch and we watched for the next several hours, celebrating. That morning I called Hugh and Carl and told them the news.

Gilles and I re-wrote our talk slightly. We added a section after discussing our prediction of pulsating DB white dwarf stars, and then we showed the light curve of the first of the class, GD 358. At the meeting our talk created quite a buzz. John Cox, one of the pioneers of modern stellar pulsation theory and one of the men the meeting was dedicated to, stood up and pointed out that in the 300-year history of research on pulsating stars, no pulsating stars had ever been predicted theoretically before being observed. His perspective was extremely important to my career. A stellar pulsation expert, who was working at the NSF, Morris Aizenman, informed me that the NSF had prepared press releases on the discovery, and the powers that be had reversed their preliminary decision and my grant would be funded after all.

It was my fifteen minutes of fame. I did some radio and TV interviews, and repeated the story over and over to various reporters. The NSF sent me a package of all the papers that ran the story; there were hundreds from around the world. The most fun I had was when my dad called. He happened to be up near Chicago getting his car worked on, he wandered into a coffee shop, picked up a Chicago newspaper, and there was his son on the front page. I remember thinking about how weird it was to have people all over the world reading about *my* science in their newspapers; I remember thinking the next day that people all over the world were wrapping their fish with stories about my science…

From that moment, I knew I would have a career in astronomy; and although I did go on to train horses as a hobby, the grocery store in the Ozarks was put on permanent hold. I was offered faculty positions at a number of places, but I held out for a chance to be part of Harlan's family at the University of Texas, to work with the folks here. I was lucky enough to join the faculty and here I am, the same person I would have been as an amateur astronomer running a grocery store in the Ozarks, where I would have been, but for a bolt of lightning.

Some advice and a warning for young players

Ed Salpeter, my professional grandfather, likes to talk about young scientists as young players—I like that image. I think people are drawn to science, particularly astronomy and space science, by the same thing that has always motivated human exploration, internal or external. It is the desire to stand somewhere no one has ever stood before, think a thought no one has ever thought before, paint an image no one has ever seen before. In science, if you are lucky, there will be moments where you will know something about the universe that no human being has ever known before; there is nothing like that feeling. You are the only human being who has ever lived who knows what you know. *Warning...* this feeling is intoxicating, and addictive!

One great thing about UT is the tremendous quality of the graduate students we have here. I have had the privilege of supervising or co-supervising more than ten Ph.D.'s so far, and have three grad students working with me at the moment, and an undergrad student. These are among the best and brightest the world has to offer. If you wonder if astronomy is for you, and you are good in science, there is one litmus test. The one sure-fire predictor of success is the fire inside. If a student burns inside to do astronomy, they will succeed. It is exciting to help them learn to do science and watch them take-off and fly on their own. As Frank Bash always points out, if you get discouraged by reading the news, just spend some time with these young people; it gives you hope for our future.

On white dwarf stars and being an astronomer

Ed Nather and I have worked together on white dwarf stars since we met at a conference at the University of Illinois in 1975. They are interesting for many reasons. Most stars in the universe are already white dwarf stars or will become white dwarf stars. This is the most common endpoint for the evolution of stars, and is the ultimate fate of our Sun. White dwarf stars contract after using up all their nuclear energy, and are about the size of the Earth, and half the mass of the Sun—they are very dense and initially very hot objects, so a lot of interesting and exotic physics goes on inside them. They have no more fuel, and they can't contract, so they cool. We have shown that if you identify the coolest white dwarf stars in a group of stars, you have found the oldest stars, and their temperature gives you a measure of the age of the group. The white dwarf stars give us an archeological record of the history of star formation; the first white dwarf stars ever formed in our galaxy are still visible. We can use them to measure the age of the galaxy and set a limit on the age of the universe.

We have used white dwarf stars as the veritable Swiss army knife of the sky: you can use them to study condensed matter physics, explore weak interaction physics, prove stellar evolution, measure the age of the galaxy, or search for extra-solar planets. Like the Swiss army knife, they are simple, so they have a lot of uses. When we run out of things to do with them, or understand them completely, I'm sure we'll move on. We keep trying to move on, but then we always come up with a new angle, or something new related to the white dwarf stars. When an area of astronomy becomes a fad and we can hear the "thundering hoof beats," as Ed likes to say, then we step aside and invent another field. Working with Ed Nather is really great; his instrumental genius and scientific vision make anything possible. It is sure a lot of fun. I like to quote the comedian, Steve Martin, "The most amazing thing of all, is I get paid for doing this!"

Cloudy night entertainment

If there is some cloud, and you can't do any serious work, but there are occasional holes, you take data just to make sure you can't do science. But be careful to throw away marginal data. As Rob Robinson always says, "The only data worse than no data is marginal data." If there is an eyepiece or imager on the telescope it is always fun to just look at planets, galaxies, and nebulae; I still have the heart of an amateur astronomer.

An occasional completely cloudy night at the mountain is greeted, particularly on a long run, with some indifference. You work on a paper, or calculation, or read some scientific paper you've been meaning to get to; but after four or five consecutive cloudy nights, some of us get stupid. I remember learning to juggle with pool balls on one cloudy stretch. Another time, after about the fifth cloudy night, my graduate students and I cleared the tables and chairs out of the dining room, took off our shoes, grabbed towels and a chalkboard eraser, and played eraser hockey. We are sliding around in our socks, just like on ice skates, body checking, and swinging our towels like hockey sticks. Nobody was ever called for "high-toweling."

One time a bunch of us were passing around a copy of "Surely You're Joking Mr. Feynman" and I noticed a passage describing how to pick locks. We gathered the necessary items and I pulled up a chair in front of the door to the kitchen, which to our frustration was always locked after dinner, while a friend read the passage aloud. After a half an hour of futzing around, bingo, the door opened. We all helped ourselves to the hidden cache of ice cream in the kitchen freezer, then relocked the door. The weather the next night was still awful. The teacher in me couldn't resist the opportunity to teach everyone else to pick locks.

Everyone learned quickly—my students were eager learners; then we started having contests to see who could pick the lock the fastest. The record was about five seconds.

Unfortunately, the fun ended several days later when someone discovered, not the missing ice cream, but that the lock was worn out. The lock was replaced and went from the three-tumbler type to five tumblers, which ended our foray into breaking and entering—temporarily. But there is no way to keep frustrated astronomers from ice cream. One of our students was thin enough to slide under the bars on the kitchen pass-through and open the door for the rest of us. After a time, he no-longer fit—maybe he'd had too much ice cream. Finally, another student, Todd Watson, went into the machine shop and built a special wrench to open the pass-through doors. Now when there is ice cream, they just leave it out.

The telescopes and the Davis Mountains

I love all the telescopes at McDonald, but my favorites are the 36-inch, and the 82-inch. After I open the 82-inch dome, I like to stand on the catwalk and watch the sunset; a view I shared many evenings with Harlan and Joan Smith when they were on the mountain. Twilight slowly transforms the majesty of the mountain skyline and the dark night sky opens the door to the limitless universe.

I still have the same feeling I did twenty years ago when I walk up the hill from the TQ to the 82-inch. It must be the same feeling a captain has as he walks up to his ship. I sailed her first as Rob's crewman, now I've returned as the captain; it is an honor and a privilege to be at the helm. You can feel the history, the spirits of the astronomers past, present, and future swirl around as you anticipate the discoveries the night may bring. I always say to myself, I can't believe they are letting *me* sail that magnificent, grand old lady through the sea of stars *tonight*.

I owe my career to the 36-inch, but that is not why I love observing on that telescope. Why I love it is because it puts you close to the sky, you can walk outside the small dome and look up into a really dark sky—most of my observing over the years is in the dark of the Moon. The night sky at McDonald is awesome. Not in the tired sense, of "Awesome!" but in the true sense that it fills you with wonder. It gives you some perspective; it is humbling. You are but a small part in a vast creation. You may be small, but when you are here and looking up you are *connected*, connected through the creation to the creator. McDonald is a very special and spiritual place for me. Even before I became a Christian, I always thought of it as my church, or more accurately my sanctuary.

As both a scientist and a Christian I am asked about conflict between my science and my faith. I see no conflict between the two, nor do most of my colleagues, whether Christian, Islamic, Jewish, Hindu, Buddhist, atheist, or whatever. It is interesting that science has recently shown us that the universe is specially "tuned" for our existence, and that there was a beginning, but we must be cautious not to take this too far. Conflicts between science and religion arise when people try to turn religion into science or, worse yet, science into religion.

The Davis Mountains are my favorite spot on the Earth. It is always fun listening to people from other countries, the far-away romantic places of my childhood, come to observe, or just to visit. They remark on what an interesting, romantic place Mt. Locke is. They are right. When I was engaged to my wife, Karen, I brought her to the top of the mountain; she hadn't been up here since her dad brought her when she was a child. It was dark as we drove up, so we turned our headlights off. We got out of the car and walked around the ring road past the TQ, to the flat spot just past the 36-inch telescope. We were picking our way along, looking down in the darkness of Mt. Locke. When we stopped, she looked up. She didn't say anything, she just cried. I knew then I was marrying the right one.

Karen and Don Winget on Mt. Locke, just above House A. Photo by Maegan Moorhead.

251

A startling cool breeze blows away the tortured clouds. Revealed, the brilliant blue sky smiles and calls; go to the domes, go to the domes... The Quarters empty and the astronomers boil out into the pristine twilight. The magnificent white domes sparkle in the eyes of the astronomers as they approach the domes. The shutters whisper open relieving the stifling heat from the dome bodies. The astronomers sing and dance checking their equipment and marveling at the beauty of their telescopes. The hearts of the giant steel and glass structures begin to pulse. One by one the stars in the heaven blink on announcing, we are here...look at us...we have many stories to tell tonight. The domes groan as they turn, framing each face of the occupants, man and man made. The telescopes pointing precisely at their beloved heavenly objects, listen silently to the tales of long, long ago...

ksw

Chapter 9 An Evening in the Dome

Anjum Mukadam, senior graduate student; Ian Yanagisawa, Board of Visitors member; Don Winget, professor, University of Texas; David Reaves, high school student; Mike Reed, professor, Southwest Missouri State; Donna Slaughter, high school teacher; Winston Crowder, Board of Visitors member; and Karen Winget. All narrators are in the 82-inch dome and at the beginning we are looking at the 82-inch telescope and discussing the new instrument, Argos. It is the 2002 July Board of Visitors meeting at McDonald Observatory.

Don: This is Anjum Mukadam; she is the senior graduate student in our group, working on a project to find new pulsating white dwarf stars, the aim of which ultimately is to find extra-solar planets around the stable white dwarf pulsators. Anjum is going to describe the instrument she and Ed Nather have constructed.

Anjum: Hi, we are using a CCD photometer we call Argos. At the end of the telescope, the prime focus, you can see a CCD Camera. There is a cable running down the side of the telescope, which carries the image from the camera to the computer in the control room. The camera sits on a focus assembly, which can move in and out to focus the images. That is basically it: just a camera that takes photographs of a piece of sky. The light enters the primary mirror and reflects right into the camera so it is very simple, there is just one reflection at the primary.

Don: This instrument is a revolution in astronomy and it is a revolution in high-speed photometry. If you think about it, it is probably the simplest instrument ever made. It is simpler than a man with an eye and an eyepiece because the only external optical surface, as Anjum said, is the primary mirror of the telescope. This is the equivalent of you looking at a primary mirror with nothing else in the way.

Karen: The CCD camera is like a video camera taking a picture of the star image on the glass, the primary mirror of the telescope.

Winston: Where are your controls for getting the proper focus?

Anjum: Inside the control room, and we have a hand-paddle and even out here in the dome. So we just push buttons, look at the images, and watch the stars grow smaller as they get more into focus.

Winston: And the smaller it is, the more in focus it is?

Anjum: Yes. And we move the telescope with the control panel down there on the main floor of the dome.

Winston: Do you have a video screen there?

Anjum: No, we have coordinates displayed so if you want to move the telescope to a particular piece of the sky, you just get the right coordinates and move it by hand. I am not sure if you have been to the 107-inch, but it is more automated. This telescope, the 82-inch, is an older telescope and is more hands-on. I kind of like it that way. There are many instruments you can put on this telescope and some of them have eyepieces. A few years ago, we had an eyepiece in our older instrument and we used to look at the image in the eyepiece and focus from the dome.

Winston: How do you capture the images that you want?

Anjum: We have a computerized data acquisition system.

Winston: You take the picture of the screen to the computer?

Anjum: The camera at the end of the telescope takes an image of the star on the mirror. Then, the images run down the cable right into the computer and we just record them.

Winston: Do you record them onto a hard disk?

Anjum: Yes, on the hard disk and then we make copies on CDs.

Winston: And what do you do with them?

Anjum: We reduce the data and get light curves, which we do the science with. We always have two copies of our data and archive it so somebody can come down twenty years later and use the data. I have personally used data that was from thirty years ago. So what we do here is very precious; you have to save *everything*.

Winston: You have used data of thirty years in age?

Anjum: Yes.

Winston: How was it recorded, by hand?

Don: Going backwards in time, before CDs it was on three and a half-inch floppies, before that five and a quarter-inch floppies, before that was digital cassette tapes, before that it was on large magnetic tapes, before that it was on really large floppies—the size of notebook paper— and they ran on the NOVA computers—before that it was on paper tapes, and before that Ed Nather just wrote the number down. Because we were capturing unique moments in time—time-series work—fifty years from now someone may have much better instruments but they will not have *this* moment in time.

Recently, Ed Nather was archiving all of our old data from the old magnetic and paper tapes. He couldn't read a lot of the old magnetic tapes, so the data is lost for all time. The paper tapes were a different story; there were no paper-tape readers anywhere, so Ed just made one. *Every* paper tape read perfectly and he got every number back!

Karen: Can you tell the story about how the camera came into being?

Don: The birth of the instrument was in Ed's mind and is a classic example of how he works—Ed is science driven. First we discussed the science we wanted to do, which was to find a lot of pulsating white dwarfs, enough of them so we could get a sample of the stable ones to look for planets. And the only way we could do that is if we could work on much fainter objects. Photomultiplier tubes counted individual photons and allowed us to work at about 17 to 17.5 magnitude. We really needed to go to 19.5. Where were we going to get this big factor? We were going to have to use larger telescopes. Anjum proved we could do high-speed photometry on the HET, which people said you couldn't do, but we could not get all night, every night, for weeks at a time on the HET, and we needed continuous data.

Ed thought about it and said, "I am going to try and devise the simplest possible system I can that is the most efficient, and wastes the least light." Argos collects between sixty to eighty percent of all the photons that reflect from the primary mirror. And like a lot of things Ed did, everybody said, "There is no way; this won't work, you have to have corrector optics even at prime focus or you will get funny images." Ed proved that the size of the "funny images" was so small that it would not affect the data. That is how Argos was born.

We told Frank Bash about the science and he was pretty excited that we could search for planets with masses and orbits similar to those in our own outer solar system. There is no other game in town for that. From space, NASA's Space Interferometry Mission will get outer giant planets around nearby stars, if it lasts long enough after launch, and Terrestrial Planet Finder will get inner terrestrial planets, when it's launched and for

$890 Million, but Argos will find outer planets like those in our own solar system. It will do it soon, and for less money.

Winston: For how much?

Don: $60,000 a year is about what it will cost to run the whole program. Argos cost $45,000. Frank was really sold on the science. He knows Ed, and he knew if Ed thought he could do it, Ed could do it. Frank didn't say, "Go write a proposal for a government grant." Frank said, "How much do you think it will cost to build this, Ed?" Don't tell Frank this, but Ed just pulled a number out of the air. Ed said, "mmm…$45,000." And Frank said, "You got it." After we walked out, Ed said, "I hope I can do it for that." I am sure Frank knew that Ed had thought about this a lot in advance, and his best guess is usually better than most detailed cost-studies by legions of accountants. Frank gave us the money and Ed and Anjum began working on it. They ordered this "off-the-shelf CCD camera," Ed worked on the software, and Anjum and Ed worked together on the hardware with the guys in Austin. They got the money last April 2002, Argos was on the telescope November 1st, and the first night was first light and it got first science. Everything worked. Immediately. And Ed did it for less than $45,000.

Winston: Well, that ought to set some records there.

Don: I am sure it does. I have never heard of an instrument getting built and put on the telescope that quickly. As Frank figured, Argos has breathed new life into the 82-inch. It is now more heavily subscribed, and occupies a unique niche in astronomy worldwide.

Ian: You might tell a little bit more on how you are using the observations to achieve your objective of looking for the planets.

Anjum: Our basic science goal is to find more stable pulsators. My masters work was on one star, R548, and I analyzed thirty years of data on this star. I was trying to measure a change in the pulsation period of the star, and I found that the change is so small that I cannot measure it. So these types of stars are extremely stable and that is what we are after. The reason why we are after them is the following:

If there is a planet around a star, you will expect the star to show some wobble, some motion around the common center of mass between the star and the planet. Since the star is such a stable pulsator, or clock, every time the star is coming towards Earth in its orbit around the common center of mass, our pulse *timings* will change. When it goes away again, our pulse timings will change again, and we can measure that and use it as a means of detecting the planet.

Don: Let me inject something there because that sounds like it is a Doppler effect, but it's not; it's more than that. As the star is moving towards you, the pulses are constantly getting to you sooner and sooner and sooner so it is a cumulative effect. You are really measuring, not a velocity, but an acceleration and that makes it more sensitive than a Doppler measurement.

That means we can pick up signatures of planets in a small fraction of the total orbit, so we are sensitive to a Jupiter-mass planet at Jupiter's distance and a Uranus-mass planet at Uranus' distance. This is well outside the typical range that planets have been detected so far and a fundamental leap in our ability to find solar systems similar to ours. And we will know long before NASA launches its mission.

Ian: So using this method, you will be able to look at a lot more possible solar systems, and the amount of observation time on each individual star is a lot less.

Don: Yes. Anjum is busy right now trying to build our sample. Go ahead and explain what you are doing.

Anjum: Well, you might have heard of surveys like the Sloan Digital Sky Survey and the Hamburg Quasar Survey. These basically result in thousands and thousands of stars. So we try to pick out candidates from those thousands that are likely to be these stable pulsators we want to look at. We observe each candidate for two hours, depending upon how bright it is, and try to determine if they are pulsators. We have found five to date [less than one year later the total is thirty-six and counting!] We have had very bad luck with the weather so far, and we should have found more than five. We hope to find at least seventy stable pulsators and we intend to monitor about thirty of these stars every year ourselves to search for planets.

I just returned from a conference in Naples and five or six groups of scientists from all around the world want to collaborate with us and observe some of our stars for planets. With so many collaborating, we will hopefully manage many more stars a year. So lets say sixty to seventy a year. That means sixty to seventy possible solar systems a year; I think that is quite nice.

Winston: Will any of them build instruments like this or will they take your information and use it in another way?

Anjum: Many people already have CCD photometers, but they are not like this. They have it at the Cassegrain focus, which means one more reflection. They are similar instruments and can do the job, just not as efficiently.

Don: Argos is being copied. In fact, Denis Sullivan is working on a copy in New Zealand right now.

Winston: You don't copyright your stuff?

Don: It is the opposite; we encourage anybody and everybody to use anything we have. Anjum is in the process of putting together a Website to list all of the candidate objects she has found and all the ones she knows are pulsating. So if somebody else wants to observe a star, that means we don't have to do it ourselves, and things will move along much faster. The beauty of astronomy, if you have the right attitude, is that there is a lot more to do than there are astronomers to do it. So anytime anybody else wants to do something in your field, that's great. You can do something else, or more of that. Ed likes to say, "It is amazing how much science gets done when you don't care who gets the credit." In this case, we will end up with a much larger sample. Ideally, we want to end up with a sample of a hundred to a hundred and twenty stars so we can say something like, "If the numbers are small, like a few percent of the systems are like our own, we will still find them." Or, "If half of all stars have planetary systems dynamically similar to our own, then we will know that." But you really need a fairly large sample in case you don't find much. Your "null results" still need to be significant.

Winston: Now, the stars you are focusing on, are they in our galaxy or are they in another galaxy?

Anjum: They are in our galaxy.

Karen: Shall we go look at the images on the computer screen?

Anjum: Sure.

[*We have now left the dome floor and are in the control room.*]

Anjum: I am going to show you some images. On the screen is an image of the star field that includes our target and comparison stars. The light curve is extracted from the time series of images and displayed as a plot. The light curve of the pulsating star looks like a wave. The peak of the wave is when the star is at its brightest and the trough of the wave is when it is at its faintest. Now, unfortunately, the clouds rolled in so you see gaps in the data, but it is very clearly a pulsator.

Winston: Absolutely!

Karen: Anjum, please explain the CCD chip a little bit.

Anjum: Well, this chip has 512 by 512 pixels so it is about a quarter-million individual detectors. It is basically similar to a digital camera but it is scientific grade, it is more sophisticated and uniform. The field of view on the chip is big enough for our target star and a few other comparison stars. If you have a very large field of view, then it takes more time to read it out. When we do time-series work, we need short integration times, like five seconds or ten seconds, typically. So if you have too large a chip, which we don't need, it will take too much time to read it out and we will lose our times sensitivity. So a small chip is very ideal for our work.

Karen: You are only using half of the chip to take the image?

Anjum: Actually, that is right. There is the other portion of the chip that is masked and when one side of the chip is receiving light, taking data, the other portion of the chip is masked. When the data side finishes the integration, or exposure, all the data is transferred to the masked half and the data side will immediately start the next integration. The masked portion will then read out in 700 milliseconds and will send the data here to the computer where it will make an image. We actually have zero dead time; we don't lose any time at all between integrations.

I used the HET some time ago and even though it is currently frame-transfer like this one, they have a 7.5-second dead time and lose observation time. So Argos is a delightful instrument for me...no dead time.

Here are some other things that we have found. This one is a 19th magnitude variable star. It is the faintest variable ever found in this class of pulsators. We have a long list of candidate stars, this was the third one I tried, and it pulsated on the very first night. So I was very happy.

Karen: Now tell us the rest of the story.

Anjum: It's not quite so happy most of the times. The last few months we have had really bad weather, clouds, high humidity, or too much wind. Something like that can kill our ability to detect the pulsations in the star. If it is too cloudy, you just don't get anything. And of course, sometimes it is very clear and beautiful but you have just chosen the wrong star and they don't pulsate.

Karen: And you watch them for a couple hours and they still don't pulsate.

Anjum: Yes, so we have had hours of data on things that don't pulsate. We just found this particular star two nights ago and it was a very joyful event. There was lots of dancing in the control room then.

Winston: Can you go back to these stars and check them again?

Anjum: Yes, I intend to do that in August; I will be back here in two weeks.

Karen: When you have observed all your candidate stars, and you know they pulsate, what do you do next to detect the planets?

Anjum: The planet detection will take a few years. You have to monitor them every year for a few years and see if you see any change in the pulse timing, in the arrival times of light from the star. It needs a few years of monitoring. Actually, there is another junior colleague of mine, Fergal Mullally; he is from Ireland and joined our group. He is visiting home at the moment so he is not here but his Ph.D. work will be monitoring, for four or five years, many of the stars that I find. Hopefully, he will be the one who will find some planets. I think I will graduate before we find any, but in a few years' time, we will have some to talk about.

Don: Here is a plot Anjum can show you on the computer screen that shows what a detection is going to look like.

Anjum: Oh, yes. This is a simulation that spans over twenty years. This is what a Jupiter around a white dwarf will look like. If there is no planet then your light curve will be a straight line but if there is a planet like a Jupiter, then this line will look like a wave. It is going to be a very easy detection because this technique is very sensitive.

Don: The thing to take away from all this is: the reason this works and is so sensitive, as Ed likes to point out, it is because *time* is the quantity we can measure most accurately as human beings. We can measure time with much greater relative precision than mass, distance, or any other fundamental quantity. We are making a measurement of time; that is why this works and why we can get such incredible precision. The other thing, as you have seen, it is really a simple instrument in conception. It is a simple idea in execution.

By the way, it was interesting to hear the politicians today, and the University leaders alike, talking about how we need to reach out to the students and the high school science teachers. We are doing this in this project today. The tall fellow over there, David Reaves, is a high school student and he is working on this project with us. Although she is not in the dome at the moment, also working with us is Donna Slaughter; she is a high school science teacher, teaching astronomy at Stony Point High School in Round Rock, Texas.

It is always important to stay ahead of the curve, by the time people are talking about something, you need to be already doing it. It was that way with the first global network of telescopes, the Whole Earth Telescope (WET). Everybody was talking about global networks, and we just did it.

Winston: You and Ed set it up.

Don: Yes, with our colleagues all around the world.

Winston: Oh, I remember when they first announced it fifteen years ago.

Karen: So, you will be around then for the planet detection in a few years.

Winston: I plan to be!

Karen: Well, it's on archival tape now, Winston. You will be here.

Winston: I will be here. I will come back and do another interview then!

Karen: Yes, we will do that. Wouldn't that be fun?

Winston: Great.

Now Sam, a BoV member, and Fern Yanagisawa, his wife, enter the control room. They are celebrating their golden wedding anniversary. Everyone sees a satellite go across the computer screen. There is a lot of chatter. Mike Reed shows the Yanagisawas the stars on the computer screen that Argos is looking at. Anjum talks with Sam Yanagasawa. Sam points out the astronomers needs to guide...

Chapter 10 Critters and Legends

Bob Tull

"Skunk Fishing" and Johnnie Floyd

One time when Johnnie and I were at the Observatory, a plane was coming in with one of our other engineers, and Johnnie volunteered to drive down and pick him up. I went along with him just for the trip. As we drove south from Ft. Davis on the road that goes to Marfa, we spotted a skunk along side the road. It was a beautiful, large, black and white kitty and it scooted off into the brush along side the road. As we passed it, Johnnie commented that he read that the beautiful black and white hairs of a skunk's tail make wonderful fishing lures.

We went down, picked up the passenger at the Marfa airport, turned around, and headed back north. As we passed the point where the skunk had been, the skunk was still there and Johnnie decided to take off after it. He got the gun out of the van, took off into the brush, and brought the skunk's tail back. He said he had placed the shot very carefully to prevent any spraying of the tail and that it would not smell too bad.

In any case, he tied the tail to the back of the van, outside where it could air out on the way back up to the dome. Well, as soon as we got back on Mt. Locke, Curt Laughlin's dog caught wind of the skunk tail and followed us back to the TQ. It was obvious that the skunk tail had to be protected from the dog in some way, so the skunk tail went to the top of the flagpole where it stayed for the next several days until Johnnie was able to transport it back to Austin.

Some months later I asked Johnnie, "Well, how did the skunk tail hairs work for the fishing lure?" He said, "Well, it turns out that fish have pretty good smell organs and they apparently avoid them."

A while ago, Johnnie Floyd's family decided to give him a 70th birthday party and Johnnie's daughter asked us if we would contribute a story about him to add to a book she was putting together. I sent her this story entitled, "Skunk Fishing." In the note Johnnie sent us very recently, thanking us for being at his birthday party, he added some new information to the story of the skunk fishing. Johnnie had housed his boat in a garage on Mt. Locke and was outfitting it in his spare time while working on the telescope. A skunk got loose in the garage and George Grubb managed to shoot the skunk in the garage while it was right under Johnnie's boat. The boat got liberally sprayed. Johnnie made the comment that after that event, the fish didn't even approach the boat anymore. So that is the story of skunk fishing.

George Grubb

Mt. Delores

There is a mountain near here named after a Mexican woman, Delores. She was engaged to marry a sheepherder, and I believe his name was José. When José took the flock out to graze, he would stay out for two or three days at a time. While he was out, Delores would go to the top of this mountain and light a fire. And, every night while José was out with the flock, he would light a fire. That was their communications. Well, Indians killed José, and Delores, until she got physically unable, would climb the mountain every night and light a fire. It wasn't long after she couldn't climb the mountain that she gave up and died. That's a neat story and shows a lot of love and a lot of tenacity.

Bear

Bear hunting used to be a big sport out here and was a necessity because the bears killed the livestock, the rancher's cows and sheep. One time C.O. Finley was bear hunting up around Mt. Livermore. The dogs treed a bear and they shot him. This bear turned out to be way bigger than any of the normal bears in this country, so they sent the head off to the Smithsonian Institute. I don't remember the scientific name for that bear but it's the only one, at least at the time the last story was written, that has been found in the United States.

Mountain lions

One night, I had gone to bed but awoken in a cold sweat hearing this screaming and growling. I grabbed a pistol and ran outside. I had two dogs; one was Sterling, a 40-pound Red Heeler. I had a rock retaining wall around the house and when I opened the door, I saw this mountain lion jump up on the retaining wall with Sterling in his mouth. I ran back in the house, traded the pistol for a shotgun and a flashlight, and took off after the mountain lion. He went around underneath House B dragging the dog. I could track him through there by blood on the grass. I got just over the saddle, the area between Mt. Fowlkes and Mt. Locke, and was looking around when I heard something under a nearby tree. That mountain lion came out from under the tree and took off running. I shot at him and he went down growling and trying to bite himself. The mountain lion was growling and the brush was crashing so I thought, well, I got him; he quit. I went down looking around for the mountain lion when I hear this noise. I turned around, looked up, and I see him. *He* is looking *down* and looking for me. So I shot him again and down he goes again. It was the same thing again, brush crashing, mountain lion growling and screaming, and I couldn't find him again. I spent a little while looking around, but my flashlight was going dead so I head back home. I went back by the tree the mountain lion had come out from under and I found my dog there. I had been so close to the mountain lion that he must have realized he couldn't stay ahead of me and carry that dog, so he put him under the tree and covered him up with a little bit of leaves and dirt.

The next morning I called Jim Espey. The Espeys are an old ranching family around here and he runs dogs after mountain lions because, like bear, they kill the livestock. Jim came up about eight o'clock with the dogs and I took him over where I had last seen the mountain lion. He put the dogs on there and in about fifteen minutes, and they treed the mountain lion across the canyon. Jim rode his mule up over there and said to me, "Well, do you want to shoot that mountain lion?" I said, "No, I don't want to shoot that mountain lion; I just don't want him killing my dog." So Jim went over and shot the mountain lion. I had shot him twice but really hadn't done too much to him. When he skinned the mountain lion out, there was one pellet under his right arm just under the skin and two pellets in his chest just under the skin. That mountain lion had been a little bit further away than I realized and was just out of the range of my shotgun. That mountain lion weighed 220 pounds and was eight and a half feet from the tip of his nose to the tip of his tail.

Since then, one morning I was out on my porch, drinking my coffee. I leaned over the rail and a mountain lion ran through my driveway. So I ran back in, got my gun, and ran back out on the porch. The mountain lion had gone to the highway but a car was coming and he ran back through my driveway. I shot him but he went on up crashing through the brush. I called Tom Brown and said, "Come over here and bring your shot gun, I need some help." At that time, Tom and I had been through police school and he thought something was going down. I said, "No, I just shot this mountain lion but he ran off up in those trees. I know he is wounded but I don't want to go in there by myself looking for a wounded lion." We both went in there and I found him dead; even though I had shot him right through the heart, he had just kept on running.

About a week after that, Curt Laughlin came out of his house, which was above my house, and there was a mountain lion sitting there looking at him. Curt called over to the shop and Fred ran over and shot that one. Another time, Eddie Webster was coming to work, a mountain lion ran out of the housing area across the road in front of him, and he got him.

Another time, in the morning, I was down in the horse pasture trying to catch my favorite horse because I was going to the cavalry demonstration. I couldn't catch my favorite horse, even with a bucket to entice him, so I caught another horse. I was coming back to the corral leading the horse through a little canyon when I looked up, and there is a mountain lion standing there. He is looking at me, swishing his tail and I am looking at him—we are only about 30 feet apart. I'm wondering, should I try and leave this mountain lion, or throw this bucket at him, or what? All of a sudden, the horse sees the mountain lion, stomps her feet, and her ears come up. She didn't get too excited so I tried to lead her off, but she would not turn her head. I didn't want to move too much because I was afraid that lion would attack so I just moved gently. That lion just turned around and went down through the trees a little bit. He looked back at us but kept on going. I went the other way.

Marlyn Krebs

Porcupines

One time, porcupines invaded the place something terrible. Down the south side of the mountain, they just killed dozens and dozens of trees by eating the bark around the trunks. We had a federal trapper in the area, Ross Graves, who lived in town, and he trapped panthers, coyotes, and all the other problem varmints. We asked Ross what could be done about the porcupines but there just isn't a whole lot you can do about it. It even got to the point that we were running over them with cars at night and they would actually flatten our tires. Eventually they just migrated through.

Skongks

The porcupines were a big thing at one time and so were skunks. One night, Gerard de Vaucouleurs arrived at the Observatory and propped open the door of the 82-inch dome while carrying in all of his stuff. Meanwhile, a skunk came in. As you go in the front door of the dome, the secretary's office is first, then the director's office, and the next office was the one de Vaucouleurs was using. The skunk went in de Vaucouleurs office and got under his desk. He is French speaking and phoned me around midnight and said, "Dere eez a skongk undare my deask." We were living in town then so I had to drive from Ft. Davis out to the Observatory. When I got there, sure enough, dere eez a skongk undare hees deask, but he sure didn't want to be. So we closed all the doors going around to the other offices but left the front door open and left the front hall lights on. I found an old bag of potato chips and spread them all the way from de Vaucouleurs' office and out the front door. That skunk just came out to eat the potato chips and went right on out the front door.

Dove

Jim Espey's place...as you are leaving Ft. Davis and go down where the cottonwoods are and turn to go up to the Observatory, way up on the right hand side of the hill is a big ranch home, big, bright-colored brick home and that was Espeys'. Down below it, he had his corrals. Of course, he had his feed there, too, and the doves would swarm to feed on it. Now, the ranchers wanted to get rid of the dove because they could eat as much feed as the cattle—there were just thousands of them. So one day, I got on one side of the feed lot, Preston got on the other, and Sid Bouclé, who owned the Mercantile Store in town, was in the back end of the pick-up on a lawn chair. I think the limit on dove was something like twenty per person, per day, but we had over ninety in the back of the pick up when we were done. We quit shooting and went into town to the old café for coffee and here were the game wardens sitting on the windowsill in front. In hunting season, they were always all over. They could see we had feathers, bloody hands and were a mess, so they yelled, "Dove hunting?" And we said, "Yeah." And they said, "How'd you do?" And we said, "We got over ninety!" They just laughed and laughed.

Another reason we went to the café was to hire Louis Johnson to put on a dove dinner for the whole community. So he cleaned and dressed them all, got two girls to wait on tables, and we had a community dove dinner down at the Louis Café. We used to do stuff like that every once in a while.

Making your own entertainment

I didn't do this but they used to have Donkey Basketball in Ft. Davis. They put straw down on the gym floor—it was asphalt tile then—and played basketball on donkeys. A company from around there brought the donkeys in and they were trained. Some of them were mean as all get out and certain ones would go down under the basket so the rider couldn't shoot. Some of the ranchers came in and, of course, it was hilarious. These cowboys riding these donkeys, no saddle, bareback, of course, and some of the donkeys just wouldn't move. That was a big show when we had the donkey basketball.

But the womanless wedding that the Lion's Club started in Ft. Davis, absolutely jammed the school. I was president of the Lion's Club at that time and all the men in the Lion's Club got together and put on this womanless wedding play. George Grubb, you know George, well, he was the groom and Ross Graves, a federal trapper and a great big guy, he was the bride. They brought John Robert Prude in and it seems to me he was the baby and the reason these two were getting married. They had to bring him in a wheelbarrow he was so big. Anyway, that was a big thing. They wanted us to put it on another night for Marfa and Alpine. You had to make your own entertainment.

Chapter 11 Harlan Stories

Harlan J. Smith,
First Texas Director of McDonald Observatory

Jim Kruger

I want to tell you something. I'm really glad my wife Julia got to meet Harlan. He was sick when she met him but he was just the most incredible guy. And really, no joke, he was the best salesman I ever met. I mean he sold NASA on building the 107-inch at McDonald Observatory for the Moon studies. If he radar-locked on a project, then it was just going to happen; he would find a way to make it happen, period, that's it. It's a done deal.

George E. Grubb

I really enjoyed working for Harlan. He was one of those soft-spoken people who could always get his point across. He would always listen to your point, too. A million times I've heard from him, "Yes George, but..." Harlan had the last say but he always listened. He would say, "I don't think that's a good idea because..." Or, "We can, until we order this..." He would always listen, and then he would say, "Yes George, but..."

He always had dinner for staff at his house and that was nice. As we got larger, that got to be a chore and he didn't have enough room for everybody at one time so he spread us over a couple of weeks, inviting just a few at a time.

Marlyn Krebs

The transition from Chicago to Texas brought Harlan Smith in. He was a great person. He was Harlan and I was Marlyn and he always liked to say "Harlan and Marlyn." He was just a wonderful person to work with. Harlan was real enthusiastic about building and growing—he had a magnificent vision for McDonald Observatory.

I remember the first time I met Harlan. He arrived at McDonald on a Sunday afternoon in this Volkswagen microbus. He, Joan, and their children just appeared on the mountain. Harlan had never been to McDonald before that day and I remember him walking around the catwalk of the 82-inch dome just looking out into the distance. I could see he was having all these ideas already...what we could do here, and what we could do there. Fortunately, a lot of his vision materialized.

Early on, the University applied for a grant from NASA to build a new instrument—the 107-inch telescope. The Board of Regents was to come out to McDonald and meet with a person from the NASA financial offices to see if they would approve or disapprove the grant. Dr. Smith asked me to be in the dome that night because the Board of Regents were going to look through the telescope and he wanted to make sure that everything went fine. This was really important to Harlan because the 107-inch was his telescope. It was his baby. They didn't tell me the name of the person coming from NASA but as it turned out, I knew her; it was Dr. Nancy Roman.

This whole group of cars drove up the mountain road and right on up to the dome. Someone got out and opened the door for this lady to get out. I was up in the 82-inch observing floor, waiting for them at the top of the stairs. This woman came walking up the stairs...she looked at me, I looked at her and she threw her arms around me and hugged me. Harlan Smith just stood there in awe, and most of the Board of Regents had the same expression. After this sudden embrace and after she walked away, Dr. Smith asked me, "How do you know her?" I said, "Well, her bedroom was right next to mine for probably four years during graduate school at Yerkes." She lived with my mother and father then and she is like a sister to me. Dr. Smith walked across the 82-inch dome floor just shaking his head. He is probably still shaking his head.

Bob Tull

Did I tell you about the one where Harlan and I were traveling together? This was 1972, and we were traveling to Geneva Switzerland to a meeting of the ESO [European Southern Observatory] for a conference on large telescopes. Harlan was to give the keynote speech on the first day of the conference. Harlan has always been very scrupulous with his money, with anybody's money...unless, of course, it is to build a telescope. For years he had driven an old VW bus for example, he would not buy a new car. He was finally forced to when that VW bus was stolen from the parking lot on campus, but that is a different story.

The point of this story is that we flew to New York together and from that point Harlan was going on Icelandic Airways because it was cheaper. He would be flying from New York to Reykjavik, Iceland, and then on to Geneva. So we parted company at New York. I went to Geneva and enjoyed the first day of the conference. Harlan wasn't there. The next day Harlan still wasn't there. He finally arrived and gave his keynote speech late.

I talked to him and discovered what the problem had been—there were two. Number 1, Harlan forgot his passport. He called Joan, his wife. She immediately went to the airport with his passport, gave it to an airline pilot who was going to New York; he flew to New York and personally handed the passport to Harlan. Number 2, the flight to Reykjavik. There was a certain amount of security in place in those days and part of the security was a psychological profile. Well, Harlan fit somebody's idea of a psychological profile and they took him into a side room, stripped him down, and inspected him before he was allowed to go on. So this was perhaps, another delay in his flight. You have seen pictures of him; he does not look suspicious.

Of course, because of Harlan's particular astronomical interests, he was always traveling and he was also always very busy in his office. Usually, these two would collide and he seldom ever left his office earlier than five or ten minutes before flight time, but he always made his flights—unless he didn't have his passport.

Tom Barnes

Harlan had this way of looking at you that just bored into you completely. You thought that all your innermost thoughts were completely transparent to him. It was most unsettling when I sat and talked to him because he would just stare at me with his unblinking gaze and serious look on his face. I had the sense that many gears were turning in his head but I didn't know what those gears were grinding out.

Harlan was also very personable. David Evans and I had a knockdown drag-out fight over some thing or other in a public meeting, and at the end of that meeting I went back to my office. Pretty soon, in my inbox from Harlan came this little scrap of paper with a Band-Aid attached to it and it said, "Tom, for one bruised ego. Harlan."

If he were here today, he'd be wearing a PEACE badge. He would definitely be doing that. He was a Quaker, through and through; so he would not be in favor of the second Gulf War, or any War.

But what would he be saying about astronomy and to the visitor of McDonald Observatory? He would take the visitor out, point at the sky and talk about stars. He would show them the Hobby-Eberly Telescope and he would talk about what it can do. He had a way of speaking to the public that was unbelievably charismatic. When you met Harlan Smith, you *knew* you met somebody—there was no doubt. Some people found him "hokey" and I heard him referred to once as the world's oldest Boy Scout. But he just spoke with enthusiasm.

John Gianforte

My name is John S. Gianforte, I am a Board of Visitors member and a voice of McDonald Observatory. Sleeping out in a tent in rural upstate New York exposed me to the night sky, both from an observational and photographic perspective. Since those days in the mid-sixties, I have expanded my activities to teaching and writing astronomy-related material as well as publishing photographs. I have also designed, built, and operated two backyard observatories.

To today's visitor, I hope you visit this great research outpost with humility, respect, and awe. For within its boundaries, we can help unravel the mysteries we have had with us since we became capable of self-awareness.

If you are a visitor one hundred years from now, in 2103, consider all that *you* know of our universe, then consider all that is *still unknown to people of your time*—my future. The difference between the two represents the fondest set of activities that could ever be undertaken by a human being—understanding how we have arrived here and what may be in store for our species in the distant future.

Dr. Harlan Smith and I met, and in 1989 we did a talk show on a Dallas radio station. I personally recorded it and offer it as my contribution to this book. Below are a few of Harlan's statements that demonstrate his genuine ability to explain some difficult concepts and answer tough questions.

Why is studying astronomy important?

Harlan: I think the most basic answer of all is there are not very many people alive who haven't looked up at the sky and wondered; why are we here, where are we in the universe, what are these little specks of protoplasm crawling around on this Earth, where do we fit in the whole scheme of things? That's really a large part of what astronomy is trying to find out. Just get the answers. How big is the universe? How old is the universe? What's in the universe? Where do we fit into it? When did our part of it come into existence? Our Sun, our planets, how did they form, how did they evolve? Are we the only life form anywhere around? These are pretty substantial questions and astronomers are trying to answer them.

Where is the McDonald Observatory?

Harlan: We are out in West Texas. By the way, anybody in this part of the world who hasn't been out there really hasn't lived yet. When you get into that country, it is indescribably beautiful. The mountains go up over eight thousand feet; most people in Texas don't know they have that kind of a mountain.

And that's a good place to put a professional astronomical telescope?

Harlan: Oh, yes it's wonderful because it's high, it's dry semi-desert and best of all, it is dark. If you walk out in Dallas, how many faint things can you see in the sky? The county we are in the middle of is bigger than the state of Connecticut and it only has a thousand people [1989]. That is heaven on Earth for astronomers. It is perfect.

Why is a large mirror and telescope important?

Harlan: Well, say you are in the desert, you are thirsty, and a rainstorm comes along. What do you do? You tip your head back and get some raindrops, right? But, that may not keep you alive. If you are smarter, you get a poncho out and spread it out so it catches the raindrops over a large area. All the water funnels down to the center of the poncho and now, you have a real drink. That's just what a big telescope lens or mirror does; it collects light from the object you are looking at over a big area and brings it to a hole in the poncho, or the focus where you can put your eye or a piece of film. Now you can study that concentrated light. This is also why they sometimes call telescopes, *light buckets*.

Word association…twenty-five words or less, instant response
PULSAR:

Harlan: *Whooohh!* How was that for one word? Pulsar, it's like a lighthouse in space that's pulsing up to 800 times a second. My twenty-five words are almost up but try this. Imagine something that has a hundred thousand times as much matter as the Earth and imagine that spinning 800 times per second. OK, that's an extreme pulsar, but if you can visualize that, you are getting started. These are scattered around in space. It is what happens to some kinds of stars when they die.

QUASAR:

Harlan: Ah! Now, you are talking about the most powerful thing in the universe. Quasars—the nearest one is about a billion light-years away—and that means the light took a billion years to get from there to here at 186,000 miles per second—that's pretty far away. Most of the other thousands of quasars we know of are much farther away than that. Now, something that far away, how can you hope to see it? It's got to be incredibly bright. In fact, quasars are the brightest things we know in the universe. They are brighter than trillions of stars. Now, what is a quasar? That's what we are trying to find out. How can anything be trillions of times as energetic as a star and still be about the same size as a big star? That's what we have been struggling to understand for the last twenty-five years.

STARS AND PLANETS—THE DIFFERENCE BETWEEN:

Harlan: OK, a planet is just a little bitty hunk of debris left over from when a star was born. The planet stays in orbit around the star and shines by reflected light. The star itself at the center puts out all the heat, light, and energy of the system. So in our case, the Sun is the Star and the Planets, like the Earth, are just solid bodies of debris; about a millionth of the original stuff goes into the planets.

NEBULAE:

John: Nebulae is of Latin origin and means cloud. A Nebula is just that, a cloud out in space. It is what we call an interstellar cloud or a cloud between the stars made up of dust and gas, mainly hydrogen gas— the most abundant element in the universe.[18]

Congressman Jake Pickle

As I remember Harlan Smith, he was *always* at the very *edge* of the *art* of interpreting the science of the universe. He was ahead of everybody, he was very well educated...a country boy, but terribly brilliant and could explain to you the things you were seeing. Harlan was also a beekeeper, he could tell you how much honey you could get, what time of the year you got it, how much it weighed, how to store the honey, he knew everything. I got to thinking this was kind of fascinating, and I went into the bee business myself. I put up some hives at my little farm and at one time I had about four different hives. I studied the bees and it was absolutely fascinating how they know exactly to come to this hive and not another hive. I did have to know when to rob the bees, or as Harlan Smith always referred to it, "You harvested the bees."

You had to get dressed with a big hood and gloves, so I had my gloves, my hood, and I got to be a beekeeper and put a hive in my backyard here in Austin. I wasn't as effective as Dr. Harlan Smith, but if I got in trouble I'd call Harlan. I said, "Harlan, lay down your telescope, will you, can you come over here some time today?" "Oh!" He said, "I'll be right over." And I said, "No." And he said, "Yes, I'm in a break, I'll do it now." He would come over to my home and whatever was wrong with my hive, he'd help me straighten it out and tell me why it worked and how it wasn't cooperating. He set me straight again.

I remember one time we were out with my bees. Harlan had it all arranged up and bees were flying everywhere. Dr. Smith, who is kind of a quite-shy man, somewhat timid—except when he would go to explaining to you in terms of the universe, then boy, he got a little bit bigger! Dr. Smith says to me, "Mr. Congressman, may I ask you a question?" And I said, "Well certainly, Dr. Smith, what do you need?" He said, "I wanted to ask you a personal question. I haven't known you that long but I must say to you, a bee has stung me down here in my pants and I need very much to attend to it. Could I go into your little

---

[18] Excerpts from Karen Denard's Evening Talk Show – KERA (Dallas) Feb. 7, 1989, Dr. Harlan Smith and John S. Gianforte, guests.

garage and take my pants down so I can find and get that bee?" I said that would be all right, so he stopped, went inside, got the little stinger, and came back out dressed again. All was quiet and peaceful…Now, if it had been me and that bee had stung me down in my pants, I'd raise hell and I'd be jumping and swinging and fighting.

So here is the world's best-known astronomer, lending his talents to the process of raising honeybees, but he had to ask me permission to go down and change his clothes to get to that bee that had stung him.

Yes, Harlan was such a gentleman and so knowledgeable. He was a very gentle soul and he was also very human because anybody who can be an expert beekeeper, he's got to be very human.

Harlan, Joan and their daughter, Hannah, enjoying a rodeo. Photo from McDonald Observatory archives.

271

Prolong

I chose not to use Epilogue here because an epilogue is the concluding narrative part. I chose Prolong because it means to extend in time or space. That is what we are going to do here--we are going on. McDonald Observatory will encounter more lives and there will be more facets to chisel into this diamond. I cannot always be involved in this oral history project, but I pray there will be someone to pick it up and carry it on.

I was inspired to this project by three people. My father, who brought me here when I was a little girl and was as exasperated as I was that we could not experience what it is like to be astronomers. Frank Bash, who wrote a note to me after I gave him "To the Domes" and appointed me Poet Laureate of McDonald Observatory. He wrote that maybe I should think about doing a book and he would love to see one about McDonald. And my husband, Don, who brought me out here as a big little girl. And yes, I did cry. I still cry every single time I come out here--and sometimes only when I think about it.

A few things surprised me while writing this book. In the beginning of this project, I thought I should collect as many oral histories as I possibly could because not every one will be interesting. That's pretty funny when I look in a drawer containing over 115 hours of narration, from more than 70 narrators, and there is not one dud. There are more, I just could not get them all interrogated and in this edition. Like I said, we will go on.

The Board of Visitors members surprised me; they are not just influential and supportive of McDonald Observatory. If you think of the Observatory community as a sandwich cookie, the Board of Visitors is the crème between the visitor who knows a little about astronomy, and the astronomer who knows too much. They are Frank and Harlan understudies when it comes to communicating astronomical knowledge and embracing the public.

Another thing that surprised me was some of the narrators' willingness to express their faith. I decided, since I was undecided about my faith in the beginning of this project, that I would only ask Frank if he believed in God. I could ask Frank, because I had the results from a survey we conducted in the Visitors Center. One of the questions the Visitor wanted to know is if astronomers believe in God. You know Frank's answer. The narrators, who offered that they believe in God, did so because they felt compelled to tell me. This does not mean that the other narrators do not believe in God, but what really surprised me was that no one felt compelled to tell me they do not believe in God.

Something I hope you realize from reading this book is that McDonald Observatory is a community. It is a community, I think, because everyone loves one another and what they are doing. Harlan Smith started it. I could not know him, but like you, I have learned about him from the people who had personal experiences with him. Frank Bash has extended that love to everyone he came into contact with. He insisted everyone put their family first and he is retiring, at this time, to do just that. The next director for McDonald Observatory must have this same affection for the Observatory, which as you now know, includes every person, every building, every telescope, every instrument, every cone and every shackle, every critter, every bug, every lightning bolt and every cloud, every drop of water, and every dark-clear path to the stars.

One last thing to leave you with; it is an image from Anita Cochran and just cracks me up when I think about it. She said, "You can always tell an astronomer. They are the ones whose heads' swivel up every time they step outside at night." Does yours swivel up at night now, too? Let me know.

Now, Dear Visitor, it is time for you to turn the page because...we must go on...

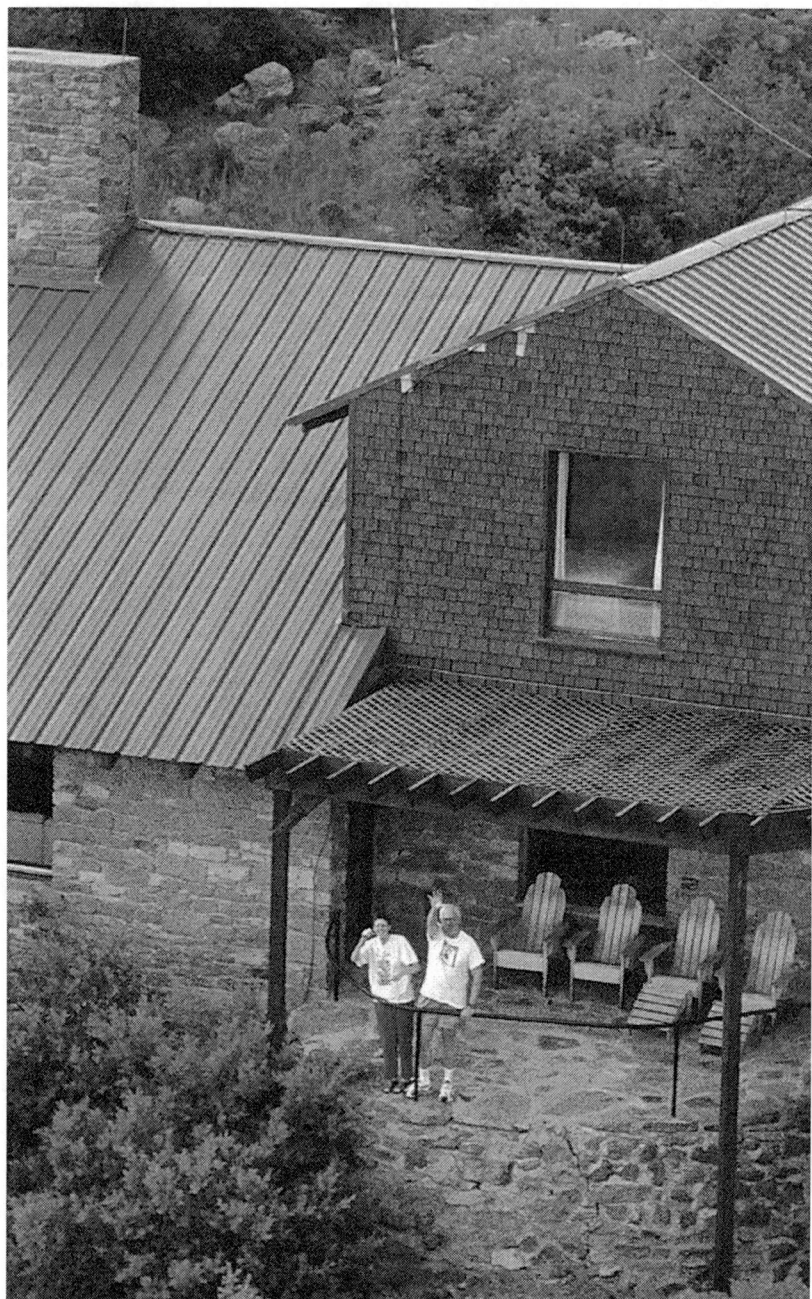

The back porch at House A. "Until next time," from Susan and Frank Bash.

Photo by Martin Harris, McDonald Observatory.

Your Stories Go Here